FRENCH LEGAL METHOD

FRENCH
LEGAL METHOD

EVA STEINER

OXFORD
UNIVERSITY PRESS

OXFORD
UNIVERSITY PRESS

Great Clarendon Street, Oxford OX2 6DP

Oxford University Press is a department of the University of Oxford.
It furthers the University's objective of excellence in research, scholarship,
and education by publishing worldwide in

Oxford New York

Auckland Bangkok Buenos Aires Cape Town Chennai
Dar es Salaam Delhi Hong Kong Istanbul Karachi Kolkata
Kuala Lumpur Madrid Melbourne Mexico City Mumbai Nairobi
São Paulo Shanghai Singapore Taipei Tokyo Toronto

Published in the United States
by Oxford University Press Inc., New York

© Eva Steiner, 2002

The moral rights of the author have been asserted
Database right Oxford University Press (maker)

First published 2002
Reprinted 2003

A catalogue record for this book is available from the British Library

Library of Congress Cataloging in Publication Data
Data available
ISBN 184–174185–X

Typeset by RefineCatch Limited, Bungay, Suffolk
Printed in Great Britain by
Antony Rowe Limited, Chippenham

Outline Contents

Contents

Preface

This book is the result of 20 years of experience as a teacher of French law, first in France at the University of Paris I-Panthéon-Sorbonne and, subsequently, since 1988, at King's College London, Law School. It is primarily intended to advance knowledge of the techniques of legal analysis employed by French jurists as well as giving assistance to those wishing to become familiar with the instruments of French law. It is hoped that a work of this nature will help the increasing number of students in this country who are involved in Anglo-French law programmes to master the concepts and techniques of French law in the course of their legal studies. Experience has shown that English law students find it extremely difficult to adapt to French legal method after having studied in English law schools. Indeed, form, structure and method are very important in the teaching of the law in France, and what makes for a good answer to a problem or essay question in France differs considerably from that in England.

Although books on French law have been published in England in recent years, none addresses exhaustively questions related to legal method, which gap this book now attempts to fill. The emergence of a new legal order within Europe has led to reflections, in this country and in other jurisdictions, about the way in which to teach law to future generations of students. It has been suggested that adroitness in thinking should play a central role in the future even, if necessary, to the detriment of erudition. It is with this context in mind that this book has been written. Thus, *French Legal Method* does not deal generally with substantive law, although when necessary it provides relevant appropriate information on substantive rules of law. However, the book can serve as an introduction to the French legal system, but with a greater emphasis on legal processes, techniques and skills rather than on legal rules and institutions.

The book can also be used as a tool for those involved in the practice and research surrounding law reform. Indeed, law reform in England increasingly concerns itself with examination of the legal method employed by Continental legal systems, particularly France, for which purpose this book may serve.

In the selection of the topics and in the structure adopted, I have taken into account the interaction between the different actors who contribute to the making of the law in a particular legal system, namely legislators, judges and academic lawyers. Bearing in mind Professor Van Caenegem's statement that in France, the judiciary, the legislature and academic writers have lived for most of the time 'in a peculiar state of equilibrium, neither ever completely dominating the others' (*Judges, Legislators and Professors*, Cambridge University Press, 1987, p. 70), I have divided the book into three interrelated parts, each of equal importance, namely, The Law-Making Process (Part I), The Method of Deciding Cases (Part II) and Legal Education (Part III).

Basic background knowledge of French legal institutions would be desirable when reading the book. Also, some knowledge of the French language is assumed although translations are generally provided throughout the book.

I am indebted to a variety of individuals and institutions for their assistance in the writing of this work:

In England:

- The editorial team at Blackstone Press for the enthusiasm they showed from the first proposal, in particular David Stott, publishing editor, for his continuous encouragement and words of praise during the writing of the book.
- The Centre of European Law at King's College London, for the confidence shown in providing me with a grant towards the cost of producing this work.
- My colleague at King's College London, Jane Henderson.

In France:

- The *Assemblée Nationale*, the Court of Cassation, the *Journal Officiel* and the *Dalloz* publishing house for allowing me to reproduce their documents in the book.
- Jean-Pierre Ancel, *Conseiller à la Cour de Cassation*, for his valued information concerning the method of deciding cases in the Court of Cassation.
- My friend and colleague Elisabeth Fortis, Professor of Criminal Law at the University of Paris X-Nanterre for her assistance in respect of my various queries on legal education.

Particular thanks are due to David Kennard for checking the language throughout the text.

Last, but not least, thanks are due to my family for their constant support in the writing of this book.

The translation into English of French legal texts, phrases and quotations are my own.

The law stated is the law as at 31 March 2002.

Eva Steiner
31 March 2002

PART I

THE LAW MAKING PROCESS

The first part of this book examines and evaluates the process of law-making in France. This process features some major differences between the French and English legal systems. In particular, the French legal system is characterised by a rigid, legalistic approach to legal sources. Authority is vested in written law and legislative sources to the detriment of judge-made law, in a system where decided cases are not binding for the future. This emphasis on written law and legislative sources has been criticised by the majority of French legal scholars as being unrealistic. As will be seen, French judges play an important part in law making through the application and interpretation of legislation.

Legislative supremacy in France can be traced back to Rousseau's *Contrat Social* in which the author lays down his famous postulate according to which law may only be the expression of the general will and can, therefore, only be generated by the elected body which that legislature represents. Rousseau's tenet was strengthened by the men of the 1789 Revolution who enacted a body of rules, still in force today, aimed at making judges subject to the legislature and at preventing them from making law. Officially, at least, rules laid down by judges have since then been denied the status of sources of law. Rousseau's heritage, coupled with the legal framework put in place during the French Revolution, thus hold the key to understanding the respective characteristics and role assigned to statute and case law in France today and these are the subject of the following chapters.

Another distinctive feature of the French legal system addressed in this first part of the book is that it is based principally on codes. This has a number of implications for the style of legislative drafting and the techniques of statutory interpretation that will also be examined here.

Part I has been divided into five chapters. Chapter 1 deals with legislation as the dominant form of law making in France, as well as in its relation to other written sources of law. It also describes the legislative process and examines the way bills are drafted. Chapter 2 looks at the process of codification, a process which has been accelerated in recent years with the setting up of the *Commission Supérieure de Codification*. Chapter 3 examines the techniques of statutory interpretation used in France and Chapter 4 gives an account of the rules concerning precedents and how they work in practice, especially in their relationship to legislation. The descriptive exercise engaged in, in Chapters 3 and 4, is mainly aimed at throwing some light on the question of whether judicial decisions do in fact make law in France. Chapter 5 gives a brief account of the process of law reform in France and serves as a conclusion to this first part.

prefatory comment regarding Chapter 1.2.2 and Box 1.1:

Since Chapter 1.2.2 was written, art. 372 of the Civil Code (Box1.1) has been restated unifying the treatment of married and unmarried parents in respect of parental responsibility. The new text of art. 372 covers the same ground, in similar length, style and effect as the previous one (new art. 372, introduced by the Loi of 4 March 2002 on parental responsibility).

1

Legislation

Quand je dis que l'objet des lois est toujours général, j'entends que la loi considère les sujets en corps et les actions comme abstraites, jamais un homme comme individu, ni une action particulière.

J.J., Rousseau, *Du Contrat Social*, Book II, Chapter VI.

This first chapter of Part I aims to establish that legislation is the primary source of law in France, that there are different types of legislation and that legislative sources are organised hierarchically. Also, this chapter is intended to familiarise readers with French legislative drafting and with the layout of a French statute. As will be seen later, much of French law – though not all of it – is codified. Codification is a particular legislative technique common to most civil law systems. It will be dealt with separately in the next chapter.

The points raised in this chapter should be considered in light of the fact that, in France, more than 100 statutes are produced in an average annual session of Parliament, to which should be added the very large number (in the thousands) of sets of rules and regulations made, each year, by ministers and various administrative bodies. This over abundance of statutory instruments has, in recent years, been a cause of concern to officials and scholars who have been at pain to point out the negative impact of such a large legislative output, especially in terms of quality of drafting, accessibility, and effectiveness.

The chapter starts with a description of the various sources of legislation known in France, followed by an examination of the French style of legislative drafting. The layout and component parts of a French statute are outlined and illustrated at the end of the chapter.

1.1 Legislative sources

For the purpose of this chapter 'legislation' or 'legislative sources' refer to written or enacted law as opposed to customary or case law. Thus, all legal written texts, including the constitution and treaties, will be regarded here as 'legislative' sources within the broadest meaning of that term.

1.1.1 General characteristics of legislation

Legislation is the primary source of French law, at least in the domain of private law. It is important, however, to note that a large body of French public law, known as 'administrative law', has been created mainly by the courts, particularly by the highest administrative court, the *Conseil d'Etat*, and looks very much like judge-produced law within the common law meaning of that expression. Despite this, emphasis on legislation remains a central feature of the French legal system. As already mentioned, this approach has a theoretical basis not only in Rousseau's works, but also, in the strong doctrine of the separation of powers inherited from the men of the French Revolution, one of whose main purposes was to protect the executive and the legislature against the judges (see Chapter 4.1.1 below). Since then, although French constitutional practice has found it necessary to adopt a more balanced distribution of powers, with judicial decisions having in practice become an important source of law, the doctrine of separation of powers, in its attempt to equate law with legislation, is still observed in many respects.

A characteristic feature of legislation in France is that it takes a variety of forms, particularly so since 1958, when the current constitution came into effect. Legislative sources can be classified under four main categories, namely:

(a) constitution

(b) treaties

(c) *lois* (parliamentary statutes)

(d) *règlements* (government regulations)

In addition, although they have not been included in the above classification, a few words should be said concerning administrative *circulaires* in view of their particular importance in French law. *Circulaires* are directives and instructions issued by relevant ministries to their agents, instructing them on how to interpret and apply new legislation. Although *circulaires* are not technically a proper legislative source, they nevertheless play an increasing role in guiding public officials and judges in their task of applying the law. In fact, judges tend to rely increasingly on the instructions contained in *circulaires* rather than on the originating statute itself. By way of illustration, the much used Circular of 14 May 1993 has provided public prosecutors and judges with a lengthy commentary on the 1992 New Penal Code with a view to guiding them in the day-to-day interpretation and application of the new criminal rules. The fear that under the cover of these instructions government departments could quietly add to or subtract from the letter or spirit of the statute they are only supposed to interpret, explains why the courts have been reluctant to ascribe to them the status of legally binding rules. Private courts, in particular, do not regard *circulaires* as being authoritative, but rather as internal measures which do not have the same legal force and effect as *lois* or *règlements* (see, in particular, *Préfet du Nord* v *Melis* (1950), D. 1951, 4). However, since the landmark decision given by the *Conseil d'Etat* in *Notre Dame de Kreisher* (1954), RPDA, p. 50, administrative courts have made a distinction between *circulaires interprétatives* and *circulaires règlementaires.* Only the latter are 'law' and are thus binding on the courts. As such, their validity can be reviewed in the same way as any other administrative acts. In particular, they can be declared illegal if they contravene a parliamentary statute (for a recent illustration, see *Syndicat des producteurs indépendants* (1997), D. 1997, 467 where the *Conseil d'Etat* struck down the Circular of 2 January 1995 issued by the Minister of Employment).

A further important aspect of French legislation is that legislative sources are also categorised in accordance with a legal hierarchy whereby a norm lower in the hierarchy must conform to norms at a level higher in that hierarchy. This is referred to as the principle of *hiérarchie des normes,* based on the Austrian Hans Kelsen's major work *Pure Theory of Law.* According to Kelsen, law consists of a hierarchy of norms with, at the top of this hierarchy, a so-called 'basic norm' from which the authority of the rest of the norms in the system is ultimately derived. It follows that each legal norm in a system is created and empowered by the norm higher than it in the legal hierarchy. All authorities responsible for enacting laws in France must abide by this principle of *hiérarchie des normes.* This is a very important aspect of the French doctrine of *Etat de Droit* whereby public authorities are required to act in accordance with legal norms, thus being subject to and not above the law. This organisation of legal norms in France assumes the form of a pyramid (as in Fig. 1.1), with constitutional laws having greater value than treaties; the latter, in turn, are superior to parliamentary statutes, which in turn have precedence over government regulations.

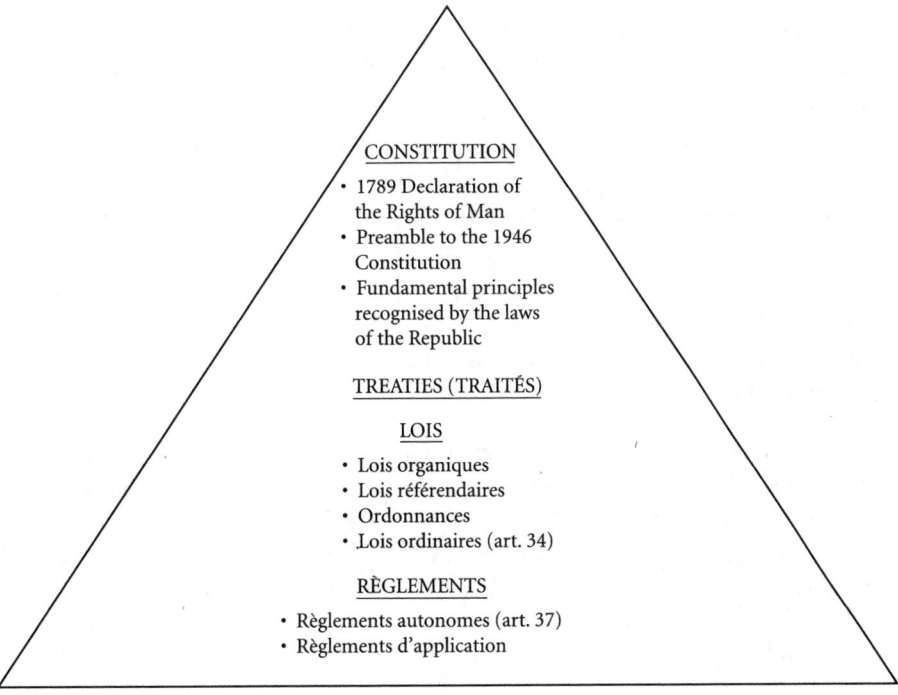

Fig. 1.1 The hierarchy of norms

This pyramid-like organisation of sources has been criticised for being unrealistic and illusory in view of the tensions and uncertainties concerning the status of EU law and international law. Indeed, French courts have not always responded in a consistent way to the conflict between internal sources of law and international agreements. Space is short here and does not allow for a full account of the legal writings and litigation that the principle of *hiérarchie des normes* has given rise to. However, a description of the essential elements and mechanisms of the hierarchical organisation of legislative sources is necessary in order to understand the significance of legislation in France. For this purpose, the different categories of legislative sources will be now outlined in decreasing order of authority.

1.1.2 Constitution

Since the 1789 Revolution, France has had an unbroken tradition of written constitutions (14 in total). The current one is the Constitution of the Fifth Republic, adopted by referendum and promulgated on 4 October 1958. The term 'constitution' must be understood broadly to include not only the main text of the Constitution, which is divided into 16 headings, but also (since the landmark *Conseil Constitutionnel* decision 71-44 DC, 16 July 1971, freedom of association, Rec. 29), its preamble which incorporates by reference a list of norms known as *bloc de constitutionnalité*. This *bloc* includes:

(a) The 1789 Declaration of the Rights of Man which affirms principles such as equality under law, freedom of speech, freedom of religion, and the presumption of innocence.

(b) The social and economic rights listed in the Preamble to the former 1946 Constitution. These rights include the right to work, to form labour unions, and to strike. Also included are the right to education and the right to health protection.

(c) The fundamental principles recognised by the laws of the Republic as referred to in the 1946 Preamble. This is a rather vague category which is not defined or illustrated by the preamble. However, the courts refer very often to this category which includes the principles of freedom of association, freedom of conscience and freedom of education.

The Constitution is at the apex of the pyramid of norms. This means that Parliament can only enact legislation in accordance with the constitutional norms, including the rights and freedoms described above. It is the *Conseil Constitutionnel,* created for this purpose in 1958, which is the exclusive authority competent to ensure conformity with the Constitution of parliamentary statutes. In this respect, since the 1971 leading case (cited above) which ascribed constitutional value to the 1789 Declaration and the 1946 Preamble, the *Conseil* has become a primary protector of civil liberties in France.

The Constitution is also superior to treaties. Although this has been the subject of a controversy among constitutional lawyers, superiority here arises out of the

Constitution, art. 54 which provides that if the *Conseil Constitutionnel* has ruled that if an international agreement contains a clause contrary to the Constitution, then the ratification of this agreement cannot take place until the Constitution has been revised. This happened in 1992, prior to ratification of the Maastricht treaty. The *Conseil* held that the treaty was contrary to the Constitution – particularly with respect to the introduction of a single European currency and a new right of non-nationals to take part in local elections – thereby requiring the amendment of the Constitution before ratification could proceed. Against the view that the Constitution is superior to treaties, it has been held by many that in a monist system such as France, international agreements, once ratified, should apply directly within the legal system, and in case of conflict, should take precedence over all the internal sources of law, including the Constitution. With regard to EU law, this approach had already been adopted by the European Court of Justice in the early ground-breaking case of *Costa* v *ENEL* (1964) ECR 585 where the Court asserted the superiority of Community law over the laws of the Member States. However, the highest administrative court in France, the *Conseil d'Etat*, recently ruled in *Sarran, Levacher et autres,* (1998), AJDA, p. 1039, that within the internal legal order, the supremacy of international agreements applies only in relation to parliamentary statutes (a point discussed at Chapter 1.1.3 below), not to constitutional provisions. It follows from what the *Conseil d'Etat* said that in the event of the Constitution being, as in *Sarran,* incompatible with some treaty provisions, the courts will not be able to set aside the Constitution in order to apply the treaty. This decision may seem paradoxical since, on the one hand, as the *Conseil d'Etat* says, a treaty takes precedence over a parliamentary statute which, on the other hand, may previously have already been declared to be in accordance with the Constitution (following the procedure of constitutional review referred to at Chapter 1.1.4 (d) below) and, as such, is technically valid. This shows to a degree that the conformity of the statute in question with the Constitution, and thus the Constitution itself, is of lower importance than the treaty and thus comes under the treaty in the hierarchy of norms.

1.1.3 Treaties

Article 55 of the Constitution provides that duly ratified treaties take precedence over domestic parliamentary statutes. Thus, in cases of conflict between the two, the treaty will prevail. However, this does not mean that the courts are empowered to strike down legislation which is incompatible with a treaty provision. Instead, the courts have the power to declare that the legislation is incompatible with the treaty and, then, apply the treaty. It is important to note that art. 55 does not distinguish between international law and EU law in its statement of the rule of superiority. Thus both international and EU law prevail over inconsistent statutes. However, it is in the area of EU law that, in the past, the rule of superiority gave rise to major difficulty in French law, especially in cases of conflict between the Treaty of Rome and a subsequent French statute, where such a statute could be held to be a deliberate attempt by Parliament to override the pre-existing treaty. Divergent views on this question were held by the Court of Cassation and by the *Conseil d'Etat*. In *Administration des Douanes* v *Société Cafés Jacques Vabre* (1975), D. 1975, 497, the Court of Cassation decided to give priority to the Treaty of Rome over a subsequent conflicting parliamentary statute introducing discriminatory customs duties and internal taxes on other Member States' products. However, following the line taken a few years earlier in *Syndicat Général des Fabricants de Semoules de France* (1968), D. 1968, 285, the *Conseil d'Etat* persisted in the view that applying art. 55 in such circumstances amounted to intervening in the province of the legislature by holding Parliament to account for adopting statutes that were contrary to pre-existing international agreements. *Syndicat Général* was eventually overruled 20 years later in *Nicolo* (1989), JCP 1989, II, 21371, where the *Conseil* agreed to examine, in accordance with art. 55, whether a 1977 statute delimiting the constituencies for elections to the European Parliament was compatible with the provisions of the Treaty of Rome. *Nicolo* was welcomed, as it brought renewed consensus to the courts over what had, until then, been a contentious issue. Although case law regarding the superiority of treaties has, in its early years, mostly related to the EC Treaty, there has been later similar resolution as in *Société Café Jacques Vabre* and *Nicolo* in favour of other international agreements, such as the 1950 European Convention on Human Rights (*René X. and Marc X.* (1992), JCP 1993, II, 21991), and the 1957 European Convention on Extradition (*Urdiain Cirizar* (1991), Leb. 347). It should also be noted that French courts have also recognised the precedence of Community regulations and directives over domestic law (in *Boisdet* (1990), AJDA, p. 863, for regulations and in *SA Rothmans International France and SA Philip Morris France* (1992), Leb. 81, for directives).

1.1.4 *Lois* (parliamentary statutes)

Loi takes a variety of forms depending on the authority empowered to enact them and the specific procedures required for their adoption. In these respects, distinctions can be drawn between:

(a) *Lois organiques*: these supplement the Constitution on matters related to the organisation of public powers such as the status of judges (Constitution, art. 65) and presidential elections (Constitution art. 6). The procedures applied for the adoption of *lois organiques* are set out in the Constitution, art. 46 and differ from the ordinary procedures preceding the passage of a bill. In particular, any *loi organique* must be referred to the *Conseil Constitutionnel* for scrutiny. This differs from the case of ordinary bills where referring a statute to the *Conseil* is not automatic.

(b) *Lois référendaires*: these are passed by means of a referendum. Any bill introduced by the government and dealing with the organisation of public powers, the social and economic policy of the nation or the ratification of a treaty may be submitted to a referendum by the President of the Republic (art. 11).

(c) *Ordonnances*: under the Constitution, art. 38, Parliament may delegate to the executive its law making power in specific areas. This delegation permits the executive to enact law, within the field of parliamentary authority, by means of *ordonnances* but for a limited period only – usually three to six months – and in order, as provided for in art. 38, to carry out its programme. As with delegated legislation in England, the advantage of *ordonnances* is that legislation can, in this way, be introduced more quickly without going through all the time-consuming legislative procedures. *Ordonnances* are passed by decision of the *Conseil des Ministres* following consultation with the *Conseil d'Etat*, acting within its function of advisory body. In order to acquire the same legal force and effect as an ordinary parliamentary statute, *ordonnances* need to be approved by Parliament. Prior to approval they have the status of *règlement* (see Chapter 1.1.5 below).

(d) *Lois ordinaires*: these refer to the ordinary legislative process in Parliament, which is briefly outlined below. Before turning to this, it should be noted that this legislative process has been characterised since 1958 by a severe restriction of Parliament's law making power and a corresponding increase in the government's involvement in parliamentary business. Indeed, one of the most striking features to arise out of the 1958 Constitution has been that Parliament no longer enjoys legislative sovereignty and now has to share its legislative function with the government. The Constitution, art. 34, gives a limited list of matters on which Parliament is authorised to legislate. These include, *inter alia*, civil liberties, nationality, civil status, criminal law and criminal procedure. According to the Constitution, art. 37, any other subject not expressly specified in art. 34 is left entirely to the discretion of the executive power. This distribution of power to legislate under arts 34 and 37 is enforced both by the *Conseil Constitutionnel* and by the *Conseil d'Etat*. As far as the former is concerned (the *Conseil d'Etat* is discussed at Chapter 1.1.5 below), it has the power, prior to their enactment, to strike down parliamentary statutes which are passed outside the areas specified in art. 34. However, in spite of the art. 34 restriction, the *Conseil Constitutionnel* chose to widen the field of application of this article by upholding parliamentary statutes that had in part strayed out of Parliament's authorised area of competence (decision 82-143 DC, 30 July 1982 *Blocages des prix et des revenus*, Rec. 57). Following a similar line, the *Conseil* has decided that Parliament is not allowed to delegate to the government other than by *ordonnances* (see (c) above) its rule making authority arising out of art. 34. A *loi* cannot, therefore, authorise the government to issue regulations in any of the areas covered by art. 34. This has been referred to as *incompétence négative* since a decision 67-31 DC, 26 January 1967, *Indépendance et inamovibilité des magistrats*, Rec. 19.

Outlined below are the main characteristics and the principal stages of the legislative process in France:

(i) The French Parliament consists of two houses, the *Assemblée Nationale* (577 members) and the *Sénat* (321 members). Before any legislative proposal, known at that stage as a *projet de loi* (governmental bill) or *proposition de loi* (private member's bill), can become a *loi* it must pass through, and be approved by, both houses and, as in England, it is possible to commence the legislative procedure in either house. If, after having been given two readings, in both houses, no agreement can be reached between the two houses, the government has the option of setting up a *commission mixte paritaire*. This is a special committee consisting of an equal number of members of both houses set up with a view to drawing up a text acceptable to both. If this too is unsuccessful, then the *Assemblée Nationale* has the final say. Before any bill can become law, its *promulgation* by the President of the Republic must take place within 15 days. The Constitution, art. 10, provides for the possibility, before promulgation, of passing back the bill to Parliament for further consideration. The President of the Republic may also, at his discretion, refer the bill to the *Conseil Constitutionel* for constitutional review (reference to the *Conseil* is also open to the Prime Minister, the presidents of both houses of Parliament and, a group of 60 members from either of the two houses). Every *loi* comes into effect following its publication in the official edition of statutes and decrees, the *Journal Officiel-Lois et Décrets* (cited as, JO).

(ii) A certain number of constitutional measures have been designed to ensure control of the legislative process by the government. These are:

(a) Governmental control of the legislative timetable and agenda of both houses (Constitution, art. 48). This means, in practice, that the government can give priority to its own bills over private members' bills.

(b) The *vote bloqué* (Constitution, art. 44 (3)). Although members of both houses may introduce any amendments they wish to any bill, the government can at any time insist on a single vote, called *vote bloqué*, to be taken on its own text, thus forcing consideration only of the amendments it has made itself.

(c) The option the government has under the Constitution, art. 49(3) to make an issue of confidence out of the rejection by Parliament of any bill or amendment it (the government) has introduced. This measure can be taken by the government when it wishes to push through controversial legislation and ensure its own majority in Parliament. The bill, when passed under this procedure, is then automatically adopted unless a vote of censure is carried. Article 49 (3) has been frequently used in recent years by successive governments.

1.1.5 *Règlements* (government regulations)

This form of legislation, in terms of the field it covers, is the French equivalent of subordinate or delegated legislation in England. However, in France, the power to issue regulations vested in ministers or other central rule-making authorities does not necessarily derive from parliamentary delegation. Here, an important distinction must be drawn between *règlements autonome* and *règlements d'application*.

The former concern the independent authority to legislate vested in the government by the Constitution, art. 37 (see Chapter 1.1.4(d) above). *Règlements autonomes* are means whereby government ministers, local authorities or other public bodies introduce particular regulations, in the form of *décrets* or *arrêtés*, which are legally binding without the need for enabling legislation. *Règlements* issued under art. 37 are thus as much legislation as the *lois* which Parliament enacts under art. 34. However, while the ordinary courts have no power to question the constitutionality of a *loi* (only the *Conseil Constitutionel* can do this, see Chapter 1.1.4.(d) above), *règlements* are subject, like most governmental actions, to scrutiny by the *Conseil d'Etat* by way of a *recours pour excès de pouvoirs*, a form of proceedings whereby the legality of administrative decisions is reviewed by an administrative court. In this respect the government must comply, as any other public body, with the principle of the hierarchy of norms. Thus, a ministerial *décret* or *arrêté* will be declared illegal, and then invalidated by the *Conseil d'Etat*, if it contravenes the Constitution, a treaty, or a parliamentary statute.

Turning now to *règlements d'application*, they usually take the form of *décrets* and can only be made in relation to particular parliamentary statutes to which they give effect by providing the detailed rules necessary for their implementation. In this respect, the enabling statute contains a specific provision stating that all or part of the details of its application are to be defined by a *'décret en Conseil d'Etat'*. A recent topical example is Loi 99-944 of 15 November 1999, art. 15, on Domestic Registered Partnerships, JO 16 November 1999, p. 16959 and Décret 99-1089 of 21 December 1999, JO 24 December 1999, p. 19216, both providing an illustration of *loi* and *décret d'application*.

Both types of *règlements* are issued in the form of statutory instruments and, as with statutes, are published in the *Journal Officiel*. Their drafting is usually left to legal advisers in the relevant ministries. They are not laid before Parliament and, in the case of *décrets*, are usually discussed and adopted in the *Conseil des Ministres*, following prior consultation with the *Conseil d'Etat* acting here, not in its judicial, but in its advisory capacity.

1.2 Legislative drafting

Legislative drafting has been the subject of much scrutiny and criticism in recent years. Working groups similar to the 1975 Renton Committee and the more recent 1992 Hansard Society Commission in England have been set up in many jurisdictions with a view to providing some guidance and making recommendations on the drafting of statutes. Similar moves aimed at rendering legislation clear and simple may be observed within the European Community specifically with the adoption in 1993 of a Resolution of the Council of the European Communities relating to the quality of drafting of Community legislation, OJ 93/C/166/01. In addition, numerous works, including guides to legislative drafting, have been written on this theme and widely published. Some authors have even suggested that the science of legislation should be taught in law schools in order to maintain a satisfactory standard in the practice of legislative drafting. French legal scholar J. Carbonnier (1995), in an authoritative sociological study on legislation, has challenged this perceived need for producing legislative drafting guides which are purportedly aimed at improving the quality of statutory instruments. He says:

A people does not need treatises on the art of legislating in order to achieve good legislation; it is rather on centuries of legislation that stood the test of time that one should rely to build up a science of legislation.

Adding to the above, Carbonnier emphasises that much of the poor quality of modern legislation comes not from its drafting but from its lack of rationalisation, a direct consequence of the constant need felt by modern parliaments to reform the law, and the fact that contemporary legislative procedures are unable to effectively deal with the effects of the inflationery tendency in overabundant legislative production. However, the intense legislative activity characteristic of modern parliaments described by Carbonnier follows directly from the increasing complexity and technicality of the law which has been stretched to meet the ever increasing demands of modern states. Drafting legislation, therefore, involves keeping a difficult balance between political reality and legislative quality.

One way the French legal system deals with such a complex task, is to assign to the *Conseil d'Etat* the role of supervising the process of legislative drafting. Apart from being the highest administrative court in France, the *Conseil d'Etat* is also, as has already been said, a consultative body to the government. It is in this latter capacity that the *Conseil* examines all bills drafted by the government and referred to it for *avis* (advice), prior to their discussion in Parliament. Although the government is not bound by the *Conseil's* suggestions, it nevertheless pays considerable attention to them. The *Conseil* draws the government's attention to defects in the bill in terms of style, terminology, coherence and context. It is also part of its function to comment on infringements of constitutional norms, international agreements, and fundamental principles of law contained within the bill. In so doing the *Conseil* acts as a filter to eliminate bad drafting and, more generally, bad law. In this respect it allows the government to foresee the legal objections that are likely to be raised during parliamentary discussion.

The French style of legislative drafting will now be described in more detail with illustrations of the way laws are designed in France. The approach which has been adopted here is to compare and contrast some of the most original features of the French style of drafting legislation with the English one. This comparison between the two systems is dealt with under the two following headings:

(a) generality v particularity

(b) simplicity v complexity

These are now considered in turn.

1.2.1 Generality v particularity

This distinction refers to the method whereby rules of law are formulated in each of the two systems. It is commonly asserted that the French have a tendency to express their rules of law in the form of general principles, in sharp contrast with the opposing English tendency to dress rules up as directed at specific situations the lawmaker wants to cover. One of the most frequently cited examples of 'generality' in French legislation is the expression, in the Civil Code, of the whole law of tort in only five articles – arts 1382–1386. However, this example is not totally accurate. Indeed, a cause of action in tort law arises not only from arts 1382–1386 but also from specific torts contained in a number of other existing statutes, intended to supplement the original code provisions. Examples of these are the Law of 5 April 1937 on the liability of teachers, the Law of 5 July 1985 on road traffic accidents, the Law of 9 September 1986 on terrorism, the Law of 31 December 1991 regarding AIDS victims, and the newly inserted arts 1386-1–1386-18 of the Civil Code on product liability.

Generality remains, however, a characteristic feature of French legislative drafting, in the manner in which legislative provisions are worded and in respect of the scope they are intended to cover. The characteristics can once more be traced back to Rousseau (*Contrat Social*, Book II, Chapter VI) for whom 'the scope of legislation is always general'. Constitutional theorist R. Carré de Malberg (1931) claims, in a similar vein, that the generality of legislation lies in the fact that statute or code provisions are, by their nature, not enacted with a view to their application in specific situations or to individuals. On the contrary, according to this author, legal provisions are intended to deal with an infinite number of legal situations, present and future, so long as these fall within the scope of the abstract provisions of the relevant enactment.

From this conception of legislation it follows that:

(a) French legal rules commonly take the form of statements of general principle encapsulated in broad language and short sentences. This creates a certain degree of solemnity, with rules of law appearing as common sayings or maxims. By way of illustration, some typical examples are given below:

Art. 2, Civil Code: la loi ne dispose que pour l'avenir; elle n'a point d'effet rétroactif.

Art. 1134, Civil Code: les conventions légalement formées tiennent lieu de loi à ceux qui les on faites.

Art. 2279, Civil Code: en fait de meubles, la possession vaut titre.

Art. 111-4, Penal Code: la loi pénale est d'interprétation stricte.

(b) French legal rules are also impersonal. This is reflected in the frequent use of indefinite pronouns, adjectives or articles in code provisions. Hence, the use of the words *un/une, on, quiconque, chacun, tout/toute*, as shown in the following examples:

Art. 6, Civil Code: on ne peut déroger par des conventions particulières aux lois qui intéressent l'ordre public et les bonnes moeurs.

Art. 223-7, Penal Code: quiconque s'abstient volontairement de prendre ou de provoquer les mesures permettant, sans risque pour lui ou pour les tiers, de combattre un sinistre de nature à créer un danger pour la sécurité des personnes est puni de deux ans d'emprisonnement et de 200 000 F d'amende.

Art. 9, Civil Code: chacun a droit au respect de sa vie privée.

The examples given above are drawn from code provisions, and it must be noted that the use of broad language is intimately related to the technique of codification (see Chapter 2). At the time of presentation of the draft Civil Code to the *Conseil d'Etat* in 1799, Portalis, one of the authors of the code, claimed: 'the role of the law is to lay down broad maxims of law; to establish fertile principles, and not to go into the detail of the issues which may arise out of a matter'. This style of writing has however become common practice in everyday legislation, even for statutes which are not codified. The much used Landlord and Tenant Law, 1989, art. 1, is a good example:

le droit au logement est un droit fondamental; il s'exerce dans le cadre des lois qui le régissent. L'exercice de ce droit implique la liberté de choix pour toute personne de son mode d'habitation grâce au maintien et au développement d'un secteur locatif et d'un secteur d'accession à la propriété ouverts à toutes les catégories sociales.

Les droits et obligations réciproques des bailleurs et des locataires doivent être équilibrés dans leurs relations individuelles comme dans leurs relations collectives.

Common lawyers unfamiliar with the process of law making in France might point out the damaging consequences that such a method of drafting may have especially with respect to legal certainty. Indeed, according to them, if only principles are enunciated in statutes, or if the terms used are too vague, then it is feared that the judge may find a way of avoiding the application of the relevant provisions to the very circumstances the legislator was wishing to cover. In this respect, the generality of French statutes and code provisions may be contrasted with the particularity observed in English legislative drafting. Particularity, in this context, means primarily that the legislative draftsman always tries to cover all situations when drafting a text. This has resulted in the so-called practice of 'catalogue' in English statutes. Particularity also implies precision when drafting legislation. The draftsman must make sure that an accurate form of expression has been used and do what is possible to avoid vagueness. The frequent resort to definition of key words in a special definition section is aimed at enhancing precision in common law statutes.

However, in response to the criticism made against the generality of French statutes, it may be pointed out that:

(a) Firstly, generality in French legislative drafting must be understood against the frequent use, in France, of subordinate legislation aimed at supplementing the parliamentary statutes to which they give effect (see Chapter 1.1.5 above). Indeed, *décrets* and *arrêtés*, when compared to the statutes they supplement, are highly specific, detailed and technical. Despite the fact that it has the adverse effect of shifting much of the legislative production from primary legislation to governmental regulations, resort to subordinate legislation means that there is less need for statutes to be detailed.

(b) Secondly, trying to exhaust all the possibilities covered by a text would reasonably appear to be an impossible task, not to say an illusory one. Here, certainty can never appear to be successfully achieved for the simple reason that the draftsman cannot foresee all the situations that may arise in future cases brought to court.

(c) Thirdly, contrary to conventional belief, the more precise and detailed the legislation, the greater the risk of inconsistency and contradiction in the law with its attendant risks of litigation. Both risks are significantly increased at times of heavy legislative production and are most obvious in systems of law which exhibit a general lack of coherence principally because they rely on a variety of dispersed and fragmentary sources rather than on general principles.

(d) Fourthly, concision, a salient characteristic of the French legislative style (discussed further in Chapter 1.2.2 below), is not necessarily exclusive of a certain degree of precision. Concision, defined as the quality of expressing the essential in a few words, can achieve this precision without the need to be detailed, unlike the majority of English statutes where details are very often redundant or needless. Articles 271 and 272 of the Civil Code provide an example of draftsmanship which illustrates a combination of concision and precision on the particularly complex question of the conditions for maintenance in divorce proceedings:

Art. 271: La prestation compensatoire est fixée selon les besoins de l'époux à qui elle est versée et les ressources de l'autre en tenant compte de la situation au moment du divorce et de l'évolution de celle-ci dans un avenir prévisible.

Dans le cadre de la fixation d'une prestation compensatoire, par le juge ou par les parties dans la convention visée à l'article 278, ou à l'occasion d'une demande de révision, les parties fournissent au juge une déclaration certifiant sur l'honneur l'exactitude de leurs ressources, revenus, patrimoine et conditions de vie.

Art. 272: Dans la détermination des besoins et des ressources, le juge prend en considération notamment:
- l'âge et l'état de santé des époux;
- la durée du mariage;
- le temps déjà consacré ou qu'il leur faudra consacrer à l'éducation des enfants;
- leur qualification et leur situation professionnelles au regard du marché du travail;
- leurs droits existants et prévisibles;
- leur situation respective en matière de pension de retraite;
- leur patrimoine, tant en capital qu'en revenu, apres la liquidation du régime matrimonial.

Article 271 deals neatly with the question of financial provision made by one of the spouses in the event of the breakdown of a marriage. It clearly states in as few words as possible the principle according to which maintenance is due, this being only in proportion to the needs of the spouse claiming it, and to the means of the spouse by whom it is payable; and, provided both spouses swear a declaration ascertaining their respective earnings, assets, and lifestyle. Article 272 then articulates the circumstances which the court may take into account when calculating the sum. This enumeration provides the court with meaningful and helpful guidance on how to calculate the sum due without being too specific, thus leaving to the courts the role of developing the criteria listed in the text with the possibility offered to the judges of adding to the list, as the French adverb *notamment* used in the text suggests. Article 272's enumeration also illustrates that the tendency towards 'catalogue', much favoured by the English legislative draftsman is not completely alien to French Law. However, the particularity of French 'catalogue' provisions is that, first an inclusive principle is stipulated, as in art. 271 above ('La prestation compensatoire . . . dans un avenir prévisible'), in advance of describing particular circumstances which may arise under this principle (as in art. 272). Therefore, a 'catalogue' in French law is not aimed at exhausting all the situations the legislator may wish to cover, but rather at providing mere illustrations of possible situations being covered by the prior stated inclusive principle which, in this way, can be extended by the courts to further appropriate situations and circumstances. A further typical example, illustrating the application of 'catalogue' to French statutes, may be found in art. 524 of the Civil Code dealing with *immeubles par destination*, a particular category of immovable property in French law:

Art. 524: Les animaux et les objets que le propriétaire d'un fonds y a placés pour le service et l'exploitation de ce fonds sont immeubles par destination. [inclusive pinciple]

Ainsi, sont immeubles par destination, quand ils ont été placés par le propriétaire pour le service et l'exploitation du fonds: [illustrated as follows]
Les animaux attachés à la culture;
Les ustensiles aratoires;
Les semences données aux fermiers ou colons partiaires;
Les pigeons des colombiers;
Les lapins des garennes;
Les ruches à miel;
(. . .)
Les pressoirs, chaudières, alambics, cuves et tonnes;
(. . .)

1.2.2 Simplicity v complexity

The late Sir William Dale (1981), an influential contributor to the international public debate on legislative drafting argued that because 'a statute is the supreme act of the Sovereign in Parliament addressed to the citizen', it was reasonable to expect of it, certain qualities associated with simplicity such as economy, directness, and orderliness. According to Dale, English statutes are complex and difficult to read precisely because they lack these qualities, consequently suffering, as he says, from 'verbal incontinence' and 'bad arrangement'. Dale favours the Continental practice of drafting legislation which, by contrast to the English, has managed to achieve the clarity and brevity necessary for simplicity, in particular by placing more emphasis on principle than on detail.

Dale's concern for simplicity in legislation is not new. Montesquieu, in his famous

The Spirit of Laws, had already expressed the need for the style of legislation to be concise, plain and simple. 'Laws should not be subtle', he said, 'they are designed for people of common understanding, not as a work of logic, but as the plain reasoning of a family father' (Book XXIX, 16). The same with J. Bentham, who, in his *Theory of Legislation* (Chapter XVII) advocated: 'The style and the method should be simple; the law ought to be a manual of instruction for each individual; and everyone should be enabled to consult it in doubtful cases without the aid of an interpreter'.

Turning to French legislative drafting today, it may be said that, following Continental practice, legislative provisions tend generally to avoid verbosity, as well as redundancy and circumlocution, and to exhibit an orderly approach to sentence structure. This can be illustrated by a simple example which contrasts the way rules governing parental responsibility are formulated in France and in England. In England, these rules are found in The Children Act, 1989, s. 2, and in France, in art. 372 of the Civil Code (see Box 1.1 on p. 21). These two texts serve an identical purpose: the allocation of parental responsibility to a child's parents. However, what is striking at first glance is that art. 372 is much shorter overall, with shorter sentences, and contains only three paragraphs in contrast with 11 subsections in s. 2 of the English Act. The principal reason for this is that art. 372 addresses only the situation of the father and mother of a child and does not deal with third parties to whom parental responsibility may be delegated. The situation of third parties is dealt with elsewhere in separate provisions. In contrast, s. 2, consisting of a patchwork of provisions where the general and the qualified are mixed together, deals with the situation of third parties together with the situation of the parents. There are further drafting defects in s. 2. For example, the expression 'parental responsibility' is repeated 11 times in the space of what is a relatively short text. Article 372, avoids such repetition by using the pronoun '*elle*' instead of '*autorité parentale*'. The overall resulting impression is that the text in s. 2 doesn't flow readily and as such is not as easily digestible and comprehensible as art. 372.

However, it would be incorrect to assume from the above that all statutory instruments in French law present similarly identical characteristics to the ones which have served as illustrations in this part of the chapter. In the area of public law, code provisions and statutes are not all free of these very characteristics that have provoked complaint about English drafting: length, complexity, detail and over repetition. Many examples can be found in the area of tax law or employment law where a large number of code provisions have become increasingly verbose, extremely technical and overly detailed, with the adverse result that paragraphs are not any more clearly identified or easy to read. By way of illustration, art. L. 122-26 of the *Code du Travail* concerning women's entitlement to maternity leave runs to 63 lines and art. 31 of the *Code Général des Impôts*, concerning the determination of gross income as a basis for tax calculation runs to seven pages!

A further well-known example of bad drafting is art. 121-3 of the New *Code Pénal* on criminal liability in situations where the defendant had no intention of committing the crime but was careless. It reads as follows:

Il n'y a point de crime ou de délit sans intention de le commettre.

Toutefois, lorsque la loi le prévoit, il y a délit en cas de mise en danger délibérée de la personne d'autrui.

Il y a également délit, lorsque la loi le prévoit, en cas de faute d'imprudence, de négligence ou de manquement à une obligation de prudence ou de sécurité prévue par la loi ou le règlement, s'il est établi que l'auteur des faits n'a pas accompli les diligences normales compte tenu, le cas échéant, de la nature de ses missions ou de ses fonctions, de ses compétences ainsi que du pouvoir et des moyens dont il disposait.

Dans le cas prévu par l'alinéa qui précède, les personne physiques qui n'ont pas causé directement le dommage, mais qui ont créé ou contribué à créer la situation qui a permis la réalisation du dommage ou qui n'ont pas pris les mesures permettant de l'éviter, sont responsables pénalement s'il est établi qu'elles ont, soit violé de façon manifestement délibérée une obligation particulière de prudence ou de diligence prévue par la loi ou le règlement, soit commis une faute caractérisée et qui exposait autrui à un risque d'une particulière gravité qu'elles ne pouvaient ignorer.

Although this text was amended for clarity in 2000, certain word groupings are still badly arranged in complex sentence structures. This is due to a succession of qualifying phrases and clauses which, to take as an example the sentence commencing 'Dans le cas prévu . . . ', distance the verb ('sont responsables') from close proximity to its subject ('les personnes physiques'). This text also displays verbosity, redundancy, tautologies, and the overuse of negatives, in short all the right ingredients for muddling a text and, thus, making it difficult to follow. As examples of tautology, in the second and third sentences of the text, 'il y a délit' (in English, 'there is an offence') makes redundant 'lorsque la loi le prévoit' ('when provided for by law'); the same may be said, in the third sentence, 'en cas de faute d'imprudence, de négligence' (in English, 'in circumstances of recklessness and negligence') which makes redundant 'n'a pas accompli les diligences normales'('who has not acted with reasonable care').

Something further to bear in mind when dealing with the objective of simplicity in legislative drafting is that, paradoxically, simplicity, and simplicity of language in particular, may result in more complexity. For example, in 1985, at the time of the legislative reform of the law concerning road traffic accidents, it was decided on the question of causation to use the broader concept of *implication* in the new statute, rather than the traditional, but more technical and difficult to assess, concept of *causalité*. The aim here was to facilitate the plaintiff's burden of proof. However, the change generated more doctrinal controversy and more litigation than had previously been the case. This illustrates clearly the paradox that efforts to achieve simplicity in drafting may still fall foul of the technical and complex nature of the law.

How, then, is one to find a way forward, in France as in other jurisdictions, for the successful achievement of simplicity in legislative drafting? One way might be to determine in advance a typical format for legislative enactment capable of striking a balance between open space on the page and the written word, using this format as a 'legislative model' for further statutes. Determining in advance a typical legislative format implies establishing a list of criteria about aspects of drafting such as the

Box 1.1 Contrasting English and French legislative drafting

Children Act 1989

Section 2. Parental responsibility for children

2. – (1) Where a child's father and mother were married to each other at the time of his birth, they shall each have parental responsibility for the child.

(2) Where a child's father and mother were not married to each other at the time of his birth –

  (a) the mother shall have parental responsibility for the child;

  (b) the father shall not have parental responsibility for the child, unless he acquires it in accordance with the provisions of this Act.

(3) References in this Act to a child whose father and mother were, or (as the case may be) were not, married to each other at the time of his birth must be read with section 1 of the Family Law Reform Act 1987 (which extends their meaning).

(4) The rule of law that a father is the natural guardian of his legitimate child is abolished.

(5) More than one person may have parental responsibility for the same child at the same time.

(6) A person who has parental responsibility for a child at any time shall not cease to have that responsibility solely because some other person subsequently acquires parental responsibility for the child.

(7) Where more than one person has parental responsibility for a child, each of them may act alone and without the other (or others) in meeting that responsibility; but nothing in this Part shall be taken to affect the operation of any enactment which requires the consent of more than one person in a matter affecting the child.

(8) The fact that a person has parental responsibility for a child shall not entitle him to act in any way which would be incompatible with any order made with respect to the child under this Act.

(9) A person who has parental responsibility for a child may not surrender or transfer any part of that responsibility to another but may arrange for some or all of it to be met by one or more persons acting on his behalf.

(10) The person with whom any such arrangement is made may himself be a person who already has parental responsibility for the child concerned.

(11) The making of any such arrangement shall not affect any liability of the person making it which may arise from any failure to meet any part of his parental responsibility for the child concerned.

Civil Code

Art. 372 L'autorité parentale est exercée en commun par les deux parents s'ils sont mariés.

Elle est également exercée en commun si les parents d'un enfant naturel, l'ayant tous deux reconnu avant qu'il ait atteint l'âge d'un an, vivent en commun au moment de la reconnaissance concomitante ou de la seconde reconnaissance.

Les dispositions de l'alinéa précédent ne font pas obstacle à celles des troisième et quatrième alinéas de l'article 374.

placement and positioning of the different elements of a statute on a page, the point size and the weight given to the letters of the text, the spacing and margins applied, as well as the use of indents and titles. This approach was considered and tested during the 1997 Canada-Ukraine Legislative Drafting Programme. While recounting his experience as Director of the Programme, R. C., Bergeron, QC (2000), describes how it was possible, during the programme, to prepare a set of legislative drafting rules and to decide on a legislative model, by carrying out a study of statutes from a 'purely logistical look at the written form'. In the course of this study, copies of recent statutes from each of the 13 Canadian governments were distributed to the Ukrainian participants, making sure than none of the statutory texts was translated so that they would not be distracted by their content. In this way, the participants were induced to look at and examine them while being unable to read them. This facilitated unbiased and constructive suggestions towards the creation of an 'ideal, easy, user-friendly model for a normative text'. In other words, in order to achieve simplicity the draftsman must consider visual presentation as being as important a feature as content when drafting a statute. Good drafting implies, as Bergeron said, that 'a normative text should never look like the first prize in a "put-as-many-words-as-you-can-on-the-page" contest'.

1.3 Layout and component parts of a statute

The layout of a French statute differs considerably from the way Acts of Parliament are arranged in Britain and other Commonwealth countries. In particular, there is not the same distinction in French statute law as that between long and short titles to be found in English law, nor does a French statute contain schedules or other marginal notes. Definition and interpretation sections are also alien to French statutes. Furthermore, the practice in France is to divide up the statute into articles as opposed to sections and, instead of numbered subsections, to use indented paragraphing (called *alinéas*) within the article. However, Acts of Parliament and French statutes do display certain similar features such as enacting formulae, parts and headings and commencement and transitional provisions.

The various components and the format of a French statute are outlined below.

1.3.1 Date

Starting at the beginning of a statute one finds the date of promulgation (see Boxes 1.2 and 1.3). Promulgation is the French equivalent of Royal Assent. The date is itself preceded by the statute number, such as, 'Loi 99-944 du 15 Novembre 1999'. In this example, the first two digits indicate the year, the following ones indicate the rank of publication of the *loi* in the JO within the given year. Statute numbers are important for citation purposes when distinguishing between *lois* promulgated the same day, for example, Loi 89-1008 of 31 December 1989 on commercial businesses and craft industries and Loi 89-1010 of 31 December 1989 on heavily indebted private individuals. Statutes dating back to the French Revolution of 1789 are cited by naming the date of their vote together with the date of their promulgation, such as the famous Loi of 16–24 August 1790 on the separation of powers, which remains in force.

1.3.2 Title

Next comes the title. As stated above, there is, in France, no difference, as is the case in England, between long and short titles. There is only one title, intended to provide a general indication of the scope of the statute (as in Box 1.2) or of the aim pursued by Parliament in enacting the law (as in Box 1.3). Other examples are the Loi of 24 August 1993 which bears the title: '*relative à la maitrise de l'immigration et aux conditions d'entrée et d'accueil des étrangers en France*' or the Loi of 15 June 2000 '*renforcant la protection de la présomption d'innocence et les droits des victimes*'. The title can also be a means of reference to the legislation it modifies. For example, the Loi of 4 January 1978 '*modifiant le Titre IX du Livre III du Code Civil*'. In this case the title is of very little help for understanding the scope or meaning of new legislation although it does enable the reader to zero in on the pre-modified text of legislation in force previously. The lack of a short title in French statutes is a practical drawback when considering that short titles are very convenient for citation purposes. To remedy this, French statutes are very often cited with reference to the Minister or Member of Parliament who initiated the bill, such as the famous *Loi Debré* (1959) on education or, *Loi Veil* (1975) on abortion or, *Loi Badinter* (1985) on road traffic accidents. Occasionally, in practice, the title of a statute is shortened such as the Loi of 2 February 1981 '*renforcant la sécurité et protégeant la liberté des personnes*' known as '*Loi sécurité et liberté*', the recent Loi of 15 November 1999 '*relative au pacte civile de solidarité*' simply called 'PACS' or, the Loi of 19 January 2000 '*relative à la réduction négociée du temps de travail*' commonly known as '*Loi sur les 35 heures*'.

Because the titles given to statutes are not, in principle, the object of a vote in Parliament, courts have decided that they do not have legal force although, on occasions, they can help to establish the general sense of a statute's content.

1.3.3 Preamble

A word should be said about the preamble. During the French Revolution, French statutes used to have a preamble explaining why they had been passed. In modern times French statutes no longer have a preamble. Today, however, draft bills are always introduced by a relatively lengthy explanatory memorandum called *exposé des motifs* which explains the reasons for and purpose of the legislation before it is discussed in Parliament. Once the statute is passed, the *exposé des motifs* no longer forms any part of the text of the statute. Instead, it becomes part of the *travaux préparatoires* (Chapter

3.3.2.1 below) and, as such, constitutes a valuable aid to interpretation. *Exposés des motifs* are further examined and discussed, together with an illustration, at Chapter 8.3.1 below.

1.3.4 Enacting formula

Next, as in English statutes, comes the enacting formula. These are introductory words which appear in every French statute stating that both houses of Parliament have passed the *loi* and that it has been promulgated by the President of the Republic. The form of words used may vary depending on whether or not both houses agreed on its adoption. In the first case the formula will be:

> '*L'Assemblée Nationale et le Sénat ont adopté*'

In the other case:

> '*L'Assemblée Nationale et le Sénat ont délibéré*' or
> '*L'Assemblée Nationale a adopté*'

Where the *loi* has been refered to the *Conseil Constitutionel* for scrutiny, the words:

> '*Vu la décision du Conseil Constitutionnel*', will be added.

Where the *loi* has been adopted by referendum, the formula is:

> '*Le Président de la République, conformément aux dispositions de l'article 11 de la Constitution, a soumis au référendum.*
>
> *Le Peuple français a adopté*'

For examples of the use of these different forms of wording, see Boxes 1.2 and 1.3.

No statute is law unless and until it is promulgated by the President of the Republic. Generally, the point at which the statute comes into effect is its publication in the *Journal Officiel*. However, a statute may state that it will come into effect at a later date.

1.3.5 Articles

French statutes are divided into articles, cited as 'article 1', 'article 2', etc.

When reading a statute, particular attention must be paid to the distinction between the actual articles of the newly enacted statute itself and the articles of the codes or previous statutes that the new statute modifies, which are confusingly also referred to as articles in the text, although bold characters in the former and open quotation mark italics in the latter are usually used to distinguish between the two (see, for example, in Box 1.2, article 2 of the Loi of 6 February 2001).

Articles are further subdivided into *alinéas*. *Alinéas* are indented paragraphs. However, sometimes, with a view to enhancing clarity, they may be cited I, II, III. When they are intended to introduce itemization, *alinéas* are sometimes, but not always,

Box 1.2 Layout and component parts of a statute: Example 1

LOIS

LOI n° 2001-111 du 6 février 2001 relative à l'adoption internationale (1)

NOR : *JUSX0004033L*

L'Assemblée nationale et le Sénat ont adopté,
Le Président de la République promulgue la loi dont la teneur suit :

Article 1ᵉʳ

Le titre VIII du livre Iᵉʳ du code civil est complété par un chapitre III intitulé : « Du conflit des lois relatives à la filiation adoptive et de l'effet en France des adoptions prononcées à l'étranger ».

Article 2

Dans le chapitre III du titre VIII du livre Iᵉʳ du code civil, sont insérés les articles 370-3 à 370-5 ainsi rédigés :

« *Art. 370-3.* – Les conditions de l'adoption sont soumises à la loi nationale de l'adoptant ou, en cas d'adoption par deux époux, par la loi qui régit les effets de leur union. L'adoption ne peut toutefois être prononcée si la loi nationale de l'un et l'autre époux la prohibe.

« L'adoption d'un mineur étranger ne peut être prononcée si sa loi personnelle prohibe cette institution, sauf si ce mineur est né et réside habituellement en France.

« Quelle que soit la loi applicable, l'adoption requiert le consentement du représentant légal de l'enfant. Le consentement doit être libre, obtenu sans aucune contrepartie, après la naissance de l'enfant et éclairé sur les conséquences de l'adoption, en particulier, s'il est donné en vue d'une adoption plénière, sur le caractère complet et irrévocable de la rupture du lien de filiation préexistant.

« *Art. 370-4.* – Les effets de l'adoption prononcée en France sont ceux de la loi française.

« *Art. 370-5.* – L'adoption régulièrement prononcée à l'étranger produit en France les effets de l'adoption plénière si elle rompt de manière complète et irrévocable le lien de filiation préexistant. A défaut, elle produit les effets de l'adoption simple. Elle peut être convertie en adoption plénière si les consentements requis ont été donnés expressément en connaissance de cause. »

Article 3

Les dispositions du deuxième alinéa de l'article 370-3 du code civil s'appliquent aux procédures engagées à compter de l'entrée en vigueur de la présente loi.

Article 4

Dans l'article 361 du code civil, après la référence : « 353-1, », est insérée la référence : « 353-2, ».

Article 5

Il est créé, auprès du Premier ministre, un Conseil supérieur de l'adoption.

Il est composé de parlementaires, de représentants de l'Etat, de représentants des conseils généraux, de magistrats, de représentants des organismes autorisés ou habilités pour l'adoption, de représentants des associations de familles adoptives, de personnes adoptées et de pupilles de l'Etat,
d'un représentant du service social d'aide aux émigrants, d'un représentant de la mission pour l'adoption internationale, ainsi que de personnalités qualifiées.

Il se réunit à la demande de son président, du garde des sceaux, ministre de la justice, du ministre chargé de la famille, du ministre des affaires étrangères ou de la majorité de ses membres, et au moins une fois par semestre.

Le Conseil supérieur de l'adoption émet des avis et formule toutes propositions utiles relatives à l'adoption, y compris l'adoption internationale. Il est consulté sur les mesures législatives et réglementaires prises en ce domaine.

Les modalités d'application du présent article sont fixées par décret.

Article 6

Le deuxième alinéa de l'article 56 de la loi n° 96-604 du 5 juillet 1996 relative à l'adoption est ainsi rédigé :

« L'autorité centrale pour l'adoption est composée de représentants de l'Etat et des conseils généraux ainsi que de représentants des organismes agréés pour l'adoption et des associations de familles adoptives, ces derniers ayant voix consultative. »

La présente loi sera exécutée comme loi de l'Etat.

Fait à Paris, le 6 février 2001.

JACQUES CHIRAC

Par le Président de la République :

Le Premier ministre,
LIONEL JOSPIN

La ministre de l'emploi et de la solidarité,
ÉLISABETH GUIGOU

La garde des sceaux, ministre de la justice,
MARYLISE LEBRANCHU

Le ministre de l'intérieur,
DANIEL VAILLANT

Le ministre des affaires étrangères,
HUBERT VÉDRINE

La ministre déléguée à la famille et à l'enfance,
SÉGOLÈNE ROYAL

---

(1) *Travaux préparatoires :* loi n° 2001-111.
Assemblée nationale :
  Proposition de loi n° 2217 ;
  Rapport de M. Jean-François Mattei, au nom de la commission des lois, n° 2265 ;
  Discussion et adoption le 28 mars 2000.
Sénat :
  Proposition de loi, adoptée par l'Assemblée nationale, n° 287 (1999-2000) ;
  Rapport de M. Nicolas About, au nom de la commission des lois, n° 164 (2000-2001) ;
  Discussion et adoption le 10 janvier 2001.
Assemblée nationale :
  Proposition de loi, modifiée par le Sénat, n° 2860 ;
  Rapport de M. Jean-François Mattei, au nom de la commission des lois, n° 2873 ;
  Discussion et adoption le 24 janvier 2001.

Source: Loi 2001-111 of 6 February 2001, JO 8 February 2001, p. 2136

Box 1.3 Layout and component parts of a statute: Example 2

LOIS

LOI n° 2000-493 du 6 juin 2000 tendant à favoriser l'égal accès des femmes et des hommes aux mandats électoraux et fonctions électives (1)

NOR : *INTX9900134L*

L'Assemblée nationale et le Sénat ont délibéré,

L'Assemblée nationale a adopté,

Vu la décision du Conseil constitutionnel n° 2000-429 DC en date du 30 mai 2000 ;

Le Président de la République promulgue la loi dont la teneur suit :

TITRE Iᵉʳ

DISPOSITIONS RELATIVES AUX ÉLECTIONS SE DÉROULANT AU SCRUTIN DE LISTE

Article 1ᵉʳ

[Dispositions déclarées non conformes à la Constitution par décision du Conseil constitutionnel n° 2000-429 DC du 30 mai 2000.]

Article 2

I. – Le premier alinéa de l'article L. 264 du même code est complété par deux phrases ainsi rédigées :

« Sur chacune des listes, l'écart entre le nombre des candidats de chaque sexe ne peut être supérieur à un. Au sein de chaque groupe entier de six candidats dans l'ordre de présentation de la liste doit figurer un nombre égal de candidats de chaque sexe. »

II. – Le quatrième alinéa (2°) de l'article L. 265 du même code est ainsi rédigé :

« 2° Les nom, prénoms, sexe, date et lieu de naissance, domicile et profession de chacun des candidats. »

Article 3

Le premier alinéa de l'article L. 300 du même code est complété par deux phrases ainsi rédigées :

« Sur chacune des listes, l'écart entre le nombre des candidats de chaque sexe ne peut être supérieur à un. Chaque liste est composée alternativement d'un candidat de chaque sexe. »

Article 4

[Dispositions déclarées non conformes à la Constitution par décision du Conseil constitutionnel n° 2000-429 DC du 30 mai 2000.]

Article 5

I. – Le premier alinéa de l'article L. 346 du code électoral est complété par deux phrases ainsi rédigées :

« Sur chacune des listes, l'écart entre le nombre des candidats de chaque sexe ne peut être supérieur à un. Au sein de chaque groupe entier de six candidats dans l'ordre de présentation de la liste doit figurer un nombre égal de candidats de chaque sexe. »

II. – L'avant-dernier alinéa (2°) de l'article L. 347 du même code est ainsi rédigé :

« 2° Les nom, prénoms, sexe, date et lieu de naissance, domicile et profession de chacun des candidats. »

Article 6

I. – Le premier alinéa de l'article L. 370 du même code est complété par deux phrases ainsi rédigées :

« Sur chacune des listes, l'écart entre le nombre des candidats de chaque sexe ne peut être supérieur à un. Au sein de chaque groupe entier de six candidats dans l'ordre de présentation de la liste doit figurer un nombre égal de candidats de chaque sexe. »

II. – Dans la dernière phrase du premier alinéa de l'article L. 372 du même code, après la référence : « L. 340, », est insérée la référence : « L. 347, ».

Article 7

L'article 9 de la loi n° 77-729 du 7 juillet 1977 relative à l'élection des représentants au Parlement européen est ainsi modifié :

1° Le premier alinéa est complété par deux phrases ainsi rédigées :

« Sur chacune des listes, l'écart entre le nombre des candidats de chaque sexe ne peut être supérieur à un. Chaque liste est composée alternativement d'un candidat de chaque sexe. » ;

2° Au début du deuxième alinéa, le mot : « Elle » est remplacé par les mots : « La déclaration de candidature » ;

3° Le cinquième alinéa (2°) est ainsi rédigé :

« 2° Les nom, prénoms, sexe, date et lieu de naissance, nationalité, domicile et profession de chacun des candidats. »

Article 8

I. – Le deuxième alinéa de l'article L. 331-2 du code électoral est complété par deux phrases ainsi rédigées :

« Sur chacune des listes, l'écart entre le nombre des candidats de chaque sexe ne peut être supérieur à un. Au sein de chaque groupe entier de six candidats dans l'ordre de présentation de la liste doit figurer un nombre égal de candidats de chaque sexe. »

II. – Le quatrième alinéa (2°) de l'article L. 332 du même code est ainsi rédigé :

« 2° Les nom, prénoms, sexe, date et lieu de naissance, domicile et profession de chacun des candidats. »

Article 9

[Dispositions déclarées non conformes à la Constitution par décision du Conseil constitutionnel n° 2000-429 DC du 30 mai 2000.]

Article 10

I. – Les articles *[Dispositions déclarées non conformes à la Constitution par décision du Conseil constitutionnel n° 2000-429 DC du 30 mai 2000]* 2 de la présente loi sont applicables en Nouvelle-Calédonie et à Mayotte.

II. – L'article 7 de la présente loi est applicable en Nouvelle-Calédonie, en Polynésie française, dans les îles Wallis et Futuna et à Mayotte.

Box 1.3 *Contd.*

Article 11

Le quatrième alinéa (1º) de l'article 7 de la loi nº 52-1175 du 21 octobre 1952 relative à la composition et à la formation de l'assemblée territoriale de la Polynésie française est ainsi rédigé :

« 1º Les nom, prénoms, sexe, date et lieu de naissance, domicile et profession des candidats ; ».

Article 12

Le deuxième alinéa (1º) de l'article 13-4 de la loi nº 61-814 du 29 juillet 1961 conférant aux îles Wallis et Futuna le statut de territoire d'outre-mer est ainsi rédigé :

« 1º Les nom, prénoms, sexe, date et lieu de naissance, domicile et profession des candidats ; ».

Article 13

Le troisième alinéa (2º) du II de l'article 14 de la loi nº 99-210 du 19 mars 1999 relative à la Nouvelle-Calédonie est ainsi rédigé :

« 2º Les nom, prénoms, sexe, date et lieu de naissance, domicile et profession de chaque candidat. »

TITRE II

DISPOSITIONS RELATIVES AUX DÉCLARATIONS DE CANDIDATURES

Article 14

I. – L'article L. 154 du code électoral est ainsi rédigé :

« *Art. L. 154.* – Les candidats sont tenus de faire une déclaration revêtue de leur signature, énonçant leurs nom, prénoms, sexe, date et lieu de naissance, domicile et profession. »

II. – Dans le premier alinéa de l'article L. 155 du même code, après le mot : « prénoms, », est inséré le mot : « sexe, ».

III. – Le premier alinéa de l'article L. 210-1 du même code est ainsi modifié :

1º Les mots : « , avant le premier tour, » sont remplacés par les mots : « , pour chaque tour de scrutin, » ;

2º Cet alinéa est complété par une phrase ainsi rédigée :

« Cette déclaration, revêtue de la signature du candidat, énonce les nom, prénoms, sexe, date et lieu de naissance, domicile et profession. »

IV. – L'article L. 298 du code électoral est ainsi rédigé :

« *Art. L. 298.* – Les candidats sont tenus de faire une déclaration revêtue de leur signature énonçant leurs nom, prénoms, sexe, date et lieu de naissance, domicile et profession. »

V. – Dans le premier alinéa de l'article L. 299 du même code, après le mot : « prénoms, », est inséré le mot : « sexe, ».

TITRE III

DISPOSITIONS RELATIVES AUX AIDES ATTRIBUÉES AUX PARTIS ET GROUPEMENTS POLITIQUES

Article 15

L'article 9-1 de la loi nº 88-227 du 11 mars 1988 relative à la transparence financière de la vie politique est ainsi rédigé :

« *Art. 9-1.* – Lorsque, pour un parti ou un groupement politique, l'écart entre le nombre de candidats de chaque sexe ayant déclaré se rattacher à ce parti ou groupement, lors du dernier renouvellement général de l'Assemblée nationale, conformément au deuxième alinéa de l'article 9,

dépasse 2 % du nombre total de ces candidats, le montant de la première fraction qui lui est attribué en application des articles 8 et 9 est diminué d'un pourcentage égal à la moitié de cet écart rapporté au nombre total de ces candidats.

« Cette diminution n'est pas applicable aux partis et groupements politiques ayant présenté des candidats exclusivement outre-mer lorsque l'écart entre le nombre de candidats de chaque sexe qui s'y sont rattachés n'est pas supérieur à un.

[Dispositions déclarées non conformes à la Constitution par décision du Conseil constitutionnel nº 2000-429 DC du 30 mai 2000.]

« Un rapport est présenté chaque année au Parlement *[Dispositions déclarées non conformes à la Constitution par décision du Conseil constitutionnel nº 2000-429 DC du 30 mai 2000]* sur les actions entreprises en faveur de la parité politique, et plus particulièrement les campagnes institutionnelles visant à promouvoir la parité et le développement de la citoyenneté. »

Article 16

Un rapport d'évaluation de la présente loi est présenté par le Gouvernement au Parlement en 2002, puis tous les trois ans. Il comprend également une étude détaillée de l'évolution de la féminisation des élections cantonales, des élections sénatoriales et municipales non concernées par la loi, des organes délibérants des structures intercommunales et des exécutifs locaux.

TITRE IV

DISPOSITIONS TRANSITOIRES

Article 17

I. – Les dispositions des articles 1er à 14 de la présente loi entreront en vigueur lors du prochain renouvellement intervenant à échéance normale des conseils et assemblées auxquels elles s'appliquent.

II. – Les dispositions de l'article 15 entreront en vigueur lors du prochain renouvellement de l'Assemblée nationale.

TITRE V

DISPOSITIONS DIVERSES

Article 18

[Dispositions déclarées non conformes à la Constitution par décision du Conseil constitutionnel nº 2000-429 DC du 30 mai 2000.]

Article 19

[Dispositions déclarées non conformes à la Constitution par décision du Conseil constitutionnel nº 2000-429 DC du 30 mai 2000.]

Article 20

[Dispositions déclarées non conformes à la Constitution par décision du Conseil constitutionnel nº 2000-429 DC du 30 mai 2000.]

La présente loi sera exécutée comme loi de l'Etat.

Fait à Paris, le 6 juin 2000.

JACQUES CHIRAC

Par le Président de la République :

Le Premier ministre,
LIONEL JOSPIN

La ministre de l'emploi et de la solidarité,
MARTINE AUBRY

Le ministre de l'intérieur,
JEAN-PIERRE CHEVÈNEMENT

Source: Loi 2000-493 of 6 June 2000, JO 7 June 2000, pp. 8560–8561

further divided into subparagraphs cited 1o, 2o, 3o. It is common practice in French statutes and codes to state one rule at a time in an article. If the rule needs to be qualified, then the general rule will first be stated, in unqualified form, before stating each qualification in *alinéas* or in separate succeeding articles. The same principle as in civil law applies to criminal law statutes where the prescribed penalty is stated in an article other than the one containing the prohibition. This style of drafting, going from the general to the particular, is typical and illustrates the deductive method applied by French lawyers at all levels.

1.3.6 Layout

In the majority of cases French statutes are merely divided up into articles, as in Box 1.2. However, in some statutes articles become, as in Box 1.3, the principal unit of subdivision following *titres,* (or sometimes, *chapitres*). In this latter case, consecutive articles dealing with the same point have a common heading, the common practice being to choose simple descriptive headings. Thus, statutes begin, though not always, with general clauses under the heading, *disposition générales*, before moving on to more specific provisions which are classified by subject matter under a heading such as *dispositions relatives à.* . . . Statutes usually end (as in Box 1.3) with *dispositions diverses et transitoires* which are the French equivalent of the miscellaneous and specific commencement provisions that are also to be found at the end of English statutes. The French format, which has also been adopted for EU legislative instruments, can be said to have the advantage of being clear, straightforward and easy to read and remember.

Chapter references

BECANE, J-C., and COUDERC, M., *La Loi* (*Collection Méthode du Droit*), Paris: Dalloz, 1994.

BERGERON, R., C., 'The Canada-Ukraine Drafting Programme', *Statute Law Review*, 2000, Vol. 21, pp. 1–11.

CARRÉ DE MALBERG, R., *La Loi, Expression de la Volonté Générale,* Paris: Sirey, 1931.

CLARENCE-SMITH, J., A., 'Legislative Drafting:English and Continental', *Statute Law Review*, pp. 14–22.

DALE, W., 'Statutory Reform: The Draftsman and the Judge', ICLQ, 1981, Vol. 30, pp. 141–164.

DUCAMIN, B., 'The Role of the Conseil d'Etat in Drafting Legislation', ICLQ, 1981, Vol. 30, pp. 882–901.

GUTMANN, D., 'L'Objectif de Simplification du Langage Legislatif', in *Les Mots de la Loi,* N. Molfessis editor, Paris: Economica, 1999, pp. 74–88.

MATHIEU, B., *La Loi,* (*Collection Connaissance du Droit*), Paris: Dalloz, 1996.

THORNTON, G., C., *Legislative Drafting,* 2nd edn, London: Butterworth, 1979.

2

Codification

C'est avec cette méthode que toutes les idées ont pu se simplifier, et être mises à la portée du peuple. C'est avec cette méthode que l'on a pu lui inspirer le plus profond attachement pour ses lois, et ne laisser dans son souvenir des lois anciennes, que la preuve de leur imperfection et de leurs abus. C'est surtout avec cette méthode que l'on a fait naître, chez les peuples civilisés, le désir de participer au même bonheur.

Bigot-Préameneu, *Recueil des Travaux préparatoires du Code Civil*, Fenet, Vol. 1, edn 1968, W-Germany: Otto Zeller Osnabrück.

French law, as with most civil law systems, is codified. There is to this day in France, dating back to the Napoleonic era, an unbroken tradition of codification. The famous *Code Civil* enacted under Napoleon in 1804 was to become a symbol of national identity and a model for other countries. It is still in force today having undergone, since its enactment, considerable reform. Although today's codes do not have the same prestige, they are still regarded as the primary source of law and they serve as essential day-to-day working instruments for French lawyers. In law schools as well, students are encouraged to become familiar, as early as possible, with the layout and component parts of the codes.

Finding the law can be greatly simplified if, instead of grappling with a mixture of legal texts, users are able to gain access to the whole of the law within a given area by consulting a single document. However, this should not mask the difficulties involved in using a code. Codes are numerous: it is anticipated that in the coming years there will be approximately 60 codes in France. Moreover, their areas very often overlap and they do not necessarily contain all of the law in a given field. Thus finding the law on a particular issue may still necessitate a certain degree of skill. Also, codes do not resemble one another; they vary in their form since they are required to fulfil different functions. This is not surprising in a country where codification of the law has stretched over a long period of time, the codes being a product of the political, historical and social circumstances existing at the time when they were drafted. The Napoleonic codes of the nineteenth century, forged in the conceptual method of legal thinking of the Enlightenment, take the form of systematic works, bringing together all the rules in a particular branch of law with the formulation of concepts and the use of logical classifications. At the time of their drafting, when France had just undergone a revolution, they were perceived as instruments with which political change and social reform could be introduced.

Today's codes do not serve the same function. They are aimed at clarifying, and making more accessible, law which has become more complex owing to the increasing number of statutes in particular areas. The most common current method of codification used is the restatement in one place of the law in a particular area which was previously to be found scattered in different documents. In 1989, the French government decided to make this type of codification official by setting up a *Commission Supérieure de Codification*. The Commission has undertaken an ambitious programme of codifying the whole of French Law. Since its creation, it has already introduced eight new codes and redesigned seven existing ones. These codes are the result of the work carried out by ministries involved in the task of producing a draft in their relevant area. It is clear that, today, codification is less an ideological enterprise than a technical exercise.

This chapter will introduce readers to the process and forms of codification in France today. In so doing, it will focus in particular upon the method and techniques used by the *Commission Supérieure de Codification*. However, in order to clarify the notion itself and to consider the difficulties it may give rise to, codification will first be addressed in a wider context. To this effect, we will be asking the following questions: What does codification mean? And, why do we codify?

2.1 What does codification mean?

Today, codification is present everywhere. It can be found not only in civil and common law systems, but also, in former socialist countries where, following the break with former political systems, a new impetus has been given to codification. The fact that codification is present in every kind of legal system, and in various forms, makes the task of defining this notion a difficult one. In fact, from earliest times, it has been used vaguely to describe the process leading to very different pieces of legislation ranging from mere compilations of legal texts to comprehensive and systematic statements of the law. Thus, the following have been included under the umbrella of codification:

(a) the collections of Roman imperial enactments of the third century A.D., such as, the famous Gregorian and Theodosian codes

(b) the vast compilation of Roman law achieved by Emperor Justinian during the sixth century A.D., known later as the *Corpus Juris Civilis*

(c) the exhaustive scientific kind of codification known to the Continent of Europe, for instance, the French, German or Swiss Civil Codes

(d) more modest enterprises such as the English consolidating statutes or the American Restatements.

There is, undoubtedly, a common underlying reason for all these types of codification and that is the restructuring of the rules of law as a coherent whole. But they differ greatly from one another in the sense that, not only have they come about at different times, but also they do not serve the same purposes and do not have the same form and scope as each other.

Adding to the difficulty in defining 'codification' is the fact that this word has been commonly used in a confusing way instead of the word 'code', as if the two terms were interchangeable. Although not totally separate, the two differ in their meaning. Codification, a concept which emerged during the legislative reform movement that took place in Europe during the eighteenth and nineteenth centuries, means a certain method of legislating and not merely the graphic expression of the written law that the term code suggests. Indeed, 'code' comes from the Latin *codex* which originally described a book made of parchment in which texts were written, replacing papyrus scrolls. Despite this difference of meaning and of origin between code and codification, the use of one term for another has persisted until today, leading to confusion between the instrument of a code and the method of codification. To illustrate this point, France has a *Code Administratif* although administrative law has never been codified overall. In fact, this so-called code is an unofficial collection of statutes and regulations relevant to administrative law and published by the private law publisher Dalloz. It may be contrasted with codes such as the *Code Civil* or the *Code Pénal* which are the end product of a true process of codification, a process which will be examined in more detail later in this chapter.

In attempting to define the notion of codification more precisely two distinct approaches may be adopted. The first one consists of drawing a sharp distinction between the civil law and the common law systems, pointing out a certain number of distinctive features that codification displays in the former, but not in the latter. The second approach looks at the functions codification fulfils and the variety of forms it takes, without reference to a particular type of legal system.

Each of these two approaches is now considered in turn.

2.1.1 The civil versus the common law approach to codification

This first approach consists of pointing out a certain number of features that are present in civil law codification, in contrast with the common law approach. It has been suggested that codification in the civil law sense is comprehensive, authoritative and systematic, characteristics which do not generally appear in the common law approach to codification.

As the German Professor Helmut Coing has put it (Stoljar: 16):

Codification, as we know it in civil law countries, must be comprehensive, which means that it must contain at least all rules and principles concerning one province of law, such as commercial law or penal law. Then it must be made with the purpose of unifying the law in a given province, ideally having in this province exclusive authority. From a technical point of view, codification must further be systematic, expressed in clear and technical terminology, lay down broad principles, and avoid casuistry.

In contrast, codification in common law systems is very often associated with consolidation which can only achieve the limited objective of bringing together in one statute what was previously to be found in many. It may also consist of the restatement in one place of pre-existing rules on a particular subject which needed to be clarified or simplified. Peter de Cruz (1995: 46) has highlighted the distinction between 'civil law codes' and 'common law codes':

In the civil law system a code is an authoritative, comprehensive and systematic collection of general clauses and legal principles divided into books or parts dealing in a logical fashion with the law relating thereto (. . .)
Confusingly, codes have been compiled in common law jurisdictions (. . . .) However the cardinal feature in a common law code is that it is based on pre-existing law (usually a combination of cases and statutes) and is neither designed nor intended to be formulations of all inclusive rules. In other words common law codes are generally enacted to consolidate the law on a particular area or to clarify an area of law which has become unsettled, obscure or confused.

This distinction between civil and common law systems when it comes to codification is further emphasised by Holland and Webb (1996: 9):

The assumption underlying a codified legal system is that it is possible to create a set of texts containing an authoritative statement of the law usually in the form of civil and criminal 'codes'. Although English lawyers also talk about 'codifying' legislation, the term is used to mean rather different things in common as opposed to civil law systems. In the common law, a codifying Act is primarily a tidying up operation (. . . .) The aim of tidying-up is one which codifying Acts share with the Continental codes. However, by contrast with the Continent, codification in England has been used as a limited means of imposing legislative coherence on a particularly problematic area of law (. . . .) What English codification has not done is to produce a complete restatement of the whole of, say, commercial or criminal law in a statutory form. Yet, it is precisely the latter approach that has been adopted in the majority of civilian systems.

If one looks at the traditional Continental codes, such as the French Civil Code or the German BGB, one might agree that these are indeed illustrations of codification intended to set out authoritatively the principles and rules of a given branch of law within a logical structure. These codes, which have been statutorily enacted, have the authority to bind the courts and claim to be comprehensive in their relevant area. In France, the Civil Code embodies in its 2,283 sections the major parts of private law, with the exclusion of commercial law which is governed by a separate code. Thus the Civil Code incorporates the law of persons, family law, succession, property law, contract law, including specific contracts such as the sale of goods, and tort law. Civil law codes are also able to provide a system, that is to say a unified approach to a body of law which implies an organic structure of interrelated norms. It is evident that such a system cannot emerge from rules which are fragmented or simply placed in juxtaposition to one another as is the case with the law which has not been codified. The systematic approach to law in a code is reflected not only in its overall presentation, which usually starts with a separate general part containing general principles intended to be used in a variety of situations, but also in the formulation of general clauses. In German law, the famous general clause in para. 242 BGB, which simply says that a debtor must perform his contract in good faith, has played an important role in allowing contract law to adapt to social and moral change. The same can be said of art. 6 of the French Civil Code which broadly states that contracts cannot be contrary to public policy and morality. Civil law codes such as the 1992 New Dutch Civil Code (NBW) and the 1994 New Civil Code of Quebec are evidence that comprehensive and systematic codification is still alive today and can be regarded as the natural product of the civil law tradition. The fact that this type of codification has flourished in civil law jurisdictions to a degree unknown to common law can in part be explained by the cast of mind of civil lawyers which, over the years, has been shaped by abstract concepts and doctrines (see Chapter 10.2.2 below).

It is arguable, however, that the features characterising civil law codification, as distinguished from common law ones, may be overstated. Firstly, experience shows that codification can never be truly comprehensive. In fact, it is unrealistic to expect that, within their field, codes should be completely self-contained. In most civil law systems, when particular branches have been codified, such as civil or criminal law, large areas still remain uncodified in the form of general unwritten principles, individual statutes, and court decisions. Secondly, consolidation and restatement of the law, as in common law systems, have, now, also become a common way of ordering and unifying the law, not only in France, but also in Germany, Italy and Spain (see Chapter 2.1.2 (b) and (c) below). Finally, like common lawyers, civil lawyers rely increasingly on generally unofficial compilations of statutes existing in a particular branch of law similar, for example, to the English Halsbury's Statutes (see Chapter 2.1.2.(a) below). Whether or not these compilations are the product of true codification is debatable, but from the point of view of comprehensiveness and accessibility they serve the same functions as proper codes.

As regards common law, comprehensive and systematic codification has not been alien to its thought and practice, as shown in the writings of Jeremy Bentham in England and the work on draft codes carried out by David Dudley Field in the United States. Furthermore, in some areas, attempts towards codification resemble the civil law method of codifying. As an example, reference has often been made to the American Uniform Commercial Code (UCC) which owes a lot to the European codes, especially in its scope, structure and style of drafting. Similarly, the Restatements of the American Law Institute have been said to be 'rather like the civil law codes in their systematic structure of abstractly formulated rules' (Zweigert and Kötz: 252). In England some Acts are real 'mini codes' in the civil law sense. For example, the Children Act 1989 brings together in a single volume, divided into various parts, all the relevant statute law with the introduction of new concepts and general principles as well as the provision of a consistent set of legal remedies available in all proceedings. In these respects it constitutes an equally elaborated type of codification similar to what current civil law codes are able to achieve.

In conclusion, what seems to distinguish civil and common law codification is that civilian systems have been able to codify successfully wide areas of law, such as civil, criminal or commercial law, a task that, owing to different historical and political circumstances, common law systems have never been able to accomplish.

2.1.2 Functional approach to codification

This approach focuses on the functions codification fulfils and the consequent forms it takes, without reference to the particular legal system.

As French Professor Tallon (1979) puts it: 'Codification may take various forms ranging from mere compilations to full-fledged codification. This diversity is perhaps the major feature of codification today'.

Four forms of codification have been identified:

(a) Compilations, designed to bring together existing legal texts, either in chronological order or by subject, without altering their form. They are usually collections of statutes, privately assembled, for the use of practitioners with a view to making the law more accessible. Their size may vary: they may cover the legislation currently in operation in a country, similar to Halsbury's Statutes in England, or they may deal with a specific branch of law, such as the French *Code Administratif*, published by Dalloz, or the commonly used *Schönfelder*'s collection of statutes in Germany, in which all the most important civil, criminal and procedural laws are to be found.

(b) Consolidation, which brings together into one statute what was previously contained in several. In England this procedure has been made official in the Consolidation of Enactments Act 1949. Consolidating legislation includes the Companies Act 1985. The aim of consolidating legislation is to simplify and clarify existing law scattered in different places, with the possibility, as provided in the 1949 Act, of corrections and minor improvements. Consolidation is widespread in other common law systems such as the United States and Canada. It is also a well established way of codifying the law in Italy where traditional codes coexist with consolidated texts called *Testi Unici*. The need to simplify its legislation and to make its institutions more transparent has also led the European Commission to promote a programme of consolidation which was elaborated by the 1992 European Council of Edinburgh. Consolidation has occurred in areas such as customs or agricultural matters where a multiplicity of amendments, not always coupled with repealing measures, have led to a tangle of legislative texts.

(c) Restatement of the law, whereby a given branch of law is set out in a single, coherent and comprehensive piece of legislation. This type of codification does not necessitate reconsideration of the relevant law with a view to reform although it may include some items of law reform. This enterprise of restating the law is not alien to the common law world as shown, for instance, by the Restatements of the American Law Institute or the English codifying statutes such as the Sale of Goods Act 1893, now 1979. The English Law Commission has also adopted this form of codification when working on a criminal law code for England and Wales. In civil law countries it has become, today, the most common form of codification. In France, it is known as *codification à droit constant* and will be discussed in more detail below.

(d) Codification-reform, which means a complete reconsideration of the law in a particular field with a view to its reform. According to this approach, codes represent a fresh start and a break with the past. This was the main form of codification in the nineteenth century. Today, this ambitious form of codification is of limited application, both in civil and common law systems where codification and law reform are generally perceived as different exercises. However, as will be examined later, codification does not hinder legislative reform and, as with ordinary statutes, codes can be amended.

This search for the meaning of codification has demonstrated that, although forms and purposes may differ, most societies have felt the need to codify their laws. This attraction to codification highlights the fact that it is perceived as a desirable way of 'making' the law. However, experience shows that successful codification is not always easy to achieve, as has been the case with the English Law Commission's attempts to codify the law, especially in the area of contract. Does this mean that the supposed merits of codification have been overrated? In order to answer this point it is first necessary to examine more closely the motives for codification.

2.2 **Why do we codify?**

Codification carries with it a certain number of advantages which have been identified primarily as accessibility/comprehensibility and consistency/certainty. These are considered in turn here. However, despite these recognised advantages considerable scepticism has been expressed about codification. This section also examines the objections raised against codification

2.2.1 Advantages of codification

2.2.1.1 Accessibility and comprehensibility

Access to and comprehension of the law are not merely technical issues. In any democratic society there should be an individual civil right of easy access to the law and to its meaning, so that ordinary citizens as well as jurors, lay magistrates, civil servants, judges and legal practitioners may have an equal opportunity to know what the law is. In a recent decision 99-421 DC, 16 December 1999, JO 22 December 1999, p. 19041, the *Conseil Constitutionnel*, in the context of codification, ascribed constitutional value to the objective of making the law more accessible and more intelligible. In this case, a bill, delegating to the government the power to enact by means of *ordonnance* nine codes drafted by the *Commission Supérieure de Codification*, was referred to the *Conseil* for scrutiny. The *Conseil* decided that the delegation by Parliament of its legislative authority was valid in as much as it enabled these codes to be enacted more rapidly without their enactment being unduly delayed by the ordinary procedures followed in Parliament when examining and debating a bill. In this respect, the *Conseil* further stressed that it was 'within the general interest' that codification of the law should be carried out rapidly, 'this being consistent with the 'constitutional objectives' of accessibility and comprehensibility of the law'. In the same vein, the Loi of 12 April 2000, art. 2, (JO 13 April 2001, p. 5646) on the rights enjoyed by citizens when dealing with administrative bodies, guarantees the right of unimpeded access to the law, stating that:

It is incumbent on the administrative bodies to ensure straightforward access to the rules they enact. Access to and publication of the law both constitute a mission of public service, responsibility for which rests with the relevant administrative bodies.

Accessibility and comprehensibility can both be reasonably achieved by codification in that codes provide users with a single, clear and agreed text. Indeed, using a code is more manageable than grappling with a multitude of texts, especially at a time of legislative proliferation. The law, or at least most of it, can be found in one single volume instead of in many statutes. Also, a code stands for clarity of layout and simplicity of style and language. A number of drafting techniques, such as the use of side-notes and cross-references, can be applied with the intention of facilitating the user's grasp of the content and meaning of the code's provisions (see Chapter 2.3 below). Finally, everyone has a common agreed text as a starting point which serves as the official and authoritative word of the State. From the point of view of constitutional principles this last aspect should enhance the relationship between the State and its citizens.

2.2.1.2 Consistency and certainty

The process of drafting a code involves making an inventory of all existing laws in a particular area with a view to rearranging them in a systematic way, eliminating inconsistencies and filling the gaps left by piecemeal legislation. Codification thus enhances consistency and certainty in the law.

A multiplicity of statutes inevitably leads to inconsistencies in terminology and in substance. Codification seeks to remove these by bringing together the statutes that exist in a particular field. By doing so contradictions and ambiguities can be more easily detected and then resolved, either by repeal or by rewriting when the drafting of the code takes place.

Codification also remedies the legal uncertainty arising out of a number of factors. A multiplicity of sources can create uncertainty when it comes to defining the scope of a particular area of law. Although codification can never be truly comprehensive, exclusive or exhaustive, it nevertheless contributes to setting the boundaries of a particular field and fills the gaps left by piecemeal legislation, making it easier for judges to find an answer to the legal issues raised in the cases before them. Also, it is sometimes difficult to know how rules on a particular point, coming from various sources, relate to each other. Codification may remedy this in that it arranges rules in an orderly and rational way. Moreover, in areas of intense legislative work uncertainty may simply come from the fact that it is unclear whether certain texts are still in force. In France, when it came to draft the *Code de l'Education*, the *Commission Supérieure de Codification* soon realised that a certain number of old texts had never been expressly repealed by the legislature and had been made obsolete by new legislation. The codification process enabled the Commission to update the law in this area by repealing these obsolete texts and restating the law accordingly.

It is in the domain of criminal justice that uncertainty is more likely to have undesirable effects. In this area, not only is uncertainty incompatible with the idea that law should be clearly stated in advance in order to give due notice and fair warning, but it also discourages the bringing of prosecutions and increases the number of submissions for 'no case to answer'.

2.2.2 Objections to codification

Against codification it has been generally argued that the current diversity of sources of law diminishes the significance of codified law. In the coming years, when an increasing amount of domestic legislation is likely to originate from the European Union, the effort put into national codification will be considerably less worthwhile. For many, the future lies instead in a return to a *jus commune*, notably through the development of uniform laws. Furthermore, a combination of state intervention, corporatism and technocracy leading, not only to constant changes in the law, but also to the development of detailed specialised legislation, have conflicted with the qualities of stability and brevity that have characterised codes until now. It has been suggested, in this light, that codification has become a 'romantic anachronism'.

More specifically, those against codification have put forward the following arguments. Codification:

(a) is not feasible

(b) leads to ossification of the law

(c) implies a relearning of the law.

2.2.2.1 Feasibility

It is true that codification is not an easy task. The work of preparing a code is time-consuming and involves a number of difficulties related, notably, to the large quantity of texts which need to be collected, selected and then translated into a logical format. In France, the use in the codification process of computer-based legal information systems has proven to be a positive development in tackling these difficulties. A codification programme, called *Magicode* (described in Catta and Tauziac, 1997) was successfully applied in the drafting of the 1996 *Code Général des Collectivités Territoriales* which lays down the rules relating to local government, and is currently being used for further codes. Dealing with a mass of material is not the only difficulty. Drafting a code implies that a consensus, as regards its layout and content, has been reached. Powerful bodies, such as the tax authorities and the Customs, may want to forcibly impose their views when it comes to drafting a code in their field. Also, once they are drafted, codes have to undergo a tortuous and complex parliamentary procedure. As an illustration of this, it took more than ten years of preparatory work in working committees and three years of parliamentary debate for the first four parts of the new French Criminal Code to be enacted in 1992 (see, however, what has been decided by the *Conseil Constitutionnel* regarding the procedure of enactment by *ordonnances* in decision 99-421 DC, 16 December 1999, cited in Chapter 2.2.1.1 above). Needless to say such a work cannot be successfully completed without strong political support and a commitment on the part of the State to provide the means whereby the codifiers may carry out their work.

2.2.2.2 Ossification of the law

It has been said that, because of its characteristics of permanence and stability, a code leads inevitably to ossification of the law. In one respect, this is not so much a drawback as a virtue. Indeed, codification acts as a brake upon Parliament's propensity to enact new rules. Furthermore, the ossification view is based on a number of misconceptions. Firstly, codes are not static. Permanence and stability do not prevent a code from being updated, nor do they prevent the process of textual amendment so long as the general framework of the code and the initial numbering is kept. The French Civil Code has gone through considerable updating and amendment since its enactment in 1804. These reforms have taken place particularly in the fields of family law, property law and company law. Recent reforms have included civil status and product liability. On each occasion the original numbering has been maintained. Where necessary, supplementary articles have been inserted, e.g. arts 1386–1 to 1386–18, which have been inserted between the original articles 1386 and 1387 in order to implement the Product Liability Directive 1985 of the Council of the European Communities. Secondly, codes are not rigid. They can be developed through judicial interpretation. Indeed, codification involves the legislative formulation of general rules with broad areas of application, which tends to facilitate an evolutive interpretation of the law. This will be examined more closely in Chapter 3.

2.2.2.3 Relearning of the law

Some authors have emphasised the intellectual labour it costs legal practitioners to adjust themselves to a sea change resulting from the enactment of a code. Amongst them H.R. Hahlo (1967: 253) has been the most critical:

Only one who has never worked with a code can believe that codification is nothing but a formal change, requiring no fundamental adjustments in approach and method. A code is not just a large statute, it is a different species of law, demanding different techniques, and these techniques have to be learnt by the legal profession. Even when a rule of common law is merely restated, the fact that it is now laid down in writing and forms part of a system of interrelated rules, affects its meaning and scope.

Suggesting that the scope and meaning of the Common law will be affected by codification is debatable. It is true that the Common law has been developed through a system of precedent which implies a particular process of reasoning from case to case. However, there is no reason why this should not be maintained once the law is codified. What codification brings to the process of law is a starting point. As has already been said, codes are not self-contained. Continental lawyers rely as much as their English counterparts on case law, and much of their time is devoted to case study. Moreover, even when case law has been translated into statutory text and incorporated within a code, this does not preclude the use of former relevant cases when interpreting the new codified provisions. Looked at overall, codification highlights the need for some general principles which, to use the words of the eminent German comparatist H. Kötz (1987: 6), 'help to organise legal thinking' and 'to allow the formation of clusters of similar cases'. These principles exist already in the common law and serve in the process of adjudication so that, according to Kötz, 'there is no major operational difference in the use of general principles whether they are put in a code or whether they are found in cases'. Kötz concludes that it is therefore 'difficult to see why the mere enactment of such principles would alter the balance of power between Parliament and the judges and thus violate basic tenet of British constitutional philosophy'.

Relearning the law seems a more valid argument when it implies that one has to become familiar with the way a code is laid out, its method and techniques of drafting as well as coping with the memorisation of new code references. Even for those accustomed to codes this may be a challenge, as suggested, with humour, by French Professor Gautier (Beignier: 107) when commenting upon the recent codification of the law on intellectual property:

Who has not recently met a practitioner in the field of intellectual property who has not taken months to work out that former art. 29 of the 1957 Act on Intellectual Property has now become art. 111-3 of the new code? Practically every month I meet one of my colleagues, lost amongst these barbaric numbers, forced to engage in mental acrobatics, whilst his memory is already saturated with large piles of legal documents.

Adjusting to codification techniques may be very demanding for lawyers in legal systems where the law is not codified. However, unless these lawyers are unwilling to add to their learning, this is not an impossible task. In any case, practitioners trying to work out what the law in France is, or law students involved in French legal studies, cannot avoid learning how to use a code. The following part of this chapter is an introduction to the structure and drafting techniques of French codes.

2.3 **Codification method and techniques in France**

As has already been said at the beginning of this chapter, codification in France has taken place in a series of stages. Over the years, alongside the Napoleonic codes intended to cover large areas such as civil or criminal law, have been added the more specialised codes introduced by the former 1948 *Commission de Codification*. To this Commission is owed a certain number of codes, such as the 1953 *Code de la Santé Publique*, and later on, the 1978 *Code de l'Organisation Judiciaire*. Codes introduced by the 1948 Commission did not require Parliament's approval although some of them were later ratified by the legislature. Since 1989 a number of new codes have been drafted by the *Commission Supérieure de Codification*; they include, for example, the *Code de la Consommation* and the *Code de la Propriété Intellectuelle*. Ideally, each code should be examined separately. Indeed, they are unique each in their own way in the sense that their content and structure depend as much on the method adopted at the time of their drafting as on the subject-matter they cover. However, lack of space makes the task impossible. Instead, this part of the chapter will focus on the characteristic features, in terms of structure and drafting techniques, present in most codes in France. The following and last part will then be devoted to the crucial role played by the 1989 Commission in the development of codification method and techniques.

2.3.1 **Structure**

As already stated, a code's strength lies in its clarity and accessibility. These concerns are particularly reflected in the structure of the codes. Codes are divided into books which in turn are subdivided into titles. The titles are divided into chapters which may in turn be subdivided into sections (but not all of them are). The chapters and sections are themselves further divided into articles. Codes generally consist of four to five books, usually beginning with a general part in which the general principles governing a particular branch of law are stated. In the choice of headings for books a pragmatic approach is taken. Instead of conceptual divisions, French codes rather opt for technical divisions which are easier to memorise. As an example, the 1996 *Code des Collectivités Territoriales* is divided as follows: book one '*Dispositions Générales*', book two '*Communes*', book three '*Départements*', book four '*Régions*' and book five '*Coopérations*'.

2.3.2 **Articles**

Articles are usually cited in an abbreviated form as 'art.'. They are divided into paragraphs each introduced by an *alinéa* (abbreviated: 'al.') which consists of an indented line at the beginning of each consecutive paragraph. When citing an article, it is very important to specify which *alinéa* is being referred to as usually each of them points to distinct grounds for action or distinct remedies. As an illustration, art. 1384 of the Civil Code is reproduced below (Box 2.1). It contains eight *alinéas*, each of

Box 2.1 Example of how articles are divided into *alinéas*

Pal. 1985. 2. Panor. 234, obs. Chabas. ◆ Mais admission du recours subrogatoire du gardien d'une chose inanimée contre le coauteur, sur le fondement de l'art. 1384, al. 1er, nonobstant le principe que seule la victime du dommage causé par une chose est recevable à invoquer le bénéfice de l'art. 1384, al. 1er. • Civ. 2e, 22 oct. 1975 : *JCP 1977. II. 18517, note Chabas et Saluden ; Gaz. Pal. 1976. 1. 192, note Plancqueel.* ◆ V. aussi notes 42 s. ss. art. 1384.

Art. 1384 On est responsable non seulement du dommage que l'on cause par son propre fait, mais encore de celui qui est causé par le fait des personnes dont on doit répondre, ou des choses que l'on a sous sa garde.

(*L. 7 nov. 1922*) « Toutefois, celui qui détient, à un titre quelconque, tout ou partie de l'immeuble ou des biens mobiliers dans lesquels un incendie a pris naissance ne sera responsable, vis-à-vis des tiers, des dommages causés par cet incendie que s'il est prouvé qu'il doit être attribué à sa faute ou à la faute des personnes dont il est responsable.

« Cette disposition ne s'applique pas aux rapports entre propriétaires et locataires, qui demeurent régis par les articles 1733 et 1734 du Code civil. »

(*L. n° 70-459 du 4 juin 1970*) « Le père et la mère, en tant qu'ils exercent le droit de garde, sont solidairement responsables du dommage causé par leurs enfants mineurs habitant avec eux. » – V. note infra.

Les maîtres et les commettants, du dommage causé par leurs domestiques et préposés dans les fonctions auxquelles ils les ont employés ;

Les instituteurs et les artisans, du dommage causé par leurs élèves et apprentis pendant le temps qu'ils sont sous leur surveillance.

(*L. 5 avr. 1937*) « La responsabilité ci-dessus a lieu, à moins que les père et mère et les artisans ne prouvent qu'ils n'ont pu empêcher le fait qui donne lieu à cette responsabilité.

« En ce qui concerne les instituteurs, les fautes, imprudences ou négligences invoquées contre eux comme ayant causé le fait dommageable, devront être prouvées, conformément au droit commun, par le demandeur, à l'instance. » – V. L. 5 avr. 1937, art. 2, infra (II. – Autres textes en matière de responsabilité civile).

Les père et mère du mineur émancipé ne sont pas responsables de plein droit, en leur seule qualité de père et de mère, du dommage que ce mineur pourra causer à autrui postérieurement à son émancipation (C. civ., art. 482).

RÉP. CIV. v^ls *Responsabilité du fait d'autrui*, par BÉNAC-SCHMIDT et LARROUMET ; *Responsabilité du fait des choses inanimées*, par BÉNAC-SCHMIDT et LARROUMET.

DALLOZ ACTION *Droit de la responsabilité 1998*, nos 899 à 948 (force majeure) ; nos 949 à 1029 (fait d'un tiers, fait de la victime) ; nos 3370 à 3386 (responsabilité du fait d'autrui) ; nos 3387 à 3411 (père et mère) ; nos 3431 à 3439 (artisans) ; nos 3440 à 3494 (maîtres et commettants) ; nos 3530 à 3568 (éducateurs) ; nos 3580 à 3690 (responsabilité du fait des choses).

BIBL. ▶ LAMBERT-FAIVRE, *RTD civ. 1998. 1* (éthique de la responsabilité). – MISTRETTA, *JCP 1998. I. 116* (responsabilité civile sportive).

I. RESPONSABILITÉ DU FAIT DES CHOSES

A. FAIT DE LA CHOSE

BIBL. Danjaume, *JCP 1996. I. 3895* (responsabilité du fait de l'information).

1° CHOSES VISÉES PAR L'ART. 1384, AL. 1er

1. La disposition de l'al. 1er de l'art. 1384 est d'une généralité absolue. Ce texte ne distingue pas les choses mobilières des choses immobiliè-res. • Req. 6 mars 1928 : *DP 1928. 1. 97, note Josserand.*

2. Exemples d'application de l'art. 1384, al. 1er, à des immeubles : • Civ. 2e, 12 mai 1966 (2 arrêts) : *D. 1966. 700, note Azard* (arbres) • 4 mars 1976 : *D. 1977. 95 ; JCP 1977. II. 18544 (3e esp.), note Mourgeon* • 15 nov. 1984 : *Gaz. Pal. 1985. 1. 296, note Chabas* (falaise) • 17 mai 1995 : *Bull. civ. II, n° 142* (falaise). ◆ Sur le cas de ruine d'un bâtiment, V. art. 1386.

3. Le principe de la responsabilité du fait des choses inanimées trouve son fondement dans la notion de garde, indépendamment du caractère

Source: Art. 1384 Civil Code, *Code Dalloz*, edn 2000, p. 1028

them referring to distinct categories of civil liability. Thus, for example, *alinéa* one starts with: '*On est responsable non seulement*' and refers to liability for things in one's care, whereas, *alinéa* five which states '*Les maîtres et les commettants*' refers to vicarious liability.

2.3.3 Numbering system

Articles are also arranged in numerical sequence with the use of either a consecutive numbering system, such as: arts 1, 2, 3, and so on of the Civil Code, or a decimal numbering system such as: art. 111-1 of the Criminal Code (on general principles governing criminal liability) which reads from right to left, article 1 of chapter 1 of title 1 of book 1, art. 421-4 of the same code (on terrorism) is article 4 of chapter 1 of title 2 of book 4. The decimal numbering system allows more flexibility when it comes to the insertion of additional articles. This is why it is used in codes which are subject to frequent amendment such as the *Code du Travail* (code of labour law) which, in fact, was the first code in France to adopt such a system. It is also the system that has been adopted by the *Commission Supérieure de Codification*. However, this system is difficult to memorise especially in complex areas of law where numbers can reach up to six digits! In this respect the consecutive numbering system is easier, apart from the fact that, when subjected to frequent amendment, it leads to a multiplicity of additions following the number of the article as shown by: arts. 235 ter GA bis, 235 ter ZA and 235 ter ZB of the *Code Général des Impôts*.

2.3.4 *Lois* and *règlements*

Most enacted codes in France consist of:

(a) a legislative part which codifies broad principles laid down in parliamentary statutes (*lois*), and where numbered provisions are generally preceded by the letter L, except in the Civil and the Criminal Codes, where the letter L does not apply;

(b) a more detailed part which embodies government decrees and regulations (*règlements*), where provisions are preceded by, either, R (decrees issued following advice given by the *Conseil d'Etat*), D (other decrees), or A (regulations called *arrêtés* issued by ministers).

Such a system, relying on two separate sets of provisions, is certainly complex, but it has been made necessary by the current 1958 Constitution, art. 37, which, as seen in the previous chapter, enables the government to enact separate legislation by way of regulations in areas which do not come under parliamentary jurisdiction. However, to facilitate accessibility, in the two respective related parts, headings and article numbers correspond. Thus, for example, art. R 226-1 of the Criminal Code is the regulation which corresponds to the legislative provision, art. 226-1. Both texts are inserted in book 2, title 2, chapter 6 of their respective parts dealing with offences against invasion of privacy. However, whereas art. 226-1 states broadly the list of offences and the penalties attached to them, art. R 226-1 gives more detail about the means by which these offences may be perpetrated.

2.3.5 Supplementary notes

Once enacted, codes are published in the *Journal Officiel*. However, this official publication is not used by practitioners, who usually opt for the unofficial publications of the codes. The reason for this is that, unlike the former, the latter contain notes and annotations intended to facilitate the user's grasp of the contents and meaning of the code's provisions. The unofficial publications which are most frequently used are the *Codes Dalloz*. They are available in book form or on CD-ROMs. They are brought up to date annually in the case of the most important codes, and periodically for the others. Articles are printed in their latest version with the date of the latest amendment to these articles in parenthesis. However, it is not stated which earlier provisions may have been repealed except in cases where articles repealed are still relevant to past situations (as, for example, in family law situations). In this case the article that has been repealed is italicised in order to distinguish it visually from the amended article. An illustration of this is art. 223 of the Civil Code (see Box 2.2).

The *Codes Dalloz* also contain, under each article, a digest of leading cases (in the code's index these are cited as J. followed by a number referring to the case citation in the digest. See the illustration in Chapter 2.3.6 below), as well as bibliographic references to academic writings (cited in bold characters under the text of the article as BIBL., followed by the reference). Case digest and bibliographic references are, however, not authoritative. They are only intended, as in art. 1165 of the Civil Code reproduced in Box 2.3 below, to provide a short cut to users wanting to get quick access to the relevant case law and academic writing.

Code provisions are also supplemented by statutes and decrees which have not been codified and which are relevant to the subject-matter. Such is the case with *Décret* 94-52 of 20 January 1994 on the procedure to be applied when wishing to change name (see Box 2.4).

2.3.6 Tables of contents and indexes

These are very helpful in assisting users in finding what they are looking for. At the end of each code, users will find:

(a) A table of contents.

(b) A chronological index listing the various statutes and decrees contained in the codes which are either in the form of articles or as supplementary laws.

(c) An alphabetical index involving the use of keywords. Once the right keyword has been identified it may be subdivided into different headings followed by a reference which is usually the number of the relevant provision and not the page number.

Box 2.2 Example of a revised article with (corresponding) repealed article: Art. 223

(L. nº 85-1372 du 23 déc. 1985, art. 3) « A l'égard du dépositaire, le déposant est toujours réputé, même après la dissolution du mariage, avoir la libre disposition des fonds et des titres en dépôt. » – *V. notes ss. art. 226, infra.*

Ancien art. 221, al. 2 *L'époux déposant est réputé, à l'égard du dépositaire, avoir la libre disposition des fonds et des titres en dépôt.*

BIBL. ▸ DAUCHY, *RTD com. 1986. 1.* – DUPUIS, D. 1988. *Chron. 39.* – D. MARTIN, D. 1989. *Chron. 135.* – RUBELLIN-DEVICHI, *RTD civ. 1985. 709.*

Art. 222 *(L. nº 65-570 du 13 juill. 1965)* Si l'un des époux se présente seul pour faire un acte d'administration, de jouissance ou de disposition sur un bien meuble qu'il détient individuellement, il est réputé, à l'égard des tiers de bonne foi, avoir le pouvoir de faire seul cet acte.

Cette disposition n'est pas applicable aux meubles meublants visés à l'article 215, alinéa 3, non plus qu'aux meubles corporels dont la nature fait présumer la propriété de l'autre conjoint conformément à l'article 1404.

BIBL. ▸ BRÉMOND, *Defrénois 1993. 465.* – SIMLER, *RTD civ. 1970. 478.*

Les propriétaires d'un immeuble avec lesquels une femme mariée a conclu un bail avec promesse d'achat, en versant une partie du prix, doivent être réputés avoir cru que cette femme avait bien le pouvoir de disposer des sommes d'argent qu'elle leur a remises et qu'elle détenait. • Lyon, 30 mai 1973 : *D. 1974. 264,* note Massip ; *JCP 1974. II. 17681,* note F. Boulanger ; *Gaz. Pal. 1974. 1. 34,* note D. Martin ; *RTD civ.* *1974. 397, obs. Nerson.* ♦ Viole l'art. 222 la cour d'appel qui ordonne la restitution d'un acompte versé par un époux agissant seul, sans rechercher si celui-ci n'était pas réputé avoir la libre disposition des fonds remis. • *Civ. 1ʳᵉ, 5 avr. 1993 : Bull. civ. I, nº 136 ; JCP éd. N 1993. II. 375,* note Henry ; *Defrénois 1993. 803, obs. Champenois.*

Art. 223 *(L. nº 85-1372 du 23 déc. 1985, art. 4)* Chaque époux peut librement exercer une profession, percevoir ses gains et salaires et en disposer après s'être acquitté des charges du mariage. – *V. notes ss. art. 226, infra.*

Ancien art. 223 (L. nº 65-570 du 13 juill. 1965) *La femme a le droit d'exercer une profession sans le consentement de son mari, et elle peut toujours, pour les besoins de cette profession, aliéner et obliger seule ses biens personnels en pleine propriété.*

BIBL. ▸ RUBELLIN-DEVICHI, *RTD civ. 1985. 721.* – SIMLER, *JCP 1989. I. 3398 ; JCP éd. N 1990. I. 258.*

1. Nature de biens communs des gains et salaires dans le régime de communauté. V. • *Civ. 1ʳᵉ, 8 févr. 1978 : Gaz. Pal. 1978. 2. 361,* note Viatte ; *JCP éd. N 1981. II. 114,* note Thuillier ; *RTD civ. 1979. 592, obs. Nerson et Rubellin-Devichi.* ♦ Sur la qualification des indemnités proches du salaire, V. note 4 ss. art. 1401. ♦ Sur la limitation des droits des créanciers concernant la saisie des gains et salaires des époux dans le régime de communauté : V. art. 1414 c. civ., réd. L. 23 déc. 1985.

2. Sur le sort des gains au Loto en régime de communauté, V. • TGI Créteil, 19 janv. 1988 : *D. 1989. 37,* note Champenois ; *JCP 1989. II. 21385,* note Simler.

3. Pouvoirs des époux : disposition à titre gratuit. L'art. 224 (ancien) donne à chaque époux le pouvoir de disposer librement de ses gains et salaires, sans qu'aucune distinction soit faite suivant le régime matrimonial adopté ou selon que la disposition a eu lieu à titre onéreux ou à titre gratuit. • Paris, 19 nov. 1974 : *D. 1975. 614, concl. Cabannes ; JCP 1976. II. 18412,* note Synvet. ♦ V. aussi • *Civ. 1ʳᵉ, 29 févr. 1984 : D. 1984. 601,* note D. Martin ; *JCP 1985. II. 20443,* note Le Guidec ; *Defrénois 1984. 1074, obs. Champenois* (libéralités consenties par le mari à une concubine). ♦ Cependant, des bons de caisse acquis avec des fonds provenant du salaire d'un des époux constituent des acquêts de communauté distincts des gains et salaires visés par l'art. 224 (ancien) ; ce texte ne leur étant pas applicable, l'art. 1422 c. civ. régit leur disposition à titre gratuit. • *Civ. 1ʳᵉ, 22 oct. 1980 : JCP 1982. II. 19757,* note Le Guidec ; *RTD civ. 1982. 132, obs. Nerson et Rubellin-Devichi.*

Source: Art. 223 Civil Code, *Code Dalloz*, edn 2000, p. 233

Box 2.3 Case digest and bibliographical references under code articles

Art. 1164 Lorsque dans un contrat on a exprimé un cas pour l'explication de l'obligation, on n'est pas censé avoir voulu par là restreindre l'étendue que l'engagement reçoit de droit aux cas non exprimés.

● SECTION VI DE L'EFFET DES CONVENTIONS À L'ÉGARD DES TIERS

Art. 1165 Les conventions n'ont d'effet qu'entre les parties contractantes ; elles ne nuisent point au tiers, et elles ne lui profitent que dans le cas prévu par l'article 1121.

RÉP. CIV. v° *Tiers*, par DECOTTIGNIES.

DALLOZ ACTION *Droit de la responsabilité 1998*, n°ˢ 298 à 309 (tiers au contrat).

BIBL. ▸ Distinction des parties et des tiers : AUBERT, *RTD civ. 1993. 263.* – GHESTIN, *JCP 1992. I. 3628* ; *RTD civ. 1994. 777.* – GUELFUCCI-THIBIERGE, *RTD civ. 1994. 275.* ▸ Étude de jurisprudence : MESTRE, *RTD civ. 1992. 90.* ▸ Prétendu principe de l'effet relatif des contrats : SAVATIER, *RTD civ. 1934. 525.* ▸ Relativité des actes juridiques : LESCOT, *JCP 1962. I. 1682.* ▸ Responsabilité dans les groupes de contrats : BOUBLI, *RD imm. 1992. 27.* – JAMIN, *D. 1991. Chron. 257.* – JOURDAIN, *D. 1992. Chron. 149* ; obs. *RTD civ. 1993. 131.* – LARROUMET, *JCP 1991. I. 3531.* ▸ Violation des droits contractuels d'autrui : STARCK, *JCP 1954. I. 1180.*

A. EFFET RELATIF DES CONTRATS

1. Groupes de contrats. Le sous-traitant n'étant pas contractuellement lié au maître de l'ouvrage, les juges ne peuvent décider que celui-ci ne dispose à l'encontre du sous-traitant que d'une action nécessairement contractuelle (violation de l'art. 1165). • Ass. plén. 12 juill. 1991, *Besse* : *Bull. civ. n° 5* ; *D. 1991. 549, note Ghestin* ; *D. 1991. Somm. 321, obs. Aubert* ; *JCP 1991. II. 21743, note Viney* ; *RTD civ. 1991. 750, obs. Jourdain* ; *ibid. 1992. 593, obs. Zenati* • Civ. 3ᵉ, 11 déc. 1991 : *Bull. civ. III, n° 319* • Civ. 1ʳᵉ, 23 juin 1992 : *ibid. I, n° 195* • 7 juill. 1992 : *ibid. I, n° 221* • Com. 4 mai 1993 : *ibid. IV, n° 173.* ◆ L'architecte n'étant pas lié contractuellement à l'entrepreneur, viole l'art. 1165 une cour d'appel qui énonce que l'action exercée par le premier contre le second a un fondement nécessairement contractuel, l'un et l'autre ayant participé à la réalisation d'une même opération immobilière, en exécution d'un groupe de contrats. • Civ. 1ʳᵉ, 16 févr. 1994 : *Bull. civ. I, n° 72* ; *Defrénois 1994. 798, obs. Delebecque.* ◆ Sur la question de la responsabilité dans les groupes de contrats, V. aussi, *supra*, Bibl.

2. La clause d'un acte de vente constatant la transmission à l'acquéreur du dépôt de garantie versé par le locataire n'est pas opposable à celui-ci, qui n'a pas été partie à l'acte de vente ; suite à la résiliation amiable du bail, l'ancien propriétaire doit donc être condamné à lui rembourser le dépôt de garantie. • Civ. 3ᵉ, 18 janv. 1983 : *Bull. civ. III, n° 14.* ◆ Également en ce sens que la restitution du dépôt de garantie pèse sur l'an-

cien propriétaire : • Douai, 6 févr. 1992 : *Bull. inf. C. cass. n° 352, 15 sept. 1992, n° 1494.* ◆ Celui qui était propriétaire d'un immeuble au moment où s'est produit le sinistre engageant sa responsabilité ne peut opposer à la victime un acte de vente postérieur, aux termes duquel l'acquéreur faisait son affaire personnelle de l'instance éventuelle. • Civ. 1ʳᵉ, 6 juin 1966 : *D. 1966. 481 (2ᵉ esp.), note Voulet.* ◆ Le bénéficiaire d'une stipulation pour autrui n'est pas fondé à se prévaloir de la clause compromissoire liant uniquement le stipulant au promettant. • Com. 4 juin 1985 : *Bull. civ. IV, n° 178* ; *RTD civ. 1986. 593, obs. Mestre.*

3. L'architecte, condamné *in solidum* avec l'entrepreneur à réparer le préjudice subi par le maître de l'ouvrage, ne saurait être admis à réclamer l'application d'une clause pénale existant dans un contrat conclu par l'entrepreneur et qui lui est étranger. • Civ. 3ᵉ, 13 nov. 1974 : *Gaz. Pal. 1975. 1. 210, note Plancqueel.*

4. Un architecte ne peut être condamné, sur le fondement de la responsabilité contractuelle de droit commun, à indemniser un syndicat de copropriétaires constitué après la construction de l'immeuble sans que les juges aient recherché l'existence d'un lien contractuel unissant l'architecte au syndicat. • Civ. 3ᵉ, 7 mai 1986 : *Bull. civ. III, n° 62* ; *RTD civ. 1987. 361, obs. Rémy.* ◆ Une société ayant accordé sa franchise à des commerçants qui ont été livrés par un fournisseur ne peut être condamnée à payer à ce dernier le prix des factures correspondantes qu'elle avait reçues sans protester, dès lors qu'elle n'a pas manifesté sa volonté de les régler. • Com. 3 juill. 1990 : *Bull. civ. IV, n° 201* ; *RTD civ. 1991.*

Source: Art. 1165 Civil Code, *Code Dalloz*, edn 2000, p. 869

The page number is provided in bold type only when the index refers to a statute or a decree which is not codified but which has been inserted into the code as a supplement to an article (such as below, in Box 2.4). For example, if one is looking for the law relating to the compensation of HIV blood-contaminated victims, the relevant keyword to look for in the *Dalloz* Civil Code index is 'SIDA' (AIDS); under 'SIDA' the following will be found (2000 edition):

SIDA
– Dignité de la personne humaine 16 (J. 29).
– Indemnisation publique, L.31 déc.1991, art. 47, **p. 1081**
– Responsabilité 1147 (J. 80); causalité 1382 (J. 39); préjudice 1382 (J. 9, 15, 89).
– Vie privée 9 (J. 38)

This means: on human rights issues see art. 16 of the Code and case citation no. 29; on State compensation see the Loi of 31 December 1991, art. 47, p. 1038 of this code; the question of HIV contamination victims is also addressed under art. 1147 of the Code in case citation no. 80; details regarding the question of causation as well as damages may be found under art. 1382 of the Code in case citations no. 39 (causation) and 9, 15, 89 (damages). Finally respect for the private life of AIDS sufferers is dealt with in case citation no. 38, under art. 9 of the Code.

2.3.7 Cross-references

One of the major difficulties with codes is that their contents are not always well defined. Codes very often overlap. This is due to the fact that various fields of law interfere with one another. For example, the law on public health may interfere with criminal law in matters of abortion or drug trafficking. In such cases the difficulty is resolved by incorporating in each code what seems to be its own relevant set of provisions with cross-references to the other code. However, when a particular provision originally contained in one code (called for this purpose, *code pilote*) needs to be included in another code (*code suiveur*), because its omission from the latter would be detrimental to the scope or the meaning of the relevant law, then, instead of a mere cross-reference, the whole provision of the 'leading' code, (*code pilote*), will be repeated in the 'following' code, (*code suiveur*). For example, the rules relating to latent defects in contract, found in the Civil Code, arts 1641 and seq., are also included in the *Code de la Consommation* because of their relevance to the domain of consumer protection. However, it is important to note that the provision concerned is only authoritative in the *code pilote* and is inserted only for information in the *code suiveur*. The technique of *code pilote* and *code suiveur* is a drafting technique which has been introduced by the *Commission Supérieure de Codification* and which is systematically applied by it when working on its codes. The drafting techniques used by the Commission will be outlined at the end of this chapter. First, however, we need to examine its role, composition and working method.

Box 2.4 Example of a non-codified *Décret*

Art. 61-1 (*L. n° 93-22 du 8 janv. 1993*) Tout intéressé peut faire opposition devant le Conseil d'État au décret portant changement de nom dans un délai de deux mois à compter de sa publication au *Journal officiel.*

Un décret portant changement de nom prend effet, s'il n'y a pas eu d'opposition, à l'expiration du délai pendant lequel l'opposition est recevable ou, dans le cas contraire, après le rejet de l'opposition. - *V. note ss. art. 61, supra.*

1. Jurisprudence antérieure à la loi du 8 janv. 1993. La rareté du nom sollicité n'est pas une condition suffisante pour établir le bien-fondé de l'opposition. • CE 14 janv. 1976 : *Rec. CE 39.* ♦ ... Pas plus que la notoriété de ce nom s'il est suffisamment répandu. • CE 20 janv. 1979 ; *Rec. CE 681* (préjudice non établi). ♦ V. aussi note 3 ss. art. 61. ♦ ... Ou encore le fait que ce nom contienne une particule nobiliaire. • CE 16 oct. 1981 : *Rec. CE 749.* ♦ Comp., admettant le bien-fondé de l'opposition lorsque le demandeur dispose d'un nom incluant une particule : • CE 9 juin 1978 : *Rec. CE 241* • 17 mai

1991 : *Rec. CE 196 ; Gaz. Pal. 1992. 1. Panor. adm. 11.*

2. Le garde des sceaux ne commet pas d'erreur manifeste d'appréciation en refusant d'autoriser une femme divorcée à prendre le nom de son mari dès lors qu'une telle mesure serait susceptible d'engendrer une confusion dommageable avec la famille de ce dernier. • CE 20 déc. 1993 : *Rec. CE 769.* ♦ Rejet de l'opposition, faute de preuve d'une confusion dommageable. • CE 6 avr. 1979 : *Rec. CE 738.*

Art. 61-2 (*L. n° 93-22 du 8 janv. 1993*) Le changement de nom s'étend de plein droit aux enfants du bénéficiaire lorsqu'ils ont moins de treize ans. - *V. note ss. art. 61, supra.*

Art. 61-3 (*L. n° 93-22 du 8 janv. 1993*) Tout changement de nom de l'enfant de plus de treize ans nécessite son consentement personnel lorsque ce changement ne résulte pas de l'établissement ou d'une modification d'un lien de filiation.

L'établissement ou la modification du lien de filiation n'emporte cependant le changement du patronyme des enfants majeurs que sous réserve de leur consentement. — *V. note ss. art. 61, supra.* - *V. NCPC, art. 1149-1 (Décr. n° 93-1091 du 16 sept. 1993).*

1. Pour une application anticipée de l'art. 61-3, V. • Versailles, 29 avr. 1993 : *D. 1993. Somm. 328,* obs. Granet-Lambrechts ; *Defrénois 1994. 327,* obs. Massip.

2. V. note 5 ss. art. 363.

Art. 61-4 (*L. n° 93-22 du 8 janv. 1993*) Mention des décisions de changement de prénoms et de nom est portée en marge des actes de l'état civil de l'intéressé et, le cas échéant, de ceux de son conjoint et de ses enfants.

Les dispositions des articles 100 et 101 sont applicables aux modifications de prénoms et de nom. - *V. note ss. art. 61, supra.*

V. Circ. 3 mars 1993 (*D. et ALD 1993. 290 ; JO 24 mars*).

Décret n° 94-52 du 20 janvier 1994, *relatif à la procédure de changement de nom.*
Art. 1er La demande de changement de nom est adressée au garde des sceaux, ministre de la justice.

2 A peine d'irrecevabilité, la demande expose les motifs sur lesquels elle se fonde, indique le nom sollicité et, lorsque plusieurs noms sont proposés, leur ordre de préférence ; elle est accompagnée des pièces suivantes :

1° La copie de l'acte de naissance du demandeur ;

2° Le cas échéant, la copie de l'acte de naissance des enfants du demandeur âgés de moins de treize ans et de ses autres enfants mineurs pour le compte desquels la demande est présentée ;

Box 2.4 *Contd.*

3° Le consentement personnel écrit des enfants mineurs du demandeur âgés de plus de treize ans ;

4° Pour chaque personne concernée, un certificat de nationalité française ou une fiche individuelle d'état civil et de nationalité française ou la copie de la manifestation de volonté d'acquérir la nationalité française ou de la déclaration d'acquisition de la nationalité française enregistrées par le juge d'instance ou du décret de naturalisation ;

5° Le bulletin n° 3 du casier judiciaire de la personne concernée si elle est majeure ;

6° Un exemplaire des journaux contenant les insertions prescrites à l'article 3 ;

7° Une fiche familiale d'état civil.

3 Préalablement à la demande, le requérant fait procéder à la publication au *Journal officiel* de la République française d'une insertion comportant son identité, son adresse et, le cas échéant, celles de ses enfants mineurs concernés et le ou les noms sollicités. S'il demeure en France, une publication est, en outre, effectuée dans un journal désigné pour les annonces légales de l'arrondissement où il réside.

4 Le garde des sceaux, ministre de la justice, instruit la demande. A cette fin, il peut demander au procureur de la République près le tribunal de grande instance du lieu de résidence de l'intéressé ou, si celui-ci demeure à l'étranger, à l'agent diplomatique ou consulaire territorialement compétent de procéder à une enquête. Il recueille, le cas échéant, l'avis du Conseil d'État.

5 L'autorisation ou le refus de changement de nom ne peut intervenir que deux mois après la date à laquelle il a été procédé à la publicité prévue à l'article 3.

6 Le refus de changement de nom est motivé. Il est notifié au demandeur par le garde des sceaux, ministre de la justice.

7 La mention prévue à l'article 61-4 du Code civil est portée en marge des actes de l'état civil des intéressés, soit d'office, soit à la demande du bénéficiaire du changement de nom, sur réquisition du procureur de la République de son lieu de naissance au vu d'une ampliation du décret autorisant le changement de nom et d'un certificat de non-opposition ou, le cas échéant, d'une copie certifiée conforme de la décision rejetant l'opposition.

8 ....

9 Les dispositions du 3° et du 4° du premier alinéa de l'article 2 et celles des articles 4 à 7 sont applicables aux demandes de changement de nom déposées avant l'entrée en vigueur du présent décret.

Les décisions portant changement de nom prises avant l'entrée en vigueur du présent décret restent soumises au délai d'opposition antérieurement applicable. – V. L. 11 *germinal an XI, art. 7, supra, ss. art. 57.*

10 Les dispositions des articles 1ᵉʳ à 7, 9 et 12 sont applicables dans les territoires d'outre-mer et dans la collectivité territoriale de Mayotte aux personnes régies par le statut civil de droit commun.

Pour l'application dans les territoires d'outre-mer et dans les collectivités territoriales de Mayotte et de Saint-Pierre-et-Miquelon des dispositions des articles 3 et 4 ci-dessus les mots : « du territoire » ou « de la collectivité » sont substitués aux mots : « de l'arrondissement » et les mots : « tribunal de première instance » sont substitués aux mots : « tribunal de grande instance ».

11 Les articles 9 et 10 du décret impérial du 8 janvier 1859 portant rétablissement du conseil du sceau des titres sont abrogés. Les autres articles de ce décret sont et demeurent abrogés.

12 Le présent décret entrera en vigueur le 1ᵉʳ février 1994.

Source: Décret 94-52 of 20 January 1994, *Code Dalloz*, edn 2000, pp. 148–149

2.4 The *Commission Supérieure de Codification*

The Commission was set up in 1989 with a view to simplifying and clarifying the law by way of codification.

2.4.1 Duties and functions of the Commission

These are set out in the Décret of 12 September 1989, art.1:

(a) to undertake a general programme of codification of the law of France

(b) to establish a method of codification, with the provision of guidelines

(c) to set up and co-ordinate working committees with responsibility for under-taking the preparation of draft codes; to provide these committees with appropriate assistance, notably by appointing a *rapporteur particulier* and, if necessary, a team of specialists

(d) to receive, examine, and then submit draft codes to the government.

At first glance there are some similarities between the 1989 Commission and the 1965 English Law Commission. Indeed, both bodies were set up, not as mere committees but as institutions with statutory existence, with a view to remedying the unsatisfactory state of the law, keeping it up to date, and making it accessible to those who are affected by it. Also, they are both advisory bodies in the sense that they are both limited to making proposals within their area of competence. However, under closer scrutiny there are significant differences between the two bodies. Although the 1965 Act refers to codification as one of the Law Commission's chief duties, the scope of its functions is much wider and concerns law reform as such. The French Commission's task is devoted wholly to restatement of the existing law in codes; law reform is not part of its agenda.

2.4.2 Composition of the Commission

The composition of the Commission reflects a strong association with the legislature, the executive and the judiciary (Box 2.5 shows the composition of the Commission). It is presided over by the Prime Minister which gives a certain authority to the institution and also reflects the will of the government to take part in the process of codification. The actual supervision of the work carried out by the Commission is entrusted to a *vice-président* appointed for four years by the Prime Minister from among the senior members of the *Conseil d'Etat*. The *vice-président* is assisted by a *rapporteur général* in his task of organising and following through the various stages of the process of codification. The Commission consists of 11 permanent members amongst whom are members of Parliament, high-ranking judges and senior government officials. There are also non-permanent members appointed for a fixed term

Box 2.5 The composition of the *Commission Supérieure de Codification*

Vice-Président : Guy BRAIBANT

Rapporteur général : Rémy SCHWARTZ

Rapporteurs généraux adjoints : Nicolas BONNAL – Luc MACHARD

Chargées de mission : Colette MÊME – Élisabeth CATTA

Secrétaire générale : Nicole GOUËFFIC

Secrétaire générale adjointe : Martine GUILLAUMOND

Secrétaire : Monique JEAN

■ *TITULAIRES*

M. Philippe SAUZAY
Conseiller d'État

M. Jean-Claude LAPLACE
Conseiller honoraire à la Cour de
cassation

M. Anne-Marie FROMENT-MEURICE
Conseillère maître à la Cour des
comptes

M. Alain VIDALIES
Député

M. Patrice GÉLARD
Sénateur

Mme Danielle RAINGEARD de la
BLÉTIÈRE
Directrice des affaires civiles et du
sceau

Mme Robert FINIELZ
Directeur des affaires criminelles et
des grâces

M. Gilbert SANTEL
Directeur général de l'administration
et de la fonction publique

M. Serge LASVIGNES
Directeur au secrétariat général du
Gouvernement

M. Jean-Paul BOLUFER
Directeur des Journaux officiels

M. Marc ABADIE
Directeur des affaires politiques,
administratives et financières de
l'outre-mer (DOM-TOM)

■ *SUPPLÉANTS*

M. Daniel CHABANOL
Conseiller d'État

M. Daniel TRICOT
Conseiller à la Cour de cassation

M. Jean-Yves BERTUCCI
Conseiller référendaire à la Cour des
comptes

M. Gérard GOUZES
Député

M. Henri de RICHEMONT
Sénateur

M. Olivier DOUVRELEUR
Sous-directeur

M. Jean-Baptiste CARPENTIER
Sous-directeur

M. Stéphane FRATACCI
Directeur adjoint au directeur général

M. Jacques ARRIGHI de CASANOVA
Maître des requêtes au Conseil d'Etat

M. Olivier GARNIER
Chef de service à la direction des
Journaux officiels

Mme Pascale COMPAGNIE
Bureau des affaires juridiques
(DOM-TOM)

who are drawn from the government departments, sections of the *Conseil d'Etat* and parliamentary commissions relevant to the field of the code under discussion. The presence of members of Parliament on the Commission is crucial as regards the successful anticipation of the issues which may well arise when it comes to parliamentary debate.

2.4.3 Working method of the Commission

Before the draft codes are examined by the Commission, they are prepared by ad hoc working committees consisting of members of the relevant ministries who may be assisted by distinguished academic lawyers. At the initial stage, after collecting and selecting the texts relevant to the area, these committees make proposals in respect of the content and layout of the code before submitting it to the Commission for its approval. At this stage, a *rapporteur particulier* liaises between the Commission and the committees. Once the content and layout have been examined and adopted by the Commission, the working committees will then start drafting the different parts of the code. The final draft will come before the Commission for approval. Once approved by the Commission, the draft is submitted to the Prime Minister. The code will then follow the procedure used for ordinary legislation, i.e. submission to the *Conseil d'Etat* for advice, followed by referral to Parliament for approval. The Commission publishes a yearly report commenting upon its activities over the past year.

2.4.4 Drafting techniques used by the Commission

These were updated in a Circular of the Prime Minister dated 30 May 1996, JO 5 June 1996, pp. 8263–8269. They can be summarised as follows:

(a) The method of codification used by the Commission is the restatement of existing law. This is described in French as *codification à droit constant* which, since the Loi of 12 April 2000, art. 3 (Law cited in Chapter 2.2.1.1 above), has become the current statutorily based method of codification in France. However, minor improvements such as the repeal of obsolete texts and bringing old provisions into line with the Constitution and with EU law are made on an informal basis by the members of the Commission.

(b) Only parliamentary statutes and regulations are codified. Thus, the following are not included:

(i)   case law

(ii)   customary law

(iii)   international law

(iv)   EU legislation.

The exclusion of international law and EU legislation from the codes is open to criticism. Indeed, it is increasingly the case that parties to a case rely as much on international/EU law as on domestic law. Therefore, it is legitimate to expect a similar degree of access for each of them. On occasions, however, the legislature introduces legislation designed to incorporate international or EU law into the relevant codes. This has occurred in 1998 with the incorporation of new arts 1386-1 to 1386-18 into the Civil Code in response to the European Product Liability Directive 1985 (see Chapter 2.2.2.2 above).

(c) The numbering system adopted by the Commission is the decimal numbering system for reasons stated at Chapter 2.3.3 above.

(d) The technique of *code pilote* and *code suiveur* (see Chapter 2.3.7 above) is generalised to all the codes drafted by the Commission.

Since its creation in 1989, the Commission has already codified some 500 statutes, comprising approximately 10,000 articles. Quick and easy access to codes has been facilitated by the creation of a special website *Legifrance*, www.legifrance.gouv.fr, where anyone can search for individual code provisions. In its codification programme for 1996–2000 the Commission anticipated the drafting of 22 new codes and the updating of 18 existing ones to take place in the next few years. However, the heavy legislative programme and pressure of time on the parliamentary timetable delayed the codification process and forced the government to resort to *ordonnances* in order to speed up the voting on a number of pending codes (see Chapter 2.2.1.1 above).

The Commission, with the active support of the government, has played a major role in reviving the process of codification over the last ten years. Its motto has become *nul n'est censé ignorer la loi*. This maxim is actually a proper rule of law, meaning that one cannot plead ignorance of the law as an excuse for its transgression. However, being formulated in ambiguous terms, this rule has often been misused as the right of citizens to know their rights and obligations. The Commission, as well as successive governments, have used it in this latter sense as a slogan in order to press the case for codification, and this says a lot about the significance attached to the process of codification in France today.

Chapter references

BEIGNIER, B., *La Codification*, Paris: Dalloz, 1996.

BRAIBANT, G., 'Utilités et Difficultés de la Codification', *Revue Droits*, 1996, Vol. 25, pp. 61–71.

CATTA, E., and TAUZIAC, V., 'L'utilisation de l'Outil Informatique', *Revue Francaise d'Administration Publique*, 1997, Vol. 82, pp. 271–283.

GAUDEMET, J., 'Codes, Collections, Compilations; les Lecons de l'Histoire', *Revue Droit*, 1996, Vol. 24, pp. 3–16.

GUY, S., 'Codifications et Consolidations Législatives à l'étranger', *Revue de Droit Public*, 1998, Vol. 3, pp. 861–890.

HAHLO, H. R., 'Here Lies the Common Law: Rest in Peace', *Modern Law Review*, 1967, Vol. 30, pp. 241–259.

HAHLO, H. R., 'Codifying the Common Law: Protracted Gestation', *Modern Law Review*, 1975, Vol. 38, pp. 23–30

KÖTZ, H., 'Taking Civil Codes less Seriously', *Modern Law Review*, 1997, Vol. 50, pp. 1–15.

OPPETIT, B., *Essai sur la Codification*, Paris: PUF, 1998.

STOLJAR, S. J., *Problems of Codification*, Canberra: Department of Law, Research School of Social Sciences, Australian National University, 1977.

TALLON, D., 'Codification and Consolidation at the Present Time', *Israel Law Review*, 1979, Vol. 14, pp. 1–12.

ZWEIGERT, K., and KÖTZ, H., *An Introduction to Comparative Law*, 3rd edn, Oxford: Clarendon Press, 1998, pp. 74–118.

3

Statutory interpretation

L'interprétation est la forme intellectuelle de la désobéissance.
       J., Carbonnier, *Droit Civil: Introduction*, 26th edn, Paris: PUF, 1999, p. 304, no. 158.

3.1 General considerations

The purpose of this chapter is to equip readers with a knowledge and understanding of the method and rules of statutory interpretation employed by French courts. Gaining familiarity with the French approach to statutory interpretation may be of particular interest, if not relevance, to foreign lawyers developing their skills and practice in a European context, especially in view of the dominant influence French law has had on the methods of statutory construction applied by the Community courts. This is particularly the case for English lawyers in view of the increased recognition given by English courts to the European Community law approach to interpretation when the need arises to apply Community legislation or to determine the meaning of domestic legislation implementing Community law.

English legal writers, when commentating on the English rules of statutory construction, have drawn attention to the shift away from the traditional canons of interpretation that have been operated in recent years by English courts in order to accommodate European Community membership. It has been suggested that there is a tendency towards convergence between the English and Continental law approaches to interpretation taking into account the path followed by English courts, long advocated by Lord Denning, to be more open and willing to adopt the broader purposive approach of Continental systems. Since the enactment of the Human Rights Act 1998, this approach has been pressed upon English judges who are now prepared to give a broader interpretation to legislation generally, not merely confining themselves to the words used by Parliament, so as to ensure consistency with human rights.

However, convergence between common and civil law systems in Europe, in particular between France and England, should not be overestimated. Despite having been brought closer, the respective methods of interpretation applied by each of the two systems still retain some inevitable characteristic features which are inextricably bound up with their respective approach to the formulation of legal rules, and, more generally, to their respective theory of legal sources. In particular, French judges have always found it appropriate to look at a legislative provision in a much wider context than their English counterparts have been willing to do. This is due in part to the fact that France has a codified system. The perceived necessity from the early days, when the codes were first established, of adapting them to rapid social transformation explains this divergence from the strict literal meaning of code provisions. Also, as described in Chapter 1, code provisions are drafted loosely and rely to a greater extent on general statements of principle rather than the more narrow and detailed legislative provisions to be found in the common law tradition. Drafting and interpretation being mutually interdependent, legal texts designed, as in France, in an open-textured manner will more likely carry within themselves the germ of further development, in the sense that the task of filling in the details of their provisions is being handed on to interpreters. In such a context, French judges have never felt they were under much pressure to be tied too closely to the wording of the statutory text and have never felt it wrong to accomplish what was necessary in order to fill the gaps, very often left there on purpose by the legislature. This accounts for the fairly liberal, mainly purposive, approach to interpretation traditionally adopted by French courts.

This approach is, as will be discussed below, one which seeks to give effect to the true spirit of legislation rather than to its letter and which is prepared to look at any extraneous material that has a bearing upon the background against which the legislation was enacted. However, it should not be assumed from the foregoing that French courts do not recognise the literal approach traditionally adopted by English courts. In fact, as will be examined, the literal approach will prevail in French law whenever the words of a statute are clear and unambiguous and address the point at issue. In the same vein, despite the emphasis placed on the spirit rather than on the letter of the law, the French approach to interpretation remains paradoxically very 'legalistic' in the sense that French courts hardly ever resolve issues of interpretation without recourse to legislative texts. Even where there are gaps in the law, French judges invariably manage, through the use of various techniques of logical deductive interpretation, to base their decision on one or more legislative texts. This approach, to a certain degree, is hardly surprising in a system which puts great emphasis, as seen in the previous chapters, on statutory and code provisions as sources of law. At the beginning of the twentieth century, legal theorist F. Gény (1919) fiercely criticised the systematic resort to legislative enactments in the French approach. According to him, this was the reflection of a true *fétichisme de la loi écrite et codifiée* symptomatic of French legal theory and practice. Gény advocated in its place an alternative approach to interpretation 'free' from constraint of the written law (see Chapter 3.2.4.3 below).

Since interpretation, in the legal context, is a form of reasoning, the subject-matter covered by this chapter inevitably overlaps with what will be said in Chapter 7 on judicial reasoning. In addition, the creation by the courts of a separate set of rules supplementing the codes through the process of interpretation, being as it is a question as much related to the judicial development of the law as to the operation of interpretation itself, has demanded that this issue be carried forward to the next chapter which deals with case law and judicial law-making.

Thus, the present chapter is broken down as follows. The first part examines the various methods used by French judges when interpreting legislation. The following part then looks at the aids to construction at their disposal. The final part is devoted to the authorities, other than the judiciary, that are authorised to interpret law in France. Indeed, although the chapter focuses mainly on judicial interpretation, mention ought to be made of the increasing role played by government departments in France in the application and interpretation of legislation.

3.2 Methods of interpretation

Nowhere, in French law, do we find any general authoritative statement concerning the law on interpreting statutes. Nor is there any form of legislation, similar to the Interpretation Acts known in some Common Law countries, intended to assist the draftsman or to guide the judge in matters of statutory interpretation. All we find in the Civil Code, arts 1156 and seq., are rules governing the interpretation of contracts. Apart from this, the general part of the new 1992 Penal Code contains an interpretation provision, art. 111-4, which sets out the principle of the restrictive construction of criminal statutes. The currently existing rules and techniques for the construction of statutes are thus the result of customary law, judicial practice and legal writing, and, apart from the above mentioned specific code provisions, can only be found in a random way among the mass of decisions that are, unfortunately, rarely explicit in this respect. Treatises and textbooks usually provide a more or less systematic and rational account of judicial practice in this area. Numerous papers, articles and important monographs have also addressed the subject and can provide an orderly account of the French rules of interpretation, although none of them can boast of being as widely used and celebrated as the English *Cross on Statutory Interpretation*. It is interesting to note, however, that French law schools regard statutory construction as part of the basic teaching of law students, and this from a very early stage in their studies. Indeed, interpretation of statutes forms part of the course '*Introduction au Droit*', which is one of the core subjects forming part of the first year syllabus in French law schools.

The French approach to statutory interpretation is usually expressed in the following three propositions and can actually be traced back as early as 1799 to Portalis's classical and visionary *Discours Préliminaire* when the famous draftsman of the Civil Code presented it to the *Conseil d'Etat*. These propositions are:

(a) *Quand la loi est claire, il faut la suivre.* Where the meaning of a statute is clear, it must be followed.

(b) *Quand elle est obscure, il faut en approfondir les dispositions pour en pénétrer l'esprit.* Where the language of a statute is obscure or ambiguous, one should construe it in accordance with its spirit rather than its letter in order to determine its legal meaning.

(c) *Si l'on manque de loi, il faut consulter l'usage ou l'équité.* Where there is a gap in the law, judges must resort to customary laws and equity when deciding a case.

Since the enactment of the Civil Code, these propositions, have been supplemented by alternative approaches such as the teleological and historical methods of interpretation that are examined in Chapter 3.2.4. This has resulted in a certain degree of flexibility in the practice of the courts which tend to favour a combination of these different methods rather than moving towards priority rules or strict canons of interpretation. In this respect, French legal writers regularly report on the difficulties they are faced with in their attempts to systematise the practice of the courts on interpretation. It is indeed difficult to find reasons in decisions by French courts which justify the choice of one approach rather than another for interpretation purposes or, more specifically, the reasoning as to why a particular provision has been interpreted restrictively rather than broadly, and vice versa.

Each of the propositions referred to above, which characterise the French approach to interpretation, must now be considered in turn. Following this, a subheading will be devoted to alternative existing methods of interpretation which are also in use in French courts.

3.2.1 *Quand la loi est claire, il faut la suivre*

If the meaning of a statute is plain and clear, then it must be followed without any recourse, here, to interpretation. This proposition is often expressed in its Latin form *interpretatio cessat in claris.* The courts have generally acknowledged this proposition in two complementary ways:

(a) by refusing to extend or to restrict the scope of a text which is clear and unambiguous, i.e. considering that what the legislature has not written the court must also not write

(b) by setting the plain meaning of a statute against the intention of the legislature, i.e. deciding, when there is conflict between the two, that the former should override the latter.

Both are illustrated below with landmark cases.

(i) In *Marchon* v *Epoux Fousset et autre* (1932) D.H. 1933, 2, a law of 9 June 1926 on commercial leases provided in art. 9 that a lessee whose tenancy had been renewed by his landlord could sell the leasehold interest in business premises to a third party provided that business activities had already taken place on those premises for a period of at least three years. Following such a sale, a landlord relied on the *travaux préparatoires* of the 1926 law to argue before the Court of Cassation that the three-year period specified by the law meant, in a case where the tenancy had been renewed, three years from the date of the renewal, not from the date of the original lease. The Court of Cassation dismissed the landlord's appeal, deciding that there was nothing in the wording of art. 9 to support his view, and that the meaning suggested by him would actually have the effect of narrowing the scope of art. 9. The Court also added that the search for the intention of the legislator through the *travaux prépara-toires*, although usually permitted when the text of a statute needed interpretation, was nevertheless forbidden where the wording of this statute was, as here, neither obscure nor ambiguous.

(ii) In *Dame Fournet* v *Chevalon* (1946), D. 1947, 90, a statute passed under the Vichy regime of 1940–41 stated that it was not possible for married couples to lodge a petition for divorce sooner than three years after the marriage took place. However, within this period, married couples could, under the terms of this statute, apply for a judgment granting judicial separation (*séparation de corps*). In 1946, after the war, legislation was introduced with a view to enabling spouses who had been unable to apply for a divorce under the previous 1941 legislation to have their judgment of *séparation de corps* automatically converted into a divorce judgment. The plaintiff argued that the new legislation did not apply to the judicial separation between her and her husband, the 1946 statute having been intended to apply only to those couples who, under the former one, were not entitled to lodge a divorce application, namely those not having yet been married for three years. In her case, she contended, an application for divorce instead of the judicial separation granted would have been possible under the 1941 statute as she had been married at that time for more than three years. The Riom Court of Appeal hearing the case did not agree with the plaintiff's view. Relying on the clear wording of the new 1946 statute, notably the use of such general terms as 'any judgment of *séparation de corps*', the Court held that the restriction suggested by the plaintiff was not permissible in this case, even though, as she rightly argued, the wording of the text was not consistent with what Parliament had intended when the new statute was introduced. In this case, judges were, once again, not prepared to depart from the clear wording of a statute in order to give effect to the intention of the legislator.

However, these solutions, based on a strict literal approach, have been qualified by the courts in a number of ways:

(i) In *Administration de l'enregistrement* v *Congrégation des Pères Augustins de l'Assomption*, (1898), S. 1899, 1, 193, a case concerning taxation matters, it had formerly been decided that applying the literal meaning of a tax statute expressed in clear terms did not necessarily mean that the interpreter had failed to give effect to the intention of the legislator. According to the Court of Cassation which heard the case, it was firstly towards the literal meaning of the relevant legislation that one should always have to look when seeking the original intention of the legislator. This solution was founded on the assumption that the words chosen by Parliament in a statute were clearly designed to reflect its intention in passing that statute.

(ii) In *Samedi Soir* v *Le Borgne*, (1952), JCP 1952, II, 7108, the court held that in circumstances where the application of the literal meaning was likely to result in an absurdity, the judge could look at the legislative intent and 'rectify' the legislative provision by means of interpretation. This principle had previously been applied, for the first time, in a famous railway case, *Bailly* v *Min. Publ.* (1930), D.H. 1930, 253. There, a decree dated 11 November 1917, on safety rules for railway and tramway passengers contained a provision, art. 78, which was drafted in French as follows:

Il est interdit aux voyageurs:
de monter ou de descendre ailleurs que dans les gares, stations, haltes ou aux arrêts à ce destiné et lorsque le train est complètement arrêté.
(it is forbidden to get on or to get off the train other than in railway stations and when the train is completely stopped).

The text, expressed in such terms, was badly drafted and when read meant in French exactly the opposite of what it was intended to mean, i.e., that passengers were forbidden to get on or get off a train before it had completely stopped. The defendant who had been prosecuted for jumping off a train before it had stopped used art. 78 in its literal meaning as a defence. The Court of Cassation, in a famous ruling, upheld the decision of the lower court to re-establish the intended meaning of art. 78 which had first resulted in the conviction of the defendant.

(iii) Sometimes, in order to keep up with social change, French courts have departed from the literal meaning of a statute, applying instead a meaning that was not originally intended by the legislator at the time when the statute was passed. In the more recent case of *Association des centres éducatifs du Limousin* v *Blieck*, (1991), D. 1991, 324, the full assembly of the Court of Cassation, in a landmark decision, held that a centre for handicapped people which had undertaken to look after a mentally handicapped person who had set fire to the plaintiff's property was to be held liable under article 1384 of the Civil Code for the damage caused by the action of this person. In this case the Court did not follow the appellant's view based on previous precedents that the relevant part of art. 1384, which provides that a person is responsible for the damage caused by the actions of others for whom he is answerable, was originally intended to be limited to the specific instances of liability detailed in the remainder of that article, i.e. parents, teachers and employers (see the text of art. 1384 at Chapter 2.3.2 above, Box 2.1). In this case, the appellant contended that a centre for mentally handicapped people did not fall under either of these categories. However, the Court of Cassation decided to depart from its previous case law based on a literal meaning of art. 1384 and to allow the injured party in this case to have an action in tort. The decision of the Court had the effect of establishing a general principle of liability for the damage caused by the action of others for whom a person is answerable, allowing thereby the application of art. 1384 to new situations that the legislator of 1804, when this text was drafted, could not have foreseen.

3.2.2 *Quand elle est obscure, il faut en approfondir les dispositions*

Where the language of a statute is ambiguous or obscure, leading to doubts about its meaning or to a conflict with other rules, judges have a duty to interpret and to search for what the legislature meant when enacting the text. This raises the question how is the intention of the legislator to be ascertained in such a case? The method used in French law to ascertain the legislative intention in ambiguous texts, is the exegetical method of interpretation. This approach is based on the assumption that any statute is an act of will and that the most rational method for interpreting this will is to investigate the legislator's intention at the time when the law was made. In this respect, there are a number of rules and techniques aiding interpretation. These are considered below under a separate heading with examples of specific applications by the courts (see Chapter 3.3).

The exegetical method has very often been confused with the literal method from which it differs significantly and must be distinguished. Both methods, it is true, are characterised by a rigid adherence to the text of a statute. However, whilst the literal approach holds that the judge should look exclusively at the words and grammar of the text of a statute in order to construe its meaning, the exegetical method looks beyond the words of the text in an attempt to determine the reasons for its enactment. *L'esprit l'emporte sur la lettre* could have been the motto for the *Ecole de l'Exégèse*, a school of thought which was at its height during the second half of the nineteenth century (see further at Chapter 9.1.3 below). It began to lose its influence at the beginning of the twentieth century, a time when the Napoleonic codes were felt to be showing their age due to the profound economic, social and political transformation through which French society was passing. These changes called for legal development, which could only be achieved, in a society still attached to the structure of the old codes, through a change in the method of code interpretation. This accounts for the decline of the exegetical method and the subsequent addition of new approaches to interpretation such as the historical and teleological methods of interpretation (see Chapter 3.2.4 above). Today, however, a time of important legislative activity, the exegetical method has again become a dominant method of statutory construction for newly enacted legislation, since there is less of a need to adapt new legislation to societal change.

3.2.3 *Si l'on manque de loi, il faut consulter l'usage ou l'équité.*

This proposition, according to which, where there is a gap in the law, the court may resort to other sources such as custom or equity, is of limited application in French law. This is particularly true of private law where codes are deemed to provide the primary source of law and the basis for court decisions, and where filling legislative gaps, without the support of any statutory text, would be seen as an encroachment on Parliament's authority. Before resorting to sources other than statutory law, when faced by situations not covered by existing rules, French courts would always, at a first stage, use techniques of logical interpretation (see Chapter 3.3.1 below) in order to extend the scope of existing rules to analogous situations arising before them. This task will usually be facilitated by the arsenal of code articles, which take the form of general statements of principles, and by the codes tendency to use general notions – known as *notions-cadres* – examples of which are *ordre public, bonnes moeurs* (art. 6, Civil Code), *bon père de famille* (art. 1728, Civil Code), *intérêt de la famille* (art. 1396, Civil Code), *exceptionnelle dureté* (in divorce law, art. 240 of the Civil Code) which are sufficiently elastic to accommodate any unforeseen situations that may arise.

Resorting to custom and equity is likely to remain the exception for two further reasons. Firstly, although local or professional custom plays a significant role in such areas as contract, property, commercial or labour law, it still remains a secondary source of French law, since most of these customary rules derive their authority from a relevant enabling statute and, thus, by their nature, do not take precedence over legislation. The second reason is concerned with the notion of equity. Equity in France has never been considered a proper source of law. French comparative scholar R. David (1972: 196) highlights this point in the following passage:

The word equity has a bad press in France; French lawyers immediately associate it with the idea of arbitrary action. 'God save us from the equity of the *parlements* [pre revolutionary courts]' is a formula that is often cited and continues to influence the thinking of lawyers and judges. Apart from the few exceptional cases where the legislator himself has referred to equity, a litigant has no chance of success if he simply argues the equity of his position before the judge. The French judge decides in law, not in equity.

It would be wrong, however, to assume from the above description that French judges never use considerations of equity, or never refer to equitable factors when deciding cases. Sometimes they do so because the law itself allows them to take considerations of equity into account. For example, in the law of contract, art. 1152 of the Civil Code allows the judge to modify a so-called 'penalty clause', whereby parties to a contract agree on a certain sum on account of damages that the defaulting party shall pay, when the agreed figure is either excessive or absurdly low. Also, under art. 1244-1 of the Civil Code, a court has absolute discretion to grant extended payment schedules to debtors in critical financial circumstances. Otherwise, recourse to equity occurs in situations where a strict application of the law would result in an unjust outcome. An illustration of this is the doctrine of the abuse of rights in property law in cases where owners, who in principle can exercise their rights freely, have been judged liable for using these rights maliciously with the sole intention of inflicting harm on another party. Also, in the context of contractual obligations, there is the doctrine of *enrichissement sans cause*. This doctrine, not being based on statute law, as is the case in German and Swiss law, is a pure creation of the courts. It allows a person to recover money paid, or the value of a benefit conferred, in circumstances where, in the absence of any contract, another person has been unjustly enriched. Since the landmark case of *Patureau* v *Boudier* (1892), D. P. 1892, 1, 596, this doctrine has been consistently applied by French courts. However, these instances of judges acting to redress injustice are exceptional, judges generally preferring to leave this matter to the legislator.

In recent years, with the creation of the *Médiateur de la République*, new grounds have been established for equity to be applied. The *Médiateur de la République* is the creation of a law dated 3 January 1973, which follows the Scandinavian institution of ombudsman (the *Médiateur* is further discussed in Chapter 5.3.3 below). The *Médiateur* is appointed by governmental decree for a period of six years. His main function consists of dealing with complaints from the general public in circumstances where it is alleged that there has been a *dysfonctionnement* or failure in the system of administrative justice (art. 1 of the 1973 Law). In this respect, he is empowered to issue recommendations to the administrative departments concerned with a view to arriving at an equitable solution for the case put to him (art. 9 al.1 of the 1973 Law). In enabling the *Médiateur* to propose solutions based on equity for the purpose of solving legal problems, the legislator implicitly recognises that the strict application of the rule of law sometimes leads to injustices which need to be remedied by the application of means other than the law itself. However, the *Médiateur's* recommendations are not 'proper' law decisions but merely suggestions, and are, therefore, not enforceable and cannot create a precedent. Furthermore, the *Médiateur*, in applying the principle of equity, must do so with moderation and caution. In this respect, successive *Médiateurs* have established and defined a set of necessary conditions which need to be met before proposing solutions based on the principle of equity. These conditions can be summarised as follows:

(a) the *Médiateur* must ensure that harm has been suffered to an exceptional gravity by the claimant

(b) the solution proposed can be financially shouldered by the administrative body concerned

(c) due vigilance must be paid to avoidance of any infringement of the rights of third parties.

Finally, also related to the notion of equity are *principes généraux de droit* (general principles of law). These principles have also been widely used by judges in French law to fill any gaps found in existing legislation which, if left unfilled would have led to injustice. *Principes généraux* are authoritative rules of law, not laid down in any text, but which have been established and applied by the courts and are binding upon them. They have their origin in the spirit as well as in the legal and constitutional traditions of the French legal system. *Principes généraux de droit* are of paramount importance in administrative law where there has never been a general code similar to the Civil Code in private law to provide support for judicial decisions. In this area they have become an independent source of law and have been mainly used as a means of ensuring protection of the individual rights of the citizen. Among the principles identified and enforced by the administrative courts are such broad principles as that of the equality of citizens before the law, as well as more specific principles such as the principle of *publicité des débats judiciaires* according to which private law cases must be heard in open court (*Dame David* (1974), D. 1975, 369). More recently the principles of *indisponibilité du corps humain* and *indisponibilité de l'état des personnes* (the principles that the human body and one's personal status are outside the scope of any transactions or other agreements) have been used by both administrative and private courts to invalidate contracts dealing with surrogate motherhood.

3.2.4 Other methods of interpretation

In addition to the literal and exegetical approaches described above there are two further options available to courts: the teleological and the historical methods. They are each in turn briefly considered here. A separate subheading outlines Gény's proposed method of interpretation, mentioned earlier (Chapter 3.1 above). Although this method has never formally been acknowledged by the courts, it has, and still retains, significance in legal scholarship.

3.2.4.1 Teleological method

Also known in France as *méthode du but social*, it is a method whereby the court seeks to identify the social purpose or objective of the legislation under consideration with a view to applying it in a way which does not conflict with this purpose. The use of the teleological approach in French law has to be considered within the broader framework of the purposive approach generally adopted by the courts. Thus identification of the objective or purpose of a text is carried out at the same time as the search for the legislative intent by consulting the *travaux préparatoires* (see Chapter 3.3.2.1 below) or sometimes, more simply, by looking at the title of the statute itself (see Chapter 1.3.2 above).

In France the name of L. Josserand is most commonly associated with teleological interpretation. In the first of his two famous essays on legal teleology, entitled *De l'Esprit des Droits et de leur Relativité*, Paris: Dalloz, 1927, Josserand argued that all rights have a social purpose, the main reason being that they arise themselves from rules of law which are, by their essence, rules of a social nature. Accordingly, rights following this view must be exercised in accordance with their social purpose and, if they are not, their exercise becomes antisocial and by extension unlawful. According to Josserand, the social purpose attached to rights explain why they are only 'relative', and this extends even to rights which have been described by the legislature as 'absolute rights', such as the right of ownership. Thus, in circumstances where a particular owner has been exercising his right in a way which adversely affects the general interest of the community, it degenerates into the reprehensible 'abuse of right of ownership' mentioned earlier (see Chapter 3.2.3 above).

Today, the teleological method is widely used by the *Conseil Constitutionnel* when interpreting statutes submitted for its scrutiny. The *Conseil* has identified a number of so-called 'objectives of constitutional value' as means of implementing constitutional principles and rights. For example, in its Decision 89-1138 of 6 March 1990, Rec. 52, the *Conseil*, acting in its capacity as supervisor of the election process, referred to the objective of 'pluralism in the expression of thought and opinion' in interpreting the 1986 legislation on the exercise of freedom of expression in the media during election campaigns. In a recent decision (cited in Chapter 2.2.1.1 above) the *Conseil* has ascribed constitutional value to the objective of 'accessibility' in the context of codification. It should also be noted that the teleological method has also become a favoured method of Community courts when interpreting Treaties and Community legislation.

3.2.4.2 The historical method of interpretation

Sometimes called *méthode évolutive*, it differs from the exegetical method in that, instead of construing a statute in the historical light of the legislative intention at the time when it was passed, seeks rather to establish an interpretation based on what would probably be the intention of Parliament if it passed the same text today. The historical method rests on the assumption that interpretation should reflect changing times. It has been used to adapt to modern times provisions of the Civil Code relating to the law of torts, especially art. 1384 al.1 dealing with liability for things in one's care. In 1804, the date of enactment of the Civil Code, this text was designed to deal only with things included in the body of the article itself, i.e. animals and dangerous buildings. However, with time, French courts have extended it to other things, notably machines and cars, when faced with developing circumstances of industrial and road traffic accidents at the turn of the twentieth century (on 1384 al.1 see Chapter 4.3.2.1 below).

3.2.4.3 The *Libre Recherche Scientifique*

In his authoritative work on legal sources and methods of interpretation, Gény (1919) advocates a 'free' but nonetheless 'scientific' approach to statutory construction which allows the interpreter to depart from the text of the statute or code when its letter fails to furnish the rule. Gény takes the view that the exegetical method is flawed. In those situations which are clearly not covered by the statute being interpreted – or by any other statute – he considers it unreasonable, if not indeed a fiction, to attempt to ascertain the intention of the legislator or to resort to a legislative text whose scope would have to be stretched to its maximum in order for it to be applied to the circumstances. What Gény implies here is that most of the time the mere citation of a statute or of a code provision as a basis for the court decision is a cover-up for judicial creation. Gény calls for an end to what he considers to be the cult of the written law in the French legal system and advises judges to depart from code and statutory provisions when appropriate and thereby engage in a 'free search' (*libre recherche*) for other sources capable of providing a solution to the case before them. This method, as proposed by Gény, is 'free' but not arbitrary. Indeed, his view is that courts should not adopt a subjective approach to interpretation. Instead, there is an obligation to give consideration to a universe of equity, reason, customary rules or, more generally, social considerations. In this sense of a defined universe as the field of operation for interpretation, Geny's system may be said to constitute the basis for a scientific method. Moreover, Gény does not completely reject formal sources from the operation of interpretation. According to him, the code should always furnish the primary rule; it is only where there is no rule available for the circumstances in the code that the judge, in his view, should feel free to depart from it. In this respect, Gény's approach has very often been categorised by quoting Ihering's famous dictum expressed in French as: '*Par le Code Civil, mais au-delà du Code Civil*' ('by the civil code, but beyond it'). Gény's *Libre Recherche Scientifique* has never had the open support of French judges and French jurists, the purported reason being that it runs counter to the traditional and official theory of legal sources which does not openly acknowledge the creative role of the courts and implicitly assumes that judges are neither able nor willing to resolve cases without assistance from legislative texts.

3.3 Aids to construction

3.3.1 Internal aids to construction

In the context of the French legal system these aids are mainly derived from the use of logic. In this respect, French law professors Aubry and Rau (1964: 311) draw a useful distinction between the grammatical interpretation of a text, considered by the interpreter, and its logical interpretation. Whilst the former helps to determine the meaning of a text by examining the vocabulary used and the grammatical structure, the latter looks at the text in relation not only to other statutes on a similar or related subject, but also to the entire body of rules existing in a given area of law. Logical interpretation proceeds from the postulate that there must be coherence and consistency between the rules of a system of law. Therefore, where there is a choice between several meanings for a statute, or where statutes are inconsistent with each other, resolution of these conflicts can be aided by examining these statutes against the wider background of other legal texts forming part of the legal system. The application of logic to legal problem solving also enables the interpreter to extend statutory provisions to areas which have not been specifically addressed, either by the text under consideration or by any other legislation. More specifically, through logical analysis the interpreter is able to deduce, from the explicit solutions given by the texts of a code or statute, the implicit solutions which are also necessarily contained within it and, by extension, can help to solve the question at issue which, as yet, has not been provided for. Such a process, of necessity demands firstly that the *ratio legis* of the text under consideration, the reasons why it has been enacted, are determined. This *ratio legis*, once determined, will then suggest an extensive or restrictive application of the rule contained in the text to the situation at hand. Various forms of logical reasoning have been developed by the courts in support of logical analysis. The most commonly used by French judges are the reasoning *a pari*, *a fortiori*, or *a contrario*. Reasoning *a pari* refers to the use of reasoning by analogy. It consists of applying a rule of law set out in a text to an unforeseen situation where the reasons which have led the legislator to adopt this rule apply with the same force to the situation under consideration and which has not been expressly provided for (*ubi eadem ratio, ibi idem jus*). A judge will employ a form of reasoning *a fortiori* where the reasons why a statute was enacted apply with greater force in the situation currently under examination. Finally, reasoning *a contrario* means that where a text expressly provides for a particular situation, it is assumed to have ruled out the opposite one (*Qui dicit de uno, de altero negat*). *Dame B. v M. and V.* (1976), D. 1976, 593, provides a suitable illustration for reasoning *a contrario* in the context of disputed parentage of a child. Here, a child whose father and mother were married to each other at the time of his conception, but divorced soon after his birth, had been subsequently registered by his mother's former lover who now claimed to be his actual biological father. The question at issue was whether or not this registration was admissible. Under the relevant provision, art. 334-9 of the Civil Code, where a child has already been registered at birth as the legitimate child of a man, this status being corroborated by circumstances showing that the child is treated and considered as such, any subsequent registration by another man is inadmissible (see below the French text of 334-9). The child's mother argued that, in this case, the child's birth certificate already mentioned the name of her then husband as the legal father of the child and this circumstance should be sufficient, under 334-9, to make inadmissible any subsequent registration of the child by another man claiming to be his father. However, the Court of Cassation, interpreting *a contrario* art. 334-9, ruled that, whereas subsequent registration is inadmissible in the case where the mention of the legal father's name already appears on the birth certificate and is corroborated by circumstances showing that the child is treated and considered as his, *a contrario*, subsequent registration is admissible where the inclusion of the name of this legal father in the birth certificate is not corroborated by such circumstances. The fact, in this case, that the legal father of the child, whose name appeared on the birth certificate, did not keep in contact with him following divorce from the mother had the effect, according to the Court of Cassation interpretation *a contrario* of 334-9, of validating the subsequent registration by the mother's former lover.

Art. 334-9: Toute reconnaissance est nulle, toute demande en recherche est irrecevable, quand l'enfant a une filiation légitime déjà établie par la possession d'état.

3.3.2 External aids to construction

Here the use of *travaux préparatoires* should be highlighted, in view of the predominant place they have in the French approach to interpretation.

3.3.2.1 *Travaux préparatoires*

Where a judge is unable to determine the meaning of a statute from the words used (as at Chapter 3.2.1 above) or, from logical interpretation (as at Chapter 3.3.1 above), then the original intention of Parliament may be sought from the legislative history of the particular statute, by consulting the *travaux préparatoires*. *Travaux préparatoires* include draft bills, statements made by the minister or other promoter of a bill (*exposés des motifs*), reports made by official parliamentary committees, amendments which were proposed and discussed and, finally, the parliamentary debates. Amendments proposed are of particular significance when it comes to ascertaining the original intention of Parliament, especially when these amendments have not been included in the text finally adopted. Indeed, where this is the case, it can be assumed that the view held by the proponent of the amendment has been rejected by the legislator and should therefore be ruled out when seeking the intention of Parliament. *Travaux préparatoires* are reported in the *Journal Officiel de la République Française-Débats Parlementaires*, a special publication of the *Journal Officiel*. They also appear as footnotes, for easy reference, under the actual published text of the statute in the *Journal Officiel-Lois et Décrets* (see Chapter 1.1.4 (d) above) as in Box 1.2 in Chapter 1. The *Journal Officiel* (*Lois et Décrets* and *Débats Parlementaires*) is available in most law schools and law court libraries, and thus makes parliamentary materials readily accessible to scholars, practitioners and judges. Students are also encouraged to look at them when assessing newly enacted legislation.

However, the use made in France of *travaux préparatoires* should not be overstated. Firstly, as has already been said, judges are not allowed to rely on *travaux préparatoires* where a text is clear (see Chapter 3.2.1 above). Secondly, recourse to parliamentary materials is only justified for newly enacted legislation and is of limited assistance in the case of older statutes where changing circumstances and the need for adaptation make knowledge of the intention of the legislator in its original context irrelevant. As shown earlier, French judges show no hesitation in adapting older statutes by using methods of interpretation that do not involve the use of *travaux préparatoires*, enabling them to take changing times into account. Thirdly, even where the words of a statute are obscure or ambiguous one may question whether *travaux préparatoires* are really of assistance in throwing light on the question of the meaning of a text. In England, this question was, the subject of controversy, especially amongst judges, prior to *Pepper v Hart*, [1993] A.C. 593, which eventually allowed the use of *travaux préparatoires* in court. The admissibility of *travaux préparatoires* in court was also once challenged in France, especially by H. Capitant (1934), in his celebrated essay on statutory construction where the author questioned the reliability of such documents, using arguments which will sound familiar to Common lawyers. According to Capitant, the main objection to the use of parliamentary materials as aids to the interpretation of a statute is that they tend to promote confusion rather than clarity. They mainly consist of a series of what are often contradictory statements of view generally given by unskilled members of Parliament, thereby resulting in more confusion than the actual words of the final legislation itself. Moreover, Capitant argues that too much attention paid to the interpretation of statements made by ministers or members in Parliament can only take place at the expense of the legal certainty provided by the written text of a statute. Also, this way of proceeding adversely affects the authority of legislation by implying that the meaning, and therefore the force, of a statute derives from the discussions which have preceded its passage.

The extent to which courts refer to *travaux préparatoires* in construing statutes is difficult to assess, the reason being that French judges hardly ever explicitly justify their decisions. However, it can be assumed that in reaching its decision a court has used *travaux préparatoires* when the judgment of this court confirms an interpretation based on *travaux préparatoires* proposed by a particular scholar at the time when the law was passed or, by the *Commissaire du Gouvernement* or the *Avocat Général* in their respective submissions to the *Conseil d'Etat* and to the Court of Cassation. Illustrations of this are *Castagné et autres* v *Epy* and, *Société générale des grandes sources d'eaux minérales francaises* v *Castagné* (1974), D. 1974, 593, both commonly referred to as the 'Perrier decisions'. Here, the Court of Cassation followed the interpretation, partly based on *travaux préparatoires*, proposed by *Avocat Général* Touffait in his celebrated *conclusions*. The question was whether or not an employer could use the general judicial remedy of *résolution judiciaire* provided for in contract law, Civil Code art. 1184, in order to terminate the contract of employment of employees who also held the position of staff representatives in a company. Dismissal of staff representatives is usually subject to the special rules provided by labour law (the then arts 22 and 24 of the Ordinance of 22 February 1945, and arts 16 and 18 of the Loi of 16 April 1946) under which their contracts can only be terminated after consultation with the *comité d'entreprise* (works council), or the *inspecteur de travail* ('works' inspector). However, prior to the 1974 *Perrier* decisions, courts used the contractual remedy provided by art. 1184 as an alternative to the labour law provisions in circumstances where allegedly staff representatives had been seriously at fault in the course of their employment. This practice of the courts became the subject of controversy between judges and legal writers, with conflicting decisions being given on this issue. In the two landmark *Perrier* cases the Court of Cassation put an end to this controversy by following the *Avocat Général*'s interpretation of the various conflicting texts at issue. The *Avocat Général* used a mixture of literal, exegetical and teleological interpretation before reaching the view that *résolution judicaire* was not an available remedy here. First, he directed the attention of the Court to the fact that art. 1184 of the Civil Code was part of Title III of this code dealing with synallagmatic contracts, a category of contracts where each party's obligation is an equivalent economic counterpart of the other. This would have the effect of excluding from the scope of art. 1184 contracts of employment which, by their nature, involve parties who are not economically equivalent. Further, the *Avocat Général* analysed meticulously the vocabulary and grammatical structure of the relevant labour law provisions. He also used the *travaux préparatoires* of those provisions, first, to make it quite obvious that it was the clear intention of Parliament to subject the dismissal of staff representatives to specific rules other than the ordinary one governing the law of contract and, second, to clarify the objective of the legislator in affording extra protection against discriminatory practice for those who serve the interests of employees. The Court of Cassation specifically referred to this latter aspect of 'extra protection' when handing down its decision.

The *Conseil Constitutionnel* has also shown a willingness to consider *travaux préparatoires* as a means of determining the meaning of a legislative text submitted for its scrutiny or as a means of monitoring whether the reasons underlying the passage of a text are consistent with constitutional rules and principles. In this respect, constitutional case law has been shown to include explicit reference to the use of *travaux préparatoires*, as revealed in a recent study carried out by P. Josse (1998) where the author shows how, out of the 395 decisions given by the *Conseil* since the date of its creation in 1958, 61 refer explicitly to *travaux préparatoires*. One typical illustration is provided by the famous decision 81-132 DC, 16 January 1982, on nationalisation, Rec.18, where the nineteenth *considerant* clause of the decision refers explicitly to the *travaux préparatoires* of the *loi* under scrutiny.

3.3.2.2 Maxims of interpretation

In addition to internal and external aids to construction, there are a number of maxims, usually expressed in Latin, which can help in interpreting statutes. Below are some of those most widely used.

(a) *Ubi lex non distinguit, nec nos distinguere debemus* means where a text is expressed in general terms, it is forbidden to introduce restrictions

(b) *Exceptio est strictissimae interpretationis* means that exceptions must be construed restrictively

(c) *Specialia generalibus derogant* means where there is a conflict between a general and a specific provision, the specific provision must prevail over the general one.

Note: the notion of 'presumption of interpretation' as an aid to construction does not exist as such in French law. However, some of the rules which, in English law, fall under the category of 'presumption' have been codified in France, e.g. penal statutes are to be constructed strictly (New Penal Code, art. 111-4), statutes do not have retrospective effect (New Penal Code, art. 112-1; Civil Code, art. 2). Furthermore, the new rule of construction in English law that legislation must be read and given effect in a way which is compatible with the European Convention on Human Rights (as per the Human Rights Act 1998, s. 3(1)), has no direct equivalent in French law, since in accordance with the French Constitution, art. 55, the European Convention on Human Rights has been incorporated into domestic law and takes precedence over any existing conflicting statute (see Chapter 1.1.3 above). Therefore, in French law, the question of ensuring consistency with the Convention is framed principally in terms of hierarchy of norms (on this hierarchy see Chapter 1.1.1 above), not interpretation. Nevertheless, in practice, in this context interpretation is still a very important issue since French courts generally interpret restrictively the guarantees and protection provided by the Convention in order to minimise alleged inconsistency with domestic legislation.

3.4 **Other authorities that can interpret the law**

Interpreting legislative provisions is mainly a task belonging to the courts when faced with problems of interpretation arising out of legal disputes. This has not always been the case in French legal history. In 1790 the *référé législatif* was introduced by the legislature which forced judges to refer a case to the legislature on questions of statutory construction. Recourse to the legislature was made obligatory where there was a persistent conflict of interpretation between the courts of appeal and the then Tribunal of Cassation. The *référé législatif*, which was nothing more than a measure adopted by the revolutionary assemblies in order to subjugate the judiciary, soon proved unworkable and was finally abolished in 1837. Today, the legislature may still, in some circumstances, be involved in the interpretation of statutes by introducing interpretative statutes intended to explain the meaning of any existing ambiguous one. In recent years, however, it has essentially been the government which, through its various departments, and by means of *réponses ministérielles*, has acted competitively with the judiciary in its role of interpreting the law. This final part, thus, briefly considers the role played by *lois interprétatives* and *réponses ministérielles* in the area of statutory construction.

3.4.1 *Lois interprétatives*

These are declaratory or explanatory statutes passed by Parliament in order to explain the meaning of an earlier statute which is unclear or disputed. *Lois interprétatives* are usually found in areas such as social security or commercial leases. These *lois* are retrospective and operate from the date on which the earlier statute has been passed. They affect all law cases which were started, but not decided, before they came into force. The Court of Cassation has decided that even cases which had already been decided at first instance prior to the passage of the *loi interprétative*, but were the subject of an appeal at the time when the *loi* had come into force, could be reviewed by the court of appeal hearing the case in the light of the new interpretation as set out in this *loi*.

3.4.2 *Réponses ministérielles*

These are written replies from government departments to questions addressed to them by members of Parliament acting on behalf of public bodies or private citizens and in which these government departments issue their own interpretation of statutes. An example of a *réponse ministérielle* is provided in Box 3.1. These *réponses* are the current replica of the Roman *rescripta* issued by Roman emperors following questions or petitions addressed to them by officials or citizens. *Réponses ministérielles* fulfil the same function as circulars (see Chapter 1.1.1 above) and, as with these, today provide one of the most significant sources of statutory interpretation in France. However, as with circulars, they are not regarded as authoritative, and are thus not

Box 3.1 An example of *réponse ministérielle*

Impôt sur le revenu
(quotient familial –
parent n'ayant pas obtenu la garde de l'enfant)

23416. – 28 décembre 1998. – **Mme Dominique Gillot** attire l'attention de **M. le ministre de l'économie, des finances et de l'industrie** sur la situation fiscale des personnes divorcées et des célibataires avec enfants n'ayant pas obtenu la garde de ces derniers. En effet, le parent n'ayant pas obtenu la garde de l'enfant ne peut prétendre à la demi-part supplémentaire (pour deux enfants, une part supplémentaire, etc., au sens de l'article 194 du code général des impôts) accordée pour la division du revenu imposable. Ce dernier bénéficie de la déductibilité de la pension alimentaire lorsqu'il est en capacité de la verser. Elle lui demande donc quelle serait l'incidence pour le budget de l'État d'une réforme visant à laisser la possibilité au parent n'ayant pas obtenu la garde de l'enfant de bénéficier de la demi-part supplémentaire au lieu et place de la déductibilité de la pension alimentaire, mesure qui marquerait la volonté des pouvoirs publics de poursuivre l'engagement pris de mettre en œuvre une politique familiale socialement plus juste.

Réponse – Conformément aux principes généraux du droit fiscal et à la jurisprudence constante du Conseil d'Etat, un enfant ne peut être à la charge que d'un seul contribuable pour le calcul de l'impôt au regard des règles du quotient familial. En cas de divorce, les enfants mineurs sont considérés comme étant à la charge du parent auquel le jugement de divorce a confié la garde. L'autre parent peut, pour sa part, déduire de son revenu global le montant de l'obligation alimentaire qu'il exécute selon les modalités fixées par le jugement de divorce ou, en cas de divorce sur demande conjointe, par la convention homologuée par le juge. Il n'est pas envisagé de modifier ces dispositions qui assurent ainsi un traitement fiscal équilibré entre les ex-époux.

Source: Réponse Ministérielle no. 23416 of 28 December 1998, JO AN 22 February 1999, p. 1068

binding on the courts. Despite this limitation, judges and parties to a case increasingly rely on them, especially when they come from the Minister of Justice. The fact that they are published in the *Journal Officiel* is manifest evidence of their significance today. The growing recourse to this practice can be accounted for by the fact that it provides a quick, easy and clear answer to a problem of interpretation. However, these *réponses* are not without their dangers. Firstly, they may be a perverse means for the government to re-introduce, in a statute, a meaning which was part of the original draft bill introduced by the relevant ministry but which was later amended by Parliament. Secondly, if the government is not satisfied with the manner in which a statute has been implemented, it may offer its 'official' interpretation with a view to redressing the situation to its perceived advantage. In this context it must be added that *réponses ministérielles* do not of themselves guarantee that an interpretation given in one case will necessarily be followed in another case. In such circumstances, legal certainty, and more specifically the protection of citizen's legitimate expectations, are at stake. This is crucial for tax law where *réponses ministérielles* are more frequently used than in any other branches of law. The fact that not only is the law changing rapidly in this area, but its implementation has also been left to the discretion of the tax authorities, taken together account for the tendency of taxpayers to address a large volume of inquiries to this administration which, by definition, is in the best position to provide an update on its own practice. In view of this situation, attempts have been made over the years to define more precisely the limits of the tax authorities' discretion in interpreting the law. This has resulted in the introduction, alongside *réponses ministérielles*, of the more formal tax law *rescrits* in a Loi of 8 July 1987. *Rescrits* are formal replies by the tax authorities to queries on their rights and duties addressed to them by taxpayers. Unlike *réponses ministérielles*, tax law *rescrits* are binding on the issuing tax authority which thus cannot go back on its written replies. Similar *rescrits* exist under a ministerial *Arrêté* of 5 July 1990 for the regulation of stock exchange transactions. These *rescrits* deal with queries addressed by private citizens to the *COB* (*Commission des Opérations de Bourse*) on the legality of particular stock exchange transactions those citizens intend to engage in.

Note: since a Loi of 15 May 1981 (*Code de l'Organisation Judiciaire*, art. L 151-1), on a reference made by a lower court, the Court of Cassation can issue a non-binding opinion (*avis*) on questions of interpretation arising out of novel and difficult question of law (a similar procedure exists in the *Conseil d'Etat* for administrative law cases). This procedure has been criticised for making the highest court a quasi-official body for dealing with statutory construction, with the effect of potentially removing from judges in the lower courts the power to interpret statutes themselves. However, this fear has proved unfounded. Since the 1981 Law was enacted, there have each year been a limited number of *avis* handed down (13 *avis* in 2000 and 1999, 20 in 1998, 16 in 1997, 11 in 1996 and 15 in 1995).

Chapter references

AGOSTINI, E., 'L'Equité', D.1978, Chr.7.

AUBRY ET RAU, *Droit Civil Francais*, 7th edn, Paris: Librairies Techniques, 1964, pp. 308–318.

AUBY, J. B., 'Le Recours aux Objectifs des Textes dans leur Application en Droit Public', *Revue du Droit Public*, 1991, Vol. 107, pp. 327–337.

BATIFOL, H., 'Questions de l'Interprétation Juridique', in *Choix d'Articles Rassemblés par ses Amis*, Paris: LGDJ, 1976, pp. 409–424.

BELL, J., and ENGLE, G., *Cross: Statutory*

Interpretation, 3rd edn, London: Butterworths, 1995.

BENNION, F., *Bennion on Statute Law*, 3rd edn, London: Longman, 1990.

CAPITANT, H., 'Les Travaux Préparatoires et l'Interprétation des Lois' in *Recueil d'Etudes sur les Sources du Droit en l'Honneur de F. Gény*, Chap. 2, Vol. 2, Paris: Sirey, 1933.

COUDERC, M., 'Les Travaux Parlementaires de la Loi ou la Remontée des Enfers', D. 1975, Chr. 249.

GÉNY, F., *Méthode d'Interprétation et Sources en Droit Privé Positif*, 2nd edn, Paris: LGDJ, 1919.

JOSSE, P., *Le Rôle de la notion de Travaux Préparatoires dans la Jurisprudence du Conseil Constitutionnel*, Paris: LGDJ, 1998.

OPPETIT, B., 'Les Réponses Ministérielles aux Questions Ecrites des Ministres', D. 1974, Chr. 107.

OPPETIT, B., 'La Résurgence du Rescrit', D. 1991, Chr. 105.

4

Case law (*jurisprudence*)

Ce mot de jurisprudence des tribunaux doit être effacé de notre langue
Robespierre adressing the Assemblée Constituante on 18 November 1790.

A description has already been given in the previous chapter of how, through the process of statutory interpretation, French judges have effectively contributed to the law-making process. This chapter looks beyond the operation of interpreting existing law and examines more generally the role French courts play in the development of the law.

In French constitutional theory precedents do not form part of the 'pyramid of norms', described earlier in Chapter 1, and do not, therefore, constitute official sources of French law. This French approach to legal sources arises out of a set of rules that will be examined in this chapter, which prevent judges from interfering with the legislature in its law making function. In practice, however, French judges routinely make rules, as judges do in other legal systems. In this respect, some branches of French law which were not originally statute based, such as administrative and private international law, have been almost entirely created out of the decisions of the judges.

The fact that judges have managed to create law in such a system as that of France where, as will be seen in this chapter, there has always been a tradition of hostility towards judicial precedent, has been described by French legal theorists as a 'true phenomenon', not to say a 'real enigma' (on the latter term see Boulanger, 1961: 421). The contradiction between the traditional post-revolutionary concept that law can only be legislative in origin and the reality of judicial law making has generated a long-running debate amongst French legal academics over whether the rules established by the judges have the force of law. This debate over whether *jurisprudence*, the French equivalent to case law, is in practice a source of law is widely acknowledged in every law treatise or academic textbook in the relevant chapter dealing with sources of law. It can be described as a 'never-ending story' where advocates and opponents of '*jurisprudence* as a source of law' argue endlessly and inconclusively about the normative power of judicial decision making. This unending search for a compromise able to reconcile the theory and practice of the judicial process is probably an impossible task taking account of the conflicting views in this perennial debate. However, investigation of the issue of whether *jurisprudence* is a 'source of law' is unavoidable as it touches upon other major problems posed by case law in France, which need to be addressed here. What is the nature of the relationship between judge-made law and legislation in a system, such as that of France, which over-emphasises enacted law? And, how in such a system can judicial law making be legitimated? It is this sort of question with which this chapter is concerned. These difficulties cannot, however, be fully addressed without first giving an account of the French rules of precedent and the way in which they operate. In particular, these rules depending as much as they do on the practice of the courts, demand that some attention be given to the factors which, in the court process, contribute to placing greater weight on certain types of precedents as opposed to others.

Thus, the chapter will be arranged as follows: the status of *jurisprudence*; factors placing greater weight on precedents; *jurisprudence* and legislation; the legitimacy of judicial law making.

It should be noted that, for the purpose of what follows in this chapter, the term *jurisprudence* will be used, depending on the context, either in its wider meaning of 'a body of rules established by the courts', or in its more restrictive meaning, namely the 'judicial doctrine of a court on a particular legal issue'.

4.1 **The status of** *jurisprudence*

The status accorded to French *jurisprudence* may be said to be the outcome of a combination of long historical tradition, legal theory and legislative provisions. The position of the judiciary in this regard and the authority of its decisions can be summarised in three interrelated propositions:

(a) Following the French doctrine of separation of powers, judges are not allowed to interfere with the legislature in its law making function.

(b) From this it follows that judges are forbidden to make law intended to govern future cases, or to use previous decisions when adjudicating legal disputes. This is encapsulated in the prohibition of *arrêts de règlement* set out in art. 5 of the Civil Code.

(c) This has consequently resulted in the absence from French law of the doctrine of *stare decisis*, with the effect that court decisions do not constitute binding precedents.

Each of these propositions will now be examined in turn.

4.1.1 **The French doctrine of separation of powers**

Set against judicial law making is the constitutional theory, derived from a rigid doctrine of separation of powers, by which law is strictly a matter for the legislature, not the judiciary. Under this doctrine, the function of judges is solely that of adjudicating by applying the law originating from Parliament to legal disputes brought before them. Montesquieu's famous work, *The Spirit of Laws* (1748), is often quoted as having been strongly influential with regard to this approach. In one of the most important chapters (Book XI, Chapter VI) of his work, Montesquieu indeed refers to every judge merely being 'the mouth that pronounces the words of the law', or to judicial decisions being 'never anything other than the exact text of the law'. However, on closer scrutiny, Montesquieu's comments did not apply to judicial decisions generally, but only to criminal rulings. In this respect, Montesquieu was particularly concerned that, if judges were given too much discretion in this area, the individual's civil liberties would be undermined (on this view see Belaid, 1974, pp.44–45). Nevertheless, Montesquieu's statements have been construed more widely by the watchdogs for the separation of powers, with the intention of confining the judicial function, as a general rule, to the role of 'saying' what the law is when resolving a legal dispute. The judicial submission to the enacted law is even enshrined in the term used in French to describe the word 'court'. This term, *juridiction*, coming from the Latin phrase *juri dictio*, means 'to say what the law is'. However, this chapter, like Chapter 7, will show that judicial reasoning is a much more complex process than the simple act of 'saying' what the law is.

It may be argued that this question of the limits of judicial power is not exclusive to France and that even in a system of binding precedent, such as in England, there has been a similar trend away from the expansion of judicial law making. However, the point of departure between the two systems is that in France's case, this question is not simply a matter for constitutional theory or political debate but has been given expression in legislative enactment. The fundamental Law of 16-24 August 1790, passed at the time of the French Revolution and still in force today, forms the basis for the French doctrine of separation of powers. It states in art. 10:

Les tribunaux ne pourront prendre directement ou indirectement aucune part à l'exercice du pouvoir législatif, ni empêcher ou suspendre l'exécution des décrets du Corps législatif, [sanctionnés par le Roi], à peine de forfaiture.

(Courts are not, on pain of 'forfaiture', permitted to take part, directly or indirectly, in the exercise of the legislative power, nor can they prevent or adjourn the execution of any decree issued by the legislature.)

The 1790 Law must be read within the context of hostility surrounding the judicial function at the time of the French Revolution, a hostility which was brought about by the actions of the royal courts of the *Ancien Régime*, the *Parlements*, whereby they competed with the king in his law making power. These *Parlements* used to issue, alongside the King's edicts and ordinances, particular decisions called *arrêts de règlement* which were authoritative rulings laying down general rules with a view to their application in analogous cases in the future. Although these *arrêts de règlement* were only applicable within each *Parlement*'s own jurisdiction, and could be overridden in the event of conflict with royal legislation, they were later perceived by the French revolutionaries as a threat to the legislature's overriding authority and were prohibited at that time and thereafter.

4.1.2 Prohibition of *arrêts de règlement*

This prohibition is, today, contained in art. 5 of the Civil Code, which reads:

Il est défendu aux juges de prononcer par voie de disposition générale et réglementaire sur les causes qui leur sont soumises.

(Judges are not permitted to adjudicate by means of general and statutory rulings in the cases brought before them.)

As will be considered again later (in Chapter 4.2.4 below), this rule does not in practice prevent judges from laying down general rules with possible application to subsequent cases, as *prima facie* the wording of art. 5 would suggest. What judges are forbidden to do in art. 5 is to act as legislators by creating for the future rules which are not related to the actual facts of the case under consideration. Thus, as long as the reasoning of the court (*les motifs de la décision*: see Chapter 7.1 and Chapter 8.2.1 below) shows the relation of the principle established by the court and the consequent solution deriving from it to the material facts of the case at hand, no case for any breach of art. 5 can be made against that court.

By way of illustration, art. 5 has been applied and enforced by the Court of Cassation in a number of instances where lower courts went beyond their mere role of adjudicating the case before them. Two examples now follow.

(i) In *Société France-Editions et Publications* v *Société Laboratoires Solac et Chambre Syndicale des Fabricants de produits pharmaceutiques* (1971), JCP 1971, II, 16932, a Sunday newspaper had advertised the merits of a product manufactured by a pharmaceutical firm without its authorisation. The firm sued the newspaper for damages and for the unauthorised advertising to be discontinued. The Court of Appeal, in its decision, forbade the newspaper any longer to advertise not only this product but also any other products which, in the future, might be manufactured and marketed by the plaintiff or by any members of the national federation of pharmaceutical manufacturers. The Court of Cassation quashed this decision on the grounds that the appeal judges had adjudicated the case by way of general justification, ruling on future potential products which were not yet manufactured, and on future possible litigants not concerned with the case before them, thus violating art. 5 of the Civil Code.

(ii) The case of *K.* v *Min. Public* (1984), JCP 1985, II, 20391, concerned the legality of an identity check carried out on the person of the defendant. The then art. 78-2 of the Code of Penal Procedure authorised the police to carry out identity checks only where this was made necessary in the interests of preventing threats to public order and to the security of individuals and their property. In this case, a court of appeal took the view that the identity check carried out by the police against the defendant, at night time and in an underground station, was justified on the grounds that the

Parisian underground, being known as a place where crimes were commonly committed, fell under the category of a place where the security of its users and of their
belongings were at risk. However, according to the Court of Cassation to which the
case was referred, the appeal judges were not empowered to base their decision on
such general grounds and should, instead, have shown that the actual conditions of
threat required by art. 78-2 regarding the legality of the operation of identity checks
were actually met in the specific situation at the material time. The court of appeal's
decision was consequently quashed as, otherwise, it would have had the effect of
creating a new general rule, going beyond this particular case, whereby any future
identity checks carried out in the underground would have been justified.

It is usually recognised in French legal theory that the corollary to art. 5 is to be
found in another provision of the Civil Code – namely, art. 1351. This rule, known as
the principle of *autorité relative de la chose jugée*, is in fact the expression in French law
of the doctrine of *res judicata*. As such, it is outwardly only concerned with the effects
of a judicial decision on the actual parties to a particular dispute who by virtue of art.
1351 are prevented from raising the same issue at a later date. However, art. 1351 has
been applied in conjunction with art. 5 to mean that courts cannot determine in
advance the outcome of subsequent similar litigation involving different parties.
Articles 5 and 1351, taken together, are the written expression of the absence of a
doctrine of binding precedent in French law.

4.1.3 No doctrine of *stare decisis*

In France judicial decisions, even when pronounced by superior courts, are not binding precedents that must be followed by judges. Courts are only bound by legislation
or *principes généraux de droit* (see Chapter 3.2.3 above). There are, however, two
principal departures from this rule.

The first one is concerned with decisions given by the *Conseil Constitutionnel*. No
appeal is recognised against these decisions which, in accordance with art. 62 of the
Constitution, are also binding on all governmental, administrative and judicial
authorities. In its decision 62-18 L, 16 January 1962, *Loi d'orientation agricole*, Rec. 31,
the *Conseil* ruled that the binding authority of its decisions applies not only to the
actual ruling itself but also to the reasons stated in the decision which led to this
ruling. The rule imposed by art. 62, to follow past decisions of the *Conseil*, also applies
to the *Conseil* itself. On many occasions the *Conseil* has reconfirmed that it was bound
by the authority of its own past decisions (see decisions, 58-90 bis AN, 5 May 1959,
Rec. 223, 85-197 DC, 23 August 1985, Rec. 70, 80-126 DC, 30 December 1980 Rec. 53,
87-1026 AN, 23 October 1987, Rec. 55 and 88-1127 AN, 20 April 1989, Rec. 32).
Although the Court of Cassation has in past cases shown a resistance towards the case
law of the *Conseil Constitutionnel*, today both administrative and private law courts
would appear to have incorporated in their own case law the interpretation of statutes
given by the *Conseil* (for the *Conseil d'Etat*, see *Syndicat unifié de la radio et de la*

télévision, (1983), Rec. 293 and, for the Court of Cassation, *Directeur Général des Impôts* v *Société Royale* (1990), Bull. civ. I, no 12, which follows the interpretation given by the *Conseil Constitutionnel* in 89-268 DC, 29 December 1989, Rec.110, on the question of the retrospective operation of a tax enactment aimed at interpreting an earlier statute).

The second departure from the rule stated above is the *Code de l'Organisation Judiciaire*, art. L131-2. The Court of Cassation, when quashing a lower court decision for not having correctly applied the law, usually sends the case back to another similar lower court for review. In the event that the second court reaches the same judgment as the first one, thereby disregarding the Court of Cassation's ruling, and if the case is then being brought for a second time before the latter, then the case has per force to be examined by the full bench (*Assemblée Plénière*) of the Court of Cassation whose decision will then have a final binding effect on the third lower court to which the case must be referred back for ultimate review. Here, the *Assemblée Plénière*'s decision, it should be noted, binds the lower court only on issues of law (as opposed to issues of fact) and only for the particular case in hand, to the exclusion of any future similar cases. This foregoing, albeit complicated, mechanism happens very rarely and is mainly justified by the fact that it is expedient, at some stage, to bring an end to all litigation.

Apart from the two above instances, the law regarding precedent in France may be summarised in the five following points:

1. Precedents do not need to be followed in subsequent similar cases. This rule applies not only to the court giving the decision but also to any other courts.

2. As a consequence, even the highest courts – Court of Cassation and *Conseil d'Etat* – are not bound by their own previous decisions.

3. And similarly, lower courts are also not bound by the decisions of superior courts.

4. Explicit reference by a court to its own *jurisprudence* when giving a decision and, more generally, citation of previous cases is not allowed when these are meant to serve as a legal basis for the court's decision. Thus, as was decided in the Highway Code case of *Thirion* v *Motte* (1958), Bull. crim., no 466, no court can give as the determinative reason for reaching its decision (here the defendant was held not guilty of the offence) the fact that, having already decided the issue in past similar cases, it is bound by the *jurisprudence* adopted in these cases. In the same vein, in the industrial injury case of *Caisse mutuelle de réassurance agricole de l'Ile-De-France et autres* v *Casimiro* (1967), JCP1968, II, 15339, the Court of Cassation quashed a lower court judgment for having decided '*conformément à sa jurisprudence*' on the method of payment of damages due to the victim. However, reference *en passant* to '*le dernier état de la jurisprudence*' (the latest precedent), as in the recent adoption case *Naïma K.*, (1999), D. 2000, 45, heard by the Court of Appeal of Aix-en-Provence, would appear to be tolerated as long as such a reference, as in this case, is not presented as the basis for the decision given. Also, it may be noted, no objection is raised when, in

formulating the reasons for a decision in a current case, judges paraphrase the reasons (*motifs de doit*) to be found in the text of past judgments in analogous cases. It is in fact this repetition of *motifs de droit* in a consistent line of cases which forms the basis for a *jurisprudence constante* (see Chapter 4.2.2 below). To summarise, what is liable to being quashed here is not the court's actual following of a precedent, but the explicit statement by this court that it is bound by a judicial precedent. The distinction between these two situations is not as purely academic as it sounds. Underlying the restriction on any explicit reference being made to a court's *jurisprudence* is the implied presumption that judges are only bound by statutory law. However, this does not preclude them from following a precedent if they so wish.

5. As a corollary to point 4, failure by a court to follow a precedent cannot constitute a valid ground for appeal. This principle was applied recently by the Court of Cassation in *Le Collinet* v *Compagnie d'assurances Rhin et Moselle* (2000), D. 2000, 593. Here, a buyer brought an action for defective goods against the seller. The case was dismissed by the lower court on the grounds that it was not brought within a '*bref délai*' (a short period of time) as provided for by art. 1648 of the Civil Code which deals with defective goods (*garantie des vices cachés*). The buyer argued in the Court of Cassation that judges in the lower court relied on a new precedent which, contrary to the previous one, no longer allowed him to escape from the brief limitation period of art. 1648 of the Civil Code. Indeed, under a precedent existing at the time when the buyer entered into the contract, it was possible for the buyer of a defective product to opt, as he had done, for an alternative course of action based on art. 1604 of the Civil Code for non-delivery by the seller of the goods agreed for in the contract (*défaut de conformité*), for which more time was allowed to commence legal proceedings. According to the buyer, failure by the lower court to apply in his case this past precedent infringed the principle of legal certainty in contractual matters. The Court of Cassation disregarded this approach and gave a reply in keeping with the established view regarding judicial precedent. It said:

It does not follow from the principle of legal certainty that a litigant has an established right to a static precedent; the fact that precedents develop forms part of the judicial process.

This decision also highlights the question of departing from precedent, with the associated frustration of not knowing whether there is any reasonable expectation that the precedent in question will be followed (see Chapter 4.2.3 below). It is of interest to note that, alongside *Le Collinet*, the Court of Cassation has, for a few years, been suggesting in its annual report (see Chapter 5.3.1 below) that the limitation period in art. 1648 at issue in the above case, rather than being left to the discretion of the judge, should be fixed by the legislature so as to avoid litigants seeking alternative courses of action when there is uncertainty as to which way the judge will rule in terms of an issue such as '*bref délai*'. According to the Court's Report, such an amendment would have the principal effect of strengthening legal certainty and parties' expectations in the contractual sphere, the very points raised by the buyer in his unsuccessful claim in *Le Collinet*.

The absence of the doctrine of *stare decisis* in France, with all the consequences flowing from this, described above, accounts for the fact that French courts never discuss the facts of prior decisions as common law judges do in their judgments. However, this does not apply to counsel who, in court, routinely refer not only to past precedents in their arguments but also to the specific facts of those precedents. Thus, it is not uncommon to hear counsel arguing in court that the facts of the present case differ from the facts of a previous one relating to a similar issue and that, therefore, the present case cannot be subsumed under the same rule as that applied in the previous case. Nor is it out of place for photocopies of previously reported judgments to be included in the *dossier* (file) submitted to the court by counsel before its deliberations.

4.2 Factors giving weight to precedents

Despite the rules and principles preventing judicial decisions from becoming binding precedents, there are, in French law, a certain number of factors which contribute to ascribing a certain degree of normative force to precedents. Although the decision affected by these factors is not formally binding, it nevertheless has a persuasive value for similar cases in the future. These factors are:

(a) the hierarchical rank of the court which gives the decision

(b) the fact that a particular interpretation or principle is repeated in a consistent line of precedents

(c) the departure from previous precedent, known in French law as *revirement de jurisprudence*

(d) the statement of a principle of general application (*arrêt de principe*) by the court giving the decision.

Each of these factors is now discussed in turn.

4.2.1 Hierarchy of courts

4.2.1.1 Higher court decisions

The hierarchical rank of the court which has given the decision is important when it comes to determining the value of a precedent. Precedent from a higher court carries more weight than precedent from a lower court. There are several explanations for this.

(i) The highly decentralised nature of the system of courts in France and the role played by the highest courts, the Court of Cassation and the *Conseil d'Etat*, should first be highlighted. Figure 4.1 provides a basic guide to the structure of the

Ordre Judiciaire (Ordinary Courts)

Ordre Administratif (Administrative Courts)

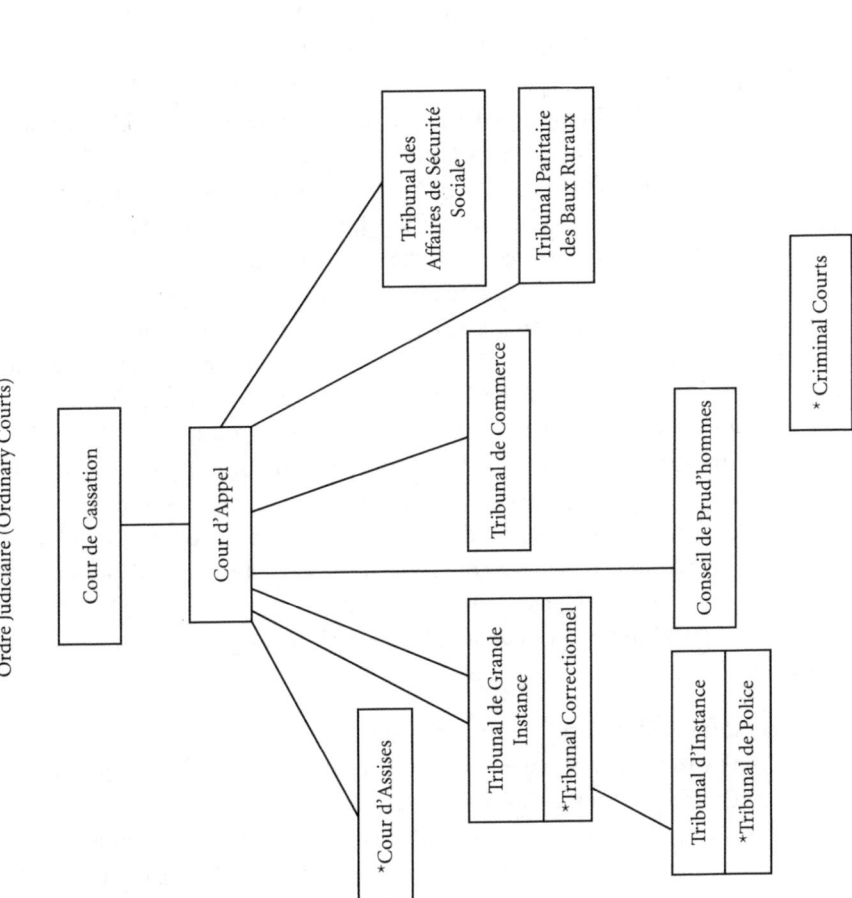

Fig. 4.1 The court structure in France

French court system. This system is characterised by the fact that courts of first instance and courts of appeal are numerous and are spread out across France. There are 191 *tribunaux de grande instance* (large civil claims courts) and 473 *tribunaux d'instance* (small civil claims courts) both hearing cases in the area of private law. At the appellate level, 35 courts of appeal have jurisdiction for hearing appeals in civil and criminal matters. At the top of the hierarchy are the Court of Cassation and the *Conseil d'Etat* whose role, within their respective province, is to ensure that the law is correctly and uniformly applied by the lower courts throughout the country. Correct and uniform application of the law, here implies, not only that the same body of law is observed in the different parts of the country, but also, that the same interpretation of the law is applied uniformly by the courts. The latter is achieved by quashing lower court decisions which do not comply with this interpretation, and by sending them back for reconsideration to another lower court.

(ii) There are more specific reasons of a psychological and sociological nature that may be applied when accounting for the greater weight accorded to higher court decisions. F. Terré (2000: 255) argues that the reason why these decisions are usually followed lies in what he calls the 'law of imitation' and the 'law of continuity'. Judges in the lower courts usually find it expedient to follow the model offered by a decision of the courts above them in the hierarchy, provided that the principle on which this decision is based is clearly stated. However, 'imitation' is also forced upon judges in the lower courts in the sense that if they do not follow higher court decisions their own decisions are likely to be reversed, with the implicit stigma attached thereto that they do not know 'their law'. As far as the law of continuity is concerned, it rests on the assumption that continuity and consistency in judicial decisions are both desirable features. From this it follows that the courts, including the highest ones, are unlikely to overrule their own established *jurisprudence* and jeopardise these two qualities without some very good reason or unavoidable necessity to do so. The foregoing accounts for the paradox that French judges, who by law are not bound by any precedents, feel more compelled than their English counterparts to follow them, especially when taking into account all the existing ways offered to English judges to escape from the constraints of *stare decisis*. In fact, the 'law of imitation' and the 'law of continuity' when taken together bind French judges as much as, probably even more than, the rule of binding precedent in the case of the English judges.

4.2.1.2 *Assemblée Plénière* and *Chambre Mixte* decisions

Decisions given by the Court of Cassation sitting in *Assemblée Plénière* or in *Chambre Mixte* have much more persuasive authority than those given by an ordinary panel of the Court. *Assemblée Plénière* and *Chambre Mixte* only convene for certain important cases, as set out in the *Code de l'Organisation Judiciaire*, art. L 131-2. According to this text, when a case gives rise to a 'question of principle, notably because of a persistent conflict of precedents between lower courts, or between the lower courts and the Court of Cassation itself', then the head of the Court may call upon the full bench of the Court of Cassation, the *Assemblée Plénière*, to adjudicate the case with a view to settling the matter. A case comes before a *Chambre Mixte*, made up of members taken from two or more divisions of the Court, either because it falls within the jurisdiction of more than one division of the Court, or when the points it raises have, in the past, resulted in conflicting decisions, or are expected to create further conflict between the divisions of the Court in the future. In both cases what implicitly underlies the legal requirement that cases have to be heard by a full court or a wider panel, is not only the preservation of uniformity in the law, but also legal certainty, equality of treatment in similar cases and the predictability of the probable application of law for the public at large. However, it may be worth noting that decisions of *Assemblée Plénière* and *Chambre Mixte* are rare in practice. Each year, there are only a handful of decisions, compared with the thousands of decisions given by the ordinary divisions of the Court of Cassation during the same period of time. Moreover, regrettably, it may also be noted that the decision to convene one of these two panels is very often taken late, and furthermore does not always settle the conflict of precedent for which the panel was called. For example, it took more than a decade for the Court of Cassation to convene a *Chambre Mixte* in *Veuve Gaudras* v *Dangereux* (1970), D. 1970, 201, on the then issue in conflict of the right of unmarried partners to obtain damages for the loss of one of the partners in a motor accident, against the responsible third party. In the context of vicarious liability, no less than five decisions of *Assemblée Plénière* were given between 1960 and 1988 on the issue of determining what art. 1384 al. 5 meant by saying 'employers being liable for the damages caused by their employees *dans les fonctions auxquelles ils les ont employés* (in the course of their employment). And even after each of these leading decisions given by the *Assemblée Plénière*, the issue remained unresolved.

4.2.1.3 Lower court decisions

It would be wrong to assume from the foregoing that there is no force or value attached to the decisions of the lower courts. In particular, lower court decisions are authoritative in the following circumstances:

(a) Until a higher court has decided on a particular issue of law, lower court decisions are valued in the sense that they help, in an anticipatory way, to predict the likely course which case law will take in the future on the issue at hand.

(b) Once a higher court has delivered a decision on a particular question, lower court decisions still retain some significance. On the one hand, where a lower court readily follows a higher court decision, this gives a greater authority to it. On the other hand, where a lower court is reluctant to follow a higher court decision, this considerably undermines the force of such a precedent and may, in some cases, lead to a superior court overruling its own decision. A classic example of such a case is *Desmares* v *Epoux Charles* (1982), D. 1982, 449. Here, the Court of Cassation issued a very strong ruling in favour of the victims of road traffic accidents wherein it excluded the possibility of the plaintiff's damages being reduced on account of his/her contributory negligence (unless the plaintiff's action in this respect had amounted to a case of *force majeure*, i.e. had been unforeseeable and unavoidable, for the defendant). Consequently, following this ruling, any driver of a vehicle having caused an accident was to be held liable for the entire damage even when contributory negligence was established. The *Desmares* decision became very unpopular amongst the lower courts, with many of them refusing to follow it. This situation led Parliament to introduce new legislation in the Loi of 5 July 1985 whose purpose was to redefine the compensation procedures for the victims of road accidents. Of more relevance here, the attitude of the lower courts also persuaded the Court of Cassation to overrule *Desmares*. This was accomplished in a series of three decisions given five years after *Desmares*, the most often cited being *Mettetal v Waeterinckx* (1987), D. 1988, 32. In this case, as in the other two, the Court of Cassation decided to restore the more traditional approach to contributory negligence by the victim, abandoned in *Desmares*, and to use it as a basis for reducing the liability of the defendant in a case where this was proved.

(c) Provided the highest courts have not yet ruled on a particular point, the appeal courts will usually follow their own previous judgments which, although not formally binding, will nevertheless be perceived as being authoritative and be followed by first instance courts within the regional jurisdiction of the relevant court of appeal.

(d) Finally, lower court decisions play a significant role as precedents on important issues not statutorily determined and on which the highest courts cannot adjudicate, the reason being that these issues are, in law, categorised as issues of fact, and, as such, are left to the discretion of the lower courts (in French to the *'pouvoir souverain des juges du fond'*). By way of illustration, there are two principal areas where lower court decisions, although not formally binding, will nevertheless provide support for subsequent similar cases:

(i)   the assessment of the quantum of damages awarded in liability cases

(ii)   the determination of sentence in criminal cases.

In both of the above matters each court of appeal has its own usual assessment which, again in both cases, is published yearly in specialised unofficial publications which are routinely consulted by professionals and judges. However, in order to avoid their decisions being quashed, lower courts have to ensure, when applying these past assessments to new cases, not to refer to them expressly in the text of their decisions (see Chapter 4.1.3(4) above).

Note: the role played by lower courts in (ii) is particularly important in view of the fact that the New Penal Code only provides for the maximum punishment to be imposed on offenders. Although aggravating circumstances are statutorily defined, extenuating circumstances are left to the discretion of the judges (art. 132-24 of the New Penal Code). Trial court decisions therefore offer in this respect a scale of penalties that can be used as a basis for evaluation when fixing sentence in subsequent similar cases.

4.2.2 Consistent line of precedents

This subheading refers to the notion known in France as *jurisprudence constante* whereby a particular interpretation or principle is repeated in a series of decisions. *Jurisprudence constante* entails greater authority being attached to a consistent line of precedents rather than to a single one. In his analysis of the respective merits of the English and Continental approaches to precedent, Goodhart (1934: 59) claimed that the French method of repeated judicial practice does not give the same certainty in the law as the binding authority of a single precedent provides in England. The reasons for this, according to Goodhart, are twofold:

Firstly, precedent which is based on practice must be of slower growth for it requires a series of cases over a considerable period of time before it can develop. Secondly, it is less definite, for it may be difficult to determine when a practice has been established.

It is surprising to note, since Goodhart's time, how commonly the certainty argument has been used in English or comparative law academic textbooks to emphasise the merits of the English system of precedent. However, the problem with the certainty argument is that it does not sufficiently take account of the various factors – factors most writers are indeed willing to acknowledge – that lessen considerably the degree of certainty attached to English precedents. Amongst these factors are the difficulty in determining the *ratio decidendi* in a binding case, the existence of important exceptions to the rule of *stare decisis* and, furthermore, the judicial practices of distinguishing and overruling. In view of these limitations, it may be seen as questionable whether there is the necessity, as in England, of laying down a strict rule requiring the precedents of particular courts to be followed. In a comparative study of the law on precedent, David (1984: 3-395) even wonders if the rule of binding precedent known in common law systems 'has ever existed'. And the eminent author adds the following for his readers' consideration: 'or, if you prefer it, there are so many limitations on and exceptions to the rule that it is binding only on those who wish to be bound by it'. David, then concludes:

The rule of precedent binds only those who are satisfied by the solution provided by the precedent, or who think that at least for the sake of certainty it is better, all things considered, to abide by that solution, it not being overtly objectionable. These two factors, which form the basis of the authority of precedent, lead judges to follow them in the vast majority of cases; they do not depend on the existence of a strict rule, which would create an antithesis between Common law and Romano-Germanic countries.

More generally, it may be said that the claim that legal certainty is better served in a system of binding precedent, as opposed to repeated judicial practice, fails to recognise that there is no such thing as 'fixed' or 'definite' precedent. Precedents evolve, developing gradually as the law in general does. As new cases are brought to their attention, judges act as fine art painters, constantly touching up the canvass on which precedents have been drawn. It is within this perspective of continuous development that the courts in France ensure that their rulings are expressed broadly in order to allow for unforeseen situations arising from changes in the social, economic and, political context which may take place following their previous decisions. *Juris-prudence constante* is therefore nothing other than the expression, in judicial terms, of the inevitable development of the law in a given legal system.

Finally, it must be noted that, even in France, a single decision is sometimes able to 'make *jurisprudence*', that is to say to establish a definite principle likely to be followed in the future. This occurs in two categories of situations which are dealt with in the following subheadings.

4.2.3 *Revirement de jurisprudence*

Revirement is a close equivalent to the concept of overruling in Anglo-American law, with this specific characteristic that *revirement* is only concerned with the departure by a highest court from its own *jurisprudence*. However, even departure from a single previous precedent, which had been perceived by the community of jurists at the time when it was decided as an *arrêt de principe* (see Chapter 4.2.4 below), is sometimes enough to mark a turning point in the course of the court's *jurisprudence*. *Revirements* are of considerable importance in relation to the degree of force and persuasiveness attaching to a precedent. Indeed, in the majority of cases they will determine for the lower courts a change in their own judicial practice. Although judges are free, in principle, to disregard such *revirements* since they are not bound by any decisions, in practice they will nevertheless generally follow them.

Because, as has been seen, precedents are not formally binding, it is not within the formal practice of French courts to state in their judgments that a previous *juris-prudence* has been overruled as this would have the effect of recognising precedents as 'authorities' in the English sense. For the same reason, the American practice of prospective overruling, whereby the court announces in advance that it will change the relevant rule – but only for future cases, is unknown in French law. This accounts for the fact that, in France, *revirements* are always implied and are sometimes difficult to identify. They are particularly difficult to identify when decisions on similar legal issues are conflicting, or where decisions extend and/or limit the application of earlier ones. However, *revirements* are easier to detect when a highest court reverses a decision of a lower one – which was based on previously established *jurisprudence* – on the grounds that the case was wrongly decided by this court. Here, as a consequence, the previous *jurisprudence* has indeed to be treated as overruled.

Revirements are rare in French law for the same reasons as those commonly put forward in most jurisdictions when dealing with the question of overruling. In this respect, the reluctance to overrule long-standing precedents is usually justified by the fact that overruling operates retrospectively, thus upsetting any previous arrange-ments made by the parties to a case under the established rules arrived at previously by the courts. Having said that, it would be wrong to assume that *revirements* are exceptional. There have been, in the past, famous examples of *revirements* on issues related to illegitimate children, at a time when these children could not be legally recognised by their natural parents. Often quoted as an example is the controversial question of whether unmarried parents were permitted at the material time to adopt their own illegitimate children; to which the Court of Cassation, after having said 'yes' in 1841, said 'no' in 1843 and finally 'yes' in *Bouleau* v *Bazouin* (1846), D.P. 1846, 1, 81. Cases such as *Desmares* (see Chapter 4.2.1.3 above), in private law, or *Nicolo* (see Chapter 1.1.3 above), in administrative law, offer further more recent illustrations of *revirements*.

4.2.4 Statement of principles of general application (*arrêts de principe*)

A decision is regarded as being particularly authoritative when a court – usually a highest court – states clearly and explicitly the principle of general application which form the basis of its decision. As will be seen in Chapter 8, it is not generally the case that French courts are explicit in their justification. That explains why these types of decisions, called *arrêts de principe*, are of particular importance, and this is notably reflected by the interest they generate in academic writing. *Arrêts de principe* are relatively limited in number, as compared with the more common *arrêts d'espèce*. The latter, unlike the former, are merely the application of established judicial practice to the material facts of a particular case and are, therefore, of limited value.

More specifically, the difference between *arrêts de principe* and *arrêts d'espèce* lies, firstly, in the nature and importance of the issues raised by the cases involved. Indeed, novel and controversial issues are areas where *arrêts de principe* are more likely to be delivered. The distinctive value ascribed to them by legal academics is also a signifi-cant factor in determining their status. Unlike *arrêts d'espèce*, *arrêts de principe* are widely reported and commented upon in all major law journals. Above all, the style in which the decision is drafted is of particular significance in indicating an *arrêts de principe*. In an *arrêt de principe* what the court is doing is to raise a particular inter-pretation to the status of a principle. What is of particular relevance here is that this principle on which the solution of the court is based is clearly stated, using broad terms to allow for its application in subsequent cases. It is this explicit statement of a principle and its capacity for generalised application which is the most important difference between *arrêts de principe* and *arrêts d'espèce*. A further aid to recognition at first glance for *arrêts de principe* is that the principle established by it is usually – although not always – enunciated in a separate proposition at the top of the judgment, in what is called a *chapeau*, literally, a 'hat'. A good illustration of a *chapeau* is *Comité d'établissement de Saint-Chamond* v *Ray* (1954), D. 1954, 217, a case concerned with the legal personality of corporate bodies. At the vey top of its judgment, the Court of Cassation states:

Attendu que la personnalité civile n'est pas une création de la loi; qu'elle appartient, en principe, à tout groupement pourvu d'une possibilité d'expression collective pour la défense d'intérêts licites, dignes, par suite, d'être juridiquement reconnus et protégés.

Arrêts de principe should not be confused with *arrêts de règlement* (see Chapter 4.1.2

above). Indeed, both types of *arrêt* are presented with a certain degree of generality in terms of the way in which the principle serving as the basis for the decision is formulated. However, what distinguishes one from another is that in *arrêt de principe*, the court links the general rule stated to the actual litigation under its consideration, whereas in *arrêt de règlement*, a precedent is created in anticipation of litigation which as yet does not exist.

The features described above characterising *arrêts de principe*, account for the fact that in the common law world they have been labelled as the 'leading cases' of French law. Indeed, the history of French case law testifies to the fact that most of them have become the source of a particular doctrine in specific areas of law which, from there, have developed into a consistent line of authorities. The following is a list, by no means comprehensive, of some of the leading decisions which have marked the history of French case law:

(i) *Blanco* (1873), D. 1873, 3, 17, the 'corner stone' of French administrative law, where it was decided that the Civil Code could no longer be used as a basis for decisions involving the liability of public bodies and officials.

(ii) *Canal de Craponne* (1876), D. 1876, 1, 193, in contract law, decided that it is not open to the courts to modify the terms of a contract agreed by the parties even in the event that circumstances have drastically changed since the conclusion of this contract (doctrine of *imprévision*).

(iii) *Cadot* (1889), Rec. 1148 marked the end of the 'Ministre-juge'. Any claim against a public body or official could, from then on, be directly brought before the administrative courts without the need to bring it first before the relevant Minister.

(iv) *Caisse Rurale Commune de Manigod* v *Administration de l'Enregistrement* (1914), D.P. 1914, 1, 257 drew a distinction between *association* and *société* on the basis that whilst the latter was a profit-making body the former was not.

(v) *Clément-Bayard* v *Cocquerel* (1915), D.P. 1917, 1, 79, marked the establishment of the doctrine of *abus de droit* in property law (see Chapter 3.2.3 above).

(vi) *Veuve Jand'heur* v *Les Galeries Belfortaises* (1930), D.P 1930,1, 57, established a presumption of responsibility for things in one's care (see Chapter 4.3.1 and 4.3.2.1 below).

(vii) *Franck* v *Connot* (1941), D.C.1942, 25, specified the criteria defining the concept of *garde* (custody) in art. 1384 al. 1 of the Civil Code (see Chapter 4.3.2.1 below).

(viii) *Comité d'Etablissement de Saint-Chamond* v *Ray* (cited in Chapter 4.2.4 above) established the test for the granting by the courts of legal personality to corporate bodies.

(ix) *Administration des Douanes* v *Soc. Cafés Jacques Vabre* (cited in Chapter 1.1.3 above) ruled on the superiority of treaties over parliamentary statutes.

(x) *Proc. Gén. C. de Cass.* v *Madame X.* (1991), D. 1991, 417 decided that any agreement between a surrogate mother and a childless couple was illegal and, as a consequence, any application for adoption following such an agreement could not be granted in court.

4.3 *Jurisprudence* and legislation

Unsurprisingly, after all that has been said, the predominant conventional view in French legal tradition on the relationship between *jurisprudence* and legislation is that the former is subordinate to the latter. However, many objections can be raised against this approach which, indeed, is routinely challenged by French legal academics. Instead of *jurisprudence* being subordinate to legislation, it would be more accurate to say that they complement one another, as will be discussed below.

4.3.1 Subordination

The view that *jurisprudence* is subordinate to legislation is supported by two principal arguments. One relates to Parliament's power to overrule judicial decisions (as was the case with the Loi of 4 March 2002, art. one, overruling the PERRUCHE decision (2000), D. 2001, 332, in respect of a wrongful life claim). The other is concerned with judges who, in the general performance of their functions, regard themselves as being primarily bound by legislation.

The first argument is at best debatable because experience has shown that in practice Parliament has a far greater tendency to overrule what it has itself previously legislated than to overrule carefully constructed rules and principles of *jurisprudence* which have developed over time. The second point, however, is more difficult to rebut in the sense that French judges, similarly to their English counterparts, do not perceive themselves as lawmakers and as a general rule do not, at least overtly, challenge legislative supremacy. This deference to the legislature is reflected in two ways:

(a) In the style adopted by judges when writing their judgments making sure, even in the case of legislative gaps, that statute or code provisions which may have been specifically extended to cover the case in hand, are stated as a basis for their decisions (see further 3.2.3 and 8.2).

(b) In courts' general unwillingness to review the constitutionality of statutes. French courts, when challenged, invariably decide that they are not empowered to review the constitutionality of existing statutes (for a clear illustration of this tendency, with respect to the Court of Cassation see, *Epoux Guillot* v *Procureur Général près la cour d'appel de Versailles* (1986), Bull. civ. I, no. 232 and, with respect to the *Conseil d'Etat* see, *Confédération nationale des associations familiales* (1990), D. 1991, 283).

However, the foundations of the subordination approach can be easily questioned by looking at legal rules in terms of the function they are supposed to fulfil, i.e. the governance of society as a whole, rather than in terms of the source from which their authority derives. Within this 'functional' perspective, *jurisprudence* and legislation do converge, at least in three respects:

(a) The rules laid down by French courts in their decisions are very often as general in character as their purportedly superior legislative counterparts and go far beyond the confines of the originating cases from which they are derived.

(b) Furthermore, they enjoy the same *de facto* authority as any statutory text. Indeed, judges follow them and citizens consider them to be as much law as legislation itself is. It is also symptomatic of this approach that in French law schools, teachers treat the relevant judicial precedents of the subject they teach as law in its own right.

An illustration of both (a) and (b) is the famous case of *Veuve Jand'heur* v *Les Galeries Belfortaises* (cited in Chapter 4.2.4 above). Here, a young girl was run over and seriously injured by one of the defendant's lorries. The issue was whether the case should be governed by art. 1384 al. 1 of the Civil Code, a text under which the defendant could be held automatically liable for damages caused by things in his care (here a car) without the necessity of establishing fault on his part (because, here, the fault was presumed). The Court of Cassation, sitting in full court, decided to apply art. 1384 al. 1 to the case, and further ruled that, henceforth, absence of fault would no longer be a defence in an action brought under 1384 al. 1. The Court said:

Attendu que la présomption de responsabilité établie par l'art 1384, al. 1 C.Civ, à l'encontre de celui qui a sous sa garde la chose inanimée qui a causé un dommage à autrui, ne peut être détruite que par la preuve d'un cas fortuit ou de force majeure ou d'une cause étrangère qui ne lui soit pas imputable.

(The presumption of liability contained in art. 1384 al. 1 and applying to the owner or custodian of an inanimate object which has caused harm, can be only rebutted by proving the equivalent of an act of God or some other external cause that cannot be attributed to the defendant.)

The rule laid down in *Jand'heur*, establishing a regime of strict liability for damage caused by things in one's care, formulated as it is, in broad terms, could easily be taken for a statute or a code provision. In fact this rule is so firmly established that no judge today would depart from it and, no counsel would argue against it in court. For 70 years – much more than the average life span of a statute in France – the *Jand'heur* precedent has been as well-established and undisputed a rule as the code provision on which it is based, art. 1384 al. 1, and from which it has become hard to distinguish.

(c) Finally, the fact that judicial decisions are often confirmed by subsequent legislation is further evidence of the convergence of function towards which both precedent and legislative rules are working. Indeed, in enacting legislation confirming a precedent, Parliament 'receives' this precedent fully into the general body of law, granting it equal status to legislation. By way of illustration is *Placet-Thirion* (1906), DP, 1907, 1, 207 (often cited as *Laurent Atthalin*, from the name of the reporting judge whose submissions were decisive to the outcome of the case) where it was decided, for the first time, that the victim of a crime has the right on his own to initiate criminal proceedings if no prosecution has been brought by the State. This right was to be confirmed later by the legislature in art. 1 al. 2 of the Code of Criminal Procedure. Another illustration is *Proc. Gén. C. de Cass.* v *Madame X.* (cited at Chapter 4.2.4 above) on the illegality of surrogacy agreements, now governed by art. 16-7 of the Civil Code.

As a final point it is interesting to note that, in recent years, the European Court of Human Rights, when interpreting the Convention on Human Rights, has pointed out the similarity that exists between legislation and case law in the context of the French legal system. In *Kruslin v France* (1990), 12 EHRR 547, the European Court, with respect to the expression 'in accordance with the law' used in art. 8 (2) of the Convention, ruled (Report, pp. 561–2) that established case law cannot be disregarded in relation to this text. It concluded that the term 'law' must, therefore, be understood not only in the formal meaning of legislative rules, but also in the substantive meaning of both written and unwritten rules. It followed clearly, according to this approach, that legislation and *jurisprudence* are both 'law' from a material (as opposed to a formal) point of view.

4.3.2 *Jurisprudence* and legislation complementing one another

The complementary nature of legislation and *jurisprudence* has been particularly emphasised by Boulanger (1953: 22); *jurisprudence*, he notes, is 'nothing other than the interpretation, the alteration and the finishing touch to enacted legislation'('*la jurisprudence c'est la loi interprétée, modifiée, complétée'*). Elsewhere Boulanger (1961: 11) further argues that precedents are 'an integral part of the legislative text itself'. This relationship between the two sources derives from the fact that Parliament is only able to enact rules of general application. It is therefore incumbent upon the judiciary to give effect to these rules by applying them to the particular circumstances of cases arising before the courts. In other words, without, and prior to, judicial adjudication, legislative rules cannot by their nature be implemented.

When considering judicial decisions as complements to legislation, French legal writers have distinguished between three categories of precedents according to the degree of creation attached to them. In this respect, the traditional classification used for custom in the theory of legal sources has been applied to precedents. Thus, as with custom, precedents can be either *secundum legem, praeter legem* or, *contra legem*.

4.3.2.1 Precedent *secundum legem*

This first category refers to the judicial function of applying and interpreting existing rules, already examined at length in the previous chapter (Chapter 3.2 above). Here, although judges sometimes engage in statutory interpretation in a creative way, they do so within boundaries fixed by the wording of statutory and code provisions. Included in this category are precedents which define the meaning and scope of statutory provisions and those which adapt those provisions to changing times. An illustration of this is the refinement and development carried out by the courts in application of art. 1384 al. 1 of the Civil Code, mentioned earlier in this chapter. With respect to responsibility for things in one's care, this text merely provides that a person is responsible for the damage caused by the action of things in his care, without giving further detail of what 'thing' (*chose* in the French text) or 'care' (*garde*) mean. These terms are so vague and broad that without judicial intervention it would have been impossible to implement art. 1384 al. 1. Thus, court decisions have been decisive in defining the scope of this text by introducing specific conditions that must be met before liability could be imposed on the owner of a thing. These conditions are:

(i) All kinds of things, as long as they are physical things, are included in the scope of art. 1384 al. 1. Thus, these may be solid, gaseous, liquid, movable or immovable objects. Moreover, it is not a necessary condition that these things be dangerous to the public, defective or, in motion when the damage occurs for art. 1384 al. 1 to be applicable (this last point was decided in *Jand'heur*, cited in Chapter 4.2.4 above).

(ii) The thing must have contributed to the occurrence of the damage or, as it is usually put by the courts, played an 'active role in the producing of the damage' for the test to apply. An illustration of this, very often heard in court, are badly signposted windows which play an 'active role' in the damage caused to the victim when hurt breaking them; the same applies to a slippery floor in a shop.

(iii) The defendant must have possessed the 'use, direction, and control' of the thing at the time of the damage in order to be held liable. This requirement has very important implications as to who is liable to pay damages to the victim. Thus, in the case of the owner of a stolen car which has caused an accident whilst being driven by the thief at the time of the accident; since the 'use, direction and control' are with the thief and not the owner, the owner is not held liable under art. 1384 al. 1 (decided in *Franck*, cited at Chapter 4.2.4 above).

4.3.2.2 Precedent *praeter legem*

This second category of precedents, as in the case of the one which follows, is concerned with the courts' power to go beyond interpretation and establish new rules alongside the existing ones. It may be said, here, that the judiciary exercises quasi-legislative power. However, unlike precedent *contra legem*, precedent *praeter legem* is supplementary to and yet consistent with legislation. It is within this category that judicial law making has been at its most creative in French law. The techniques which have been used by the courts to establish new rules, within the restrictions of the system, have differed as regards civil and administrative courts. The former tend to refer to some relevant enactment to form the basis for judicial construction. Two examples will illustrate this.

(i) In the area of contractual liability, courts have gone considerably beyond the scope of art. 1147 of the Civil Code by adding a distinction – once proposed by Demogue in his *Traité des Obligations* (1925) – between *obligation de moyen* (where the debtor is bound to no more than the exercise of reasonable care) and *obligation de résultat* (where the debtor's obligation is not merely to show due diligence, but to achieve the end result which he has promised). Further subcategories are derived from this fundamental distinction. The courts have thus 'discovered' in specific contracts, such as the contract of transport and the medical contract, a so-called implied *obligation de sécurité*. In a contract of transport it consists of the obligation of the '*transporteur de conduire le voyageur sain et sauf à destination*' – the transport company to bring the traveller safe and sound to his destination (*Compagnie Générale Transatlantique* v *Zbidi Hamida Ben Mahmoud* (1911), D.P. 1913, 1, 249). In a medical contract it imposes on a doctor the '*engagement de donner à son client des soins consciencieux, attentifs, conformes aux données acquises de la science*' – an obligation to give his client a standard of care and attention which is both conscientious and consistent with the latest techniques (*Dr Nicolas* v *Epoux Mercier* (1936), D.P. 1936, 1, p. 88).

(ii) In property law, courts have used arts 544 (on the the right of ownership) and 1382 (fault in civil liability) of the Civil Code to form the basis for the creation of the associated doctrines of abuse of rights and *troubles anormaux de voisinage* in the particular context of private nuisance between neighbours.

As far as the administrative courts are concerned, because of the absence of any general code similar to the Civil Code in their area of operation, precedent *praeter legem* arises out of the application of the rules that have been established by previous case law as well as from the use, in their decisions, of unwritten *principes généraux de droit* (on this notion see generally Chapter 3.2.3 above; also, see *Aramu* (1945), D. 1946, 158, which confirms the existence of unwritten binding general principles in the area of administrative law).

4.3.2.3 Precedents *contra legem*

Within this category are precedents which run counter to statutory provisions and effectively replace them. This is achieved in two ways:

(a) either directly, by establishing a rule which contradicts an express legislative provision, or

(b) indirectly, resisting new legislation by setting a new precedent.

A well-known illustration of 'direct' precedent *contra legem* is the case law relating to *don manuel*, in the law of gifts. Article 931 of the Civil Code provides that, for gifts *inter vivos* to be legally binding, a written record of the gift must be drawn up by a notary. Despite this code requirement, courts have for long decided that the gift *inter vivos* of any movable property can be made, without formal recording by a notary, by manual transfer only. This includes, following the latest case law, the transfer of money to a bank account and the remittance of a cheque. An example of 'indirect' precedent *contra legem* is *Proc. Gén. Paris* v *Bassilika* (1992), D. 1993, 36. In 1986, Parliament passed legislation amending the then art. 78-2 al. 2 of the Code of Criminal Procedure in order to loosen the conditions, required by that text, for the purpose of carrying out identity checks with a view to facilitating the deportation of illegal immigrants. The newly revised text of the code was worded in such a way that identity checks could effectively be carried out at any time against anyone. The Court of Cassation, in *Bassilika*, adopted a narrow interpretation of the new legislation, deciding that identity checks could only be made when, because of the behaviour of the subject, police officers had grounds for suspecting that a crime was actually in the process of being committed, a condition which was neither written in the amended art. 78-2, nor obviously intended by the legislator. In response, further legislation was introduced by the government in 1993 with the sole intention of putting an end to such a precedent. In its new amended version, art. 78-2 al. 2 specifically provided that identity checks could take place 'whatever the behaviour' of the person whose identity was to be checked by the police. This text is currently still in force in its 1993 amended version.

4.4 Legitimacy of judicial law making

This chapter has already outlined how French legal theorists have struggled with the question of whether *jurisprudence* is a source of law, given the constraints of the French doctrine of separation of powers and the code prohibition on making law that is intended to govern future cases. In view of democratic values, a new focus to the debate has centred on the question of the legitimacy of judicial law making. So the question has become not so much whether *jurisprudence* is a source of law but rather, what is the source of legitimacy for *jurisprudence*. While authors like Dupeyroux (1960) persists in holding the view that *jurisprudence* when it equates to law making is nothing else that an 'abusive source of law', thus denying any legitimacy to judicial law making, others have attempted, more or less successfully, to validate judge-made law, taking various directions in their effort to do so. These are outlined and briefly discussed below.

4.4.1 *Jurisprudence* as custom

This approach was first advocated by Planiol in his *Traité Elémentaire de Droit Civil*, 1922, Vol. 1, p. 6 and Gény in *Méthodes d'Interprétation* (cited at Chapter 3.2.4.3 above). It rests on the assumption that *jurisprudence* is not, in itself, an independent source of law and that precedent only amounts to law because, with the passage of time, it develops into custom. Thus, for Planiol, 'court decisions, alongside codes and statutes, reformulate a new law of customary nature'. The main objection to the '*jurisprudence* as custom' approach is that, unlike custom, the formation of *jurisprudence* is not spontaneous and necessitates an act of volition which is the active involvement of a judge (Belaid, 1974). Also, custom, to be recognised as such, must have existed for a certain period of time before it can be recognised as law, whereas a precedent can be established by a single decision.

4.4.2 Implicit acceptance

According to some authors such as Waline (1950), what justifies judicial law making is the implicit acceptance of precedents by the legislature. Through its silence and inaction the legislature implicitly accepts that precedents are law. This is further confirmed by the fact that, very often, the legislature adopts a precedent by converting it into legislation. The main argument put forward against this analysis is that it is a fiction to say that Parliament, through its inaction, approves of a precedent, since most of the members of Parliament are generally unaware of the content of judicial decisions!

4.4.3 Consensus

Maury (1950) and, more recently, Jestaz (1987), have argued that it is a consensus of opinion amongst the legal community which validates judicial law making. According to Maury this consensus is formed out of a recognition of the validity of precedents arising out of their acceptance by the legal community and the public at large or, even, out of the absence of any opposition to them. Thus, in this view judges, in following precedents, and practitioners, in using them in court, both 'adhere' to the binding character of precedent. The main critique voiced against this approach is that this sort of consensus may be a factor of legal stability, which is certainly desirable, but one which cannot serve to give validity to a rule established by precedent, particularly when, as in France, constitutional theory and code provisions, militate against such a form of law making.

4.4.4 Duty to adjudicate (art. 4 of the Civil Code)

It would appear that the legitimacy of judicial law making lies in the very operation of adjudication itself. This view is supported by a reading of art. 4 of the Civil Code, another important provision relating to the judicial function. Article 4 states that judges cannot use, as a pretext for failing to adjudicate, the fact that there is a gap in the law or that the law is ambiguous. This text has always been used by the Court of Cassation as a means of avoiding a 'non-judgment' (*déni de justice*), in cases heard by lower courts. Thus, for example, a court cannot refuse to return a judgment, as in *Société Barlier* v *Sociétés Sovatra et autres* (1999), Gaz. Pal. 1999, 2, Somm. 689, where two creditors A and B were suing a defendant C for the same sum of money claimed to be owing, on the grounds that 'it was impossible for the court to choose between A and B'. Similarly, in the earlier criminal case of *Baesens et autres* (1984), D. 1985, 1, the Court of Cassation using art. 4, decided to quash a decision of acquittal by a trial court given on the grounds that the law used as the basis for the prosecution was obscure and its meaning uncertain.

Therefore, under art. 4, judges have a legal duty to adjudicate, vigorously enforced by the highest courts, and this duty stands even where there is no law at all! Since, in and by the nature of such circumstances, judges are forced to 'make' the rule to support the solution adopted, there is finally a clear validation of precedent in French law. As suggested by Terré (2000: 256), referring to art. 4, '*la jurisprudence tire sa force dans la mission du juge*' (jurisprudence draws its force from the very mission of the judicial function itself).

Chapter references

AGOSTINI, E., 'L'Equité', D.1978, Chr. 7.

ATIAS, C., 'L'ambiguïté des Arrêts dits de Principe en Droit Privé', JCP, 1984, I, 3145.

ATIAS, L., 'L'image Doctrinale de la Cour de Cassation', D. 1993, Chr.133.

BACH, L. 'Jurisprudence' *Répertoire de Droit Civil*, 2000, Vol. 6.

BEIGNIER, B., 'Les arrêts de Règlements', *Revue Droits*, 1989, Vol. 9 (La Fonction de Juger), pp. 45–55.

BELAID, S., *Essai Sur le Pouvoir Créateur de la Jurisprudence*, Paris: LGDJ, 1974.

BOULANGER, J., 'Notations sur le Pouvoir Créateur de la Jurisprudence Civile', RTDC, 1961, Vol. 59, pp. 417–441.

BOULANGER, J., 'Jurisprudence' in *Répertoire de Droit Civil*, 1st edn, 1953.

CROSS, R., and HARRIS, J. W., *Precedent in English Law*, 4th edn, Oxford: Clarendon Press, 1991.

DAVID, R., 'Sources of Law', *International Encyclopedia of Comparative Law*, 1984, Vol. 2, 3–386 to 3–396.

DUPEYROUX O., 'La Jurisprudence, Source Abusive du Droit', in *Mélanges Offerts à J. Maury*, Vol. 2, Paris: Dalloz/Sirey, 1960.

ESMEIN, P., 'La Jurisprudence et la loi', RTDC, 1952, Vol. 50, pp. 17–23.

GOODHART, A.L., 'Precedent in English and Continental Law', *The Law Quarterly Review*, 1934, Vol. 50, pp. 40–65.

JESTAZ, P., 'La Jurisprudence: Réflexions sur un Malentendu', D. 1987, Chr. 11.

JESTAZ, P., 'La Jurisprudence, Ombre Portée du Contentieux', D. 1989, Chr. 149.

LARHER-LOYER, C., 'La Jurisprudence d'Appel', JCP1989, I, 3407.

MacCORMICK D.N., and SUMMERS, R.S., *Interpreting Precedents*, Ashgate/Dartmouth, 1997, especially Chapter 4 by Troper, M., and Grzegorczyk, C., 'Precedent in France', pp. 103–140.

MAURY, J., 'Observation sur la Jurisprudence en tant que Source de Droit' in *Le Droit Privé Francais au Milieu du XXe siècle, Etudes Offertes à G. Ripert*, Vol. 1, Paris: LGDJ, 1950.

SAUVEL, T., 'Essai sur la Notion de Précédent', D. 1955, Chr. 93.

TERRÉ, F., *Introduction Générale au Droit*, 5th edn, Paris: Dalloz, 2000 (Chapter 'Jurisprudence', pp. 245–260).

VOIRIN, P., 'Les Revirements de Juris-

Appendix to Chapter 4

Where to find cases

4.5 General points

4.5.1 Case reporting

As with any other legal system, the way precedents operate in France depends much on being able to gain access to cases relevant to the issue under consideration. Unreported cases have little chance of developing into precedents.

Access to precedents is achieved in France through a system of case reporting which, as will be seen, is essentially private and is largely a matter of choice and discretion on the part of the courts themselves or that of the editor of the particular series of reports in his charge. This system is by no means comprehensive. Although decisions handed down by the highest courts constitute the vast majority of decisions published in law reports, only a small percentage of the thousands given each year by these courts are published. In recent years one can observe a tendency in French law reports to publish a greater number of court of appeal and lower court decisions than formerly. However, these still represent only a small proportion and are, in the majority of cases, reported in summary form. Unreported decisions (cited as *inédit*) can be obtained in transcript form directly from the court itself. Additionally, a high percentage of unreported court decisions have become accessible through computerised systems such as Juris-Data (see Chapter 4.7.1 below). The use of on-line legal information systems has, in recent years, given rise in France to a substantial growth in the number of readily available judgment reports. However, in contrast with what has happened in England, this growth has not degenerated into a situation whereby courts have been burdened with a weight of sometimes inappropriate and unnecessary authority, deployed by advocates in the argument of a case, with the consequence that it has caused a reduction in the efficiency of litigation. In England, this situation has prompted the Lord Chief Justice to issue, with immediate effect on 9 April 2001, a practice direction laying down a number of rules as to what material should be cited in court, and this with a view to limiting the citation of previous authority to cases that were relevant and useful to the court. The difference in the circumstances of the French and the English legal systems lies in the status attached to case law. The absence of the rule of *stare decisis* in French law, with its corollary that court decisions are not 'authorities' in a technical sense, prudence et leurs Conséquences', JCP 1959, I, 1467.

WALINE, M., 'Le Pouvoir Normatif de la Jurisprudence', in *La Technique et les Principes du Droit Public. Etudes en l'Honneur de G. Scelle*, Vol. 2, Paris: LGDJ, 1950.

ZENATI, F., *La Jurisprudence*, Paris: Dalloz, 1991.

renders meaningless the establishment of a system of standard rules for the citation of authority in court.

4.5.2 Case citation

French decisions are not, in the vast majority of cases, cited by the names of the parties. The way in which French decisions are cited is, first, to specify the name of the court, in abbreviated form, followed by the full date of the decision. It is important when dealing with French case law to pay particular attention to the full date, as more than one decision can be given by the same court during the same year, month or even day! Also, it is essential to know the abbreviated form of the court's name. Here is some guidance on the main abbreviations used in case citations.

The decisions of the Court of Cassation are cited by the name of the division (*chambre*) which has heard the case followed by the date of the decision. The Court of Cassation sits in six divisions, namely:

(a) *chambre criminelle*, cited as Crim., (criminal cases)

(b) *première chambre civile*, cited as Civ. 1re, (family law, contracts)

(c) *deuxième chambre civile*, cited as Civ. 2e, (divorce, torts, civil procedure)

(d) *troisième chambre civile*, cited as Civ. 3e, (property, leases, construction law)

(e) *chambre commerciale et financière*, cited as Com., (commercial and business law)

(f) *chambre sociale*, cited as *Soc.*, (employment, social security).

Thus, an example of citation of a Court of Cassation decision would be:

'Com., 7 janvier 1992'.

Court of appeal decisions are cited by the name of the town in which the court is situated, sometimes prefaced by CA for *Cour d'Appel*, followed by the date, such as:

'Paris, 24 février 1998 or, CA Paris, 24 février 1998'.

In administrative law, in addition to the name of the court and the date, cases are also referred to by the plaintiff's name such as:

'CE [for, *Conseil d'Etat*] 20 octobre 1989, *Nicolo*' [name of the plaintiff].

A similar method of citation applies to leading private law cases, in a slightly different form. Thus:

'Arrêt Franck, Ch. Réunies, [for, Chambres Réunies, the former name for the current *Assemblée Plénière* of the Court of Cassation], 2 décembre 1941'.

What follows is a brief description of the style used for correctly citing cases which are to be found in the most widely used French law reports.

4.6 Law reports

4.6.1 Official reports

There is only one official source of law reports in the French legal system: the *Bulletins de la Cour de Cassation*. These *Bulletins* date back to 1798 and consist of two separate monthly series of publications. One is the *Bulletin criminel* (cited: *Bull. crim.*), for cases heard by the single criminal 'chamber' of the Court of Cassation. The other is *Bulletin civil* (cited *Bull. civ.*) for civil cases. The latter is bulkier than the former, the reason being that it is divided into five parts (cited: *I, II, III, IV* and *V*) to reflect the five civil 'chambers' of the Court of Cassation (see Chapter 4.5.2 above). In addition, the *Bulletin civil* contains a preliminary part reporting the decisions handed down in *Assemblée Plénière* (cited as Ass. Plén) and *Chambre Mixte* (cited as Ch. Mixte). In each of the *Bulletins* cases are reported chronologically and are numbered consecutively. They are also reported in full but, unlike private law reports, decisions are not annotated or commented on. The complete form of case citation in the *Bulletins* is made up of:

(a) the 'chamber' of the court that has delivered the decision

(b) the date

(c) the series (criminal or civil)

(d) the number of that part of the *Bulletin* in which the decision can be found (for civil cases only)

(e) the number of the case as designated by the *Bulletin*.

Thus:

'Civ. 1re, 24 mars 1998, *Bull. civ. I*, no. 124',

is the decision of the first civil chamber of the Court of Cassation, dated 24 March 1998 and reported in the *Bulletin civil*, first part, with the number 124.

The Court of Cassation itself decides what decisions need to be published amongst the thousands it delivers each year. The decisions selected for publication are those which are likely to have some relevance in the formation of precedents.

4.6.2 Semi-official reports

These are mainly:

(a) *Recueil des décisions du Conseil d'Etat*, also called *Recueil Lebon* (cited: *Rec.* or, *Leb.*, followed by page number), is published by Dalloz under the patronage of the *Conseil d'Etat*. *Lebon* publishes most of the decisions given by the *Conseil d'Etat* (cited CE), the decisions of the *Tribunal des Conflits* (cited Trib. Confl.), as well as important judgments given by the lower administrative courts. Every year there are six issues, each divided into five parts corresponding to the different categories of administrative courts. Within each part, cases are classified in chronological order. At the end of the annual collected volume a *table analytique* is provided listing the decisions reported within it in the given year, arranged according to subject-matter, together with a short digest of other decisions which could not be reported in full in the main body of the volume itself. Also, since cases decided by the administrative courts are cited by the name of the plaintiff, case search is considerably facilitated by the alphabetical table of the plaintiffs' names which is also provided. Here is an example of case citation in the *Recueil Lebon*:

'CE 19 novembre 1975, *Cuny, Rec. 817*'.

(b) *Recueil des décisions du Conseil Constitutionnel* (cited *Rec.*, followed by page number) is published by *Dalloz* under the patronage of the *Conseil Constitutionnel*. Each annually published single volume contains the full text, in chronological order, of the decisions given by the *Conseil*. At the end of the volume there is an analytical table of cases, classified by subject-matter, with a separate synopsis in English to give foreign readers easy access to French constitutional case law. The citation of the *Conseil Constitutionnel*'s decisions is made up of the roll number of the decision within the year, followed by letters indicating in abbreviated form the nature of the *Conseil*'s involvement e.g. AN (for *élections législatives*), DC (for *declaration de conformité*) or L (for *examen de forme législative*), the full date, the reference to the subject-matter of the statute submitted for scrutiny (optional), and the name of the *Recueil* in abbreviated form followed by the page number, such as:

'91-290 DC du 9 mai 1991, *Statut de la Corse, Rec. 50*'.

It may be noted that the quickest and most effective way to access the *Conseil Constitutionnel* decisions is on the *Conseil*'s website (see below under 'Internet' at Chapter 4.8.) where a list of the *Conseil*'s decisions is provided in chronological order for a given year (with the full text of the most important decisions), along with a comprehensive set of bibliographical references to commentaries made on those decisions.

4.6.3 Private reports

Private reports are known in France as *recueils de jurisprudence*. The most widely used are:

(a) *Recueil Dalloz-Sirey* (cited: *D.* followed by year) *Dalloz* and *Sirey* were originally two separate series named after their founders, Désiré Dalloz and Jean-Baptiste Sirey, until they finally merged in 1965. Prior to its merger with Sirey, Dalloz went through a series of changes since its establishment in 1845. From 1924 to 1941 the series was split into a monthly publication, *Dalloz périodique* (cited: *D.P.* followed by the relevant part of the yearly volume, either 1 or 2), which later became *Dalloz critique* (cited: *D.C.*), and a weekly one, *Dalloz hebdomadaire* (cited: *D.H.*) later renamed

Dalloz analytique (cited: *D.A.*). *Recueil Dalloz-Sirey* is today a weekly publication consisting of five parts, each separately numbered:

(i) *Chroniques* (cited; *chron.* or, *chr.*, followed by page number), consisting of articles on topical issues written by academics or practitioners)

(ii) *Jurisprudence* (sometimes, but not always, cited: *J.*, followed by page number), where cases are fully reported with elaborate commentaries called *notes*

(iii) *Sommaires commentés* (cited: *somm.*, followed by page number), consisting of case summaries with a short following commentary

(iv) *Informations rapides* (cited: *I.R.* or, *Inf. rap.*, followed by page number), case summaries with no commentary

(v) *Legislation* (cited: *L.*, followed by page number), where selected recent statutory instruments are reported.

Here is an example of case citation in the *Dalloz*:

'Civ. 1ere, 29 novembre 1994, *D.* 1995, 122, note L. Aynes',

meaning the decision given by the first civil chamber of the Court of Cassation on 29 november 1994 to be found in *Recueil Dalloz* year 1995 at page 122 in the *jurisprudence* part with a note by L. Aynes.

In the *Dalloz*, case search is facilitated by the existence of annual tables made up of a classification of cases by subject arranged in alphabetical order, together with a separate chronological index of decisions.

(b) *Semaine juridique*, or *Juris-classeur périodique* (cited: *Sem. Jur.* or *JCP* followed by year), published since 1929, is, like *Dalloz* a very important weekly law report. It is issued as a general publication (cited as *G*) as well as being published in two special-ised titles: *Notariale et Immobilière* (cited: *N*) and *Entreprise et Affaires* (cited: *E*). Unlike *Dalloz*, issues of the JCP do not have page numbers. Instead, learned articles, cases and statutes are individually and consecutively numbered in their respective parts (see example below). The general presentation and content of the general publication is similar to *Dalloz*, with five parts:

(i) *Doctrine* (cited as *I*, followed by number of item): academic writing

(ii) *Jurisprudence* (cited *II*): cases in full with commentaries sometimes called *observations* (cited as *obs*) instead of *note*

(iii) *Textes* (cited *III*): legislation

(iv) *Sommaires de Jurisprudence* (cited: *IV*): case summaries. Before 1998 these *sommaires* were called *Tableaux de jurisprudence*

(v) *Informations* (cited *Act.* Followed by the number of the weekly JCP journal where they appeared): miscellaneous, such as short analyses (called: *aperçu rapide*), new bills, book reviews . . .

Example of citation in the JCP:

'Crim.11 février 1998, *JCP* 1998, *II*, 10084, obs. A. Coche',

meaning a decision given by the Criminal Chamber of the Court of Cassation on 11 February 1998 to be found in the *Semaine Juridique*, general publication, year 1998, part *jurisprudence*, item number 10084, with a note by A. Coche.

The most important cases appear at the same time both in the *Dalloz* and in the JCP but they are not commented upon by the same author, which allows readers to compare and contrast the views and approaches taken on these decisions from separate perspectives. As with *Dalloz*, the *Semaine Juridique* also provides a subject index and a chronological index of cases in the format of tables.

(c) *La Gazette du Palais* (cited: *Gaz. Pal.* or, *GP* followed by year) is a law report primarily intended for practitioners, as reflected in its style of presentation and its content. As with the two former reports already described, *Gazette du Palais* contains academic writing (*doctrine*), legislation, *jurisprudence* and case summaries (classified either under the heading of *sommaires et décisions* or, under *sommaires annotés* or, *panoramas*), each part being separately numbered. However, learned articles and case notes are shorter, with a more practical approach to legal issues. *Gazette du Palais* appears three times a week in the form of a journal. However, it should be noted that every two months, subscribers receive a very handy blue coloured paperback issue to replace the weekly journals. Citations must indicate the year and the semester (1 or 2), as well as the page, such as:

'CA Douai, 11 janvier 1995, *Gaz. Pal.* 1995, 2, 543'.
(Decision given by the Court of Appeal of Douai on 11 January 1995, reported in the *Gazette du Palais* for the year 1995, second semester, part *jurisprudence*, page 543.)

The *Gazette du Palais* tables are much more detailed than the tables to be found in *Dalloz* or *Semaine Juridique*. In particular these tables include, in their digests, references to decisions published in approximately 30 other law reports and specialist reviews. These tables appear in a separate publication, initially every six months, and then consolidated in a further publication every three years under the name of *tables triennales*, also subheaded *répertoire universel de la jurisprudence, de la doctrine et de la législation*. These tables serve as a legal encyclopaedia in which cases are classified and summarised by subject-matter. They provide a complete statement of case law in a concise form and are one of the most useful sources for legal research.

4.6.4 Specialised reviews

Alongside traditional *recueils* are specialised reviews which, though mainly consisting of a number of leading articles, also feature, in their specialist area, brief case notes, or a special section devoted to case analysis. The most prestigious are: *Revue trimestrielle de droit civil* (cited: *RTDC* or, *RTDciv* or, *Rev. trim. dr. civ.*), *revue du droit public et de la science politique* (cited: *RDP* or, *Rev. dr. publ.*), *Revue française de droit constitutionnel* (cited: *RFDC* or, *RFDconst.*), *Revue de sciences criminelles et de droit pénal comparé* (cited: *Rev. sc. crim.*), *Actualité juridique de droit administratif* (cited: *AJ* or *AJDA*), *Répertoire du Notariat Defrénois* (cited: *Rep. Not* or, *Defrénois* or, *Déf.*).

4.6.5 *Grands Arêts* series

This series of casebooks, published by *Dalloz*, is a valuable and accessible source of leading cases in the core areas of law. Each book in the series provides, for its designated area of law, the full text of leading decisions with detailed commentaries and numerous references to past cases. They are regularly updated. The main ones are:

(a) L. Favoreu, L. Philip, *Les Grandes Décisions du Conseil Constitutionnel*, 10th edn, 1999

(b) F. Terré, Y. Lequette, *Les Grands Arrêts de la Jurisprudence Civile*, 10th edn, 1994

(c) M. Long and others, *Les Grands Arrêts de la Jurisprudence Administrative*, 12th edn, 1999

(d) J. Pradel, A. Varinard, *Grands Arrêts du Droit Criminel*, 2 Vol., 2nd edn, 1997 (Vol. 1), 1998 (Vol. 2)

(e) R.M. Chevallier, J. Boulouis, *Grands Arrêts de la Cour de Justice des Communautés Européennes*, 2 Vol., 6th edn, 1994, (Vol. 1), 4th edn, 1997, (Vol. 2).

(f) V. Berger, *Jurisprudence de la Cour Européenne des Droits de l'Homme*, 6th edn, 1998.

4.6.6 Newspapers

French newspapers do not publish case reports within the body of their papers as *The Times* does in England. However, *Le Monde*, in its column headed *société*, does, though not regularly, provide some coverage of cases heard by the courts. This coverage only reports information on cases in journalistic style with a view to keeping its readers abreast of current developments. In this respect it cannot be compared to ordinary law reports as described above and thus cannot be considered a reliable source of case law.

4.7 Electronic database and internet

4.7.1 On-line legal information systems

The most widely used on-line legal information systems available in France are: *Juris-Data* and, *Jurifrance.*

(a) *Juris-Data*

  Juris-Data was created in 1971 by *Editions Techniques*, today known as *Editions du*

Juris-classeur, (publisher of the law journal *Semaine Juridique*). This is a fee-based service. Access is via *Minitel* (a screen based information retrieval system available through France Telecom) by keying in 3613 JURISDATA or through a networked personal computer equipped with the necessary software. It stores 500,000 legal documents, of which approximately 90 per cent are drawn from case law. It includes 140,000 case reports of the Court of Cassation's judgments reported in the *Bulletin* since 1960, 33,000 decisions of the *Conseil d'Etat* reported in the *Lebon* since 1980, 299,000 unreported private law court of appeal decisions since 1980, and 33,000 unreported judgments of private law lower courts. The database also includes a fair amount of administrative court decisions, which have been selected by the courts themselves: 13,750 administrative court of appeal decisions and, 9,600 administrative lower court judgments. Search technique is by way of keywords or phrases (BAIL), legal concepts (ERREUR SUR LA SUBSTANCE), code or statute provisions (ARTICLE 1 LOI 5 JUILLET 1985), date of the case (17-9-2000), name of the parties (JAND'HEUR), name of the court (CASSATION) or, *Juris-Data* case number (no. 024 055). The database does not rely on full-text research but rather on *abstrats*, or abstracts, and summaries. *Abstrats* are short paragraphs consisting of a series of keywords aimed at identifying the subject of a case, such as:

Responsabilité civile. Fait d'autrui. C.civ., art. 1384 al.1, Fondement (oui), Handicapé mental, Centre d'aide par le travail, Mode de vie, Controle, Organisation, Circulation, Liberté, Forêt, Incendie, Réparation.

(Case of *Association des centres éducatifs du Limousin et autre* v *Blieck* cited in Chapter 3.2.1 above)

However, decisions in full-text format can be ordered via *Minitel* by specifying the *Juris-Data* reference number attributed to each case, or through the Internet on the following site reference: **www.juris-classeur.com**. Decisions ordered can be sent by fax. *Juris-Data* cases are also regularly commented upon briefly in the *Semaine Juridique* (JCP) law report.

(b) *Jurifrance*

Jurifrance is, with *Légifrance* (see Chapter 2.4.4 (d) above), part of the official service provision, whose operating license has been granted by the French government to the concessionary company ORT (part of the Reuters group). Unlike *Légifrance*, *Jurifrance* is a fee-based service. Access is also available via *Minitel* by keying in 3613 JRF. It is probably the most extensive database for French case law. The database also stores a wide range of legislative material including *lois*, *décrets*, *arrêtés* published in the *Journal Officiel* since 1945, as well as the full text of each code, the *travaux préparatoires* of bills since 1988, *réponses ministérielles* since 1988 and, EU legislation since 1953.

Case law database includes:

(i) Court of Cassation decisions published in the *Bulletin* since 1960

(ii) unreported cases of the Court of Cassation since 1986

(iii) summaries and abstracts of selected court of appeal and lower court decisions since 1980

(iv) all *Conseil d'Etat* decisions reported in the *Recueil Lebon* since 1967, as well as all *Conseil d'Etat* unreported cases since 1986

(v) all decisions given by the administrative courts of appeal since 1989 and a selection of decisions given by the lower administrative courts since 1971

(vi) all decisions given by the *Conseil Constitutionnel* since its creation in 1958

(vii) all decisions given by the Court of Justice of the European Communities since 1954.

4.7.2 CD-ROM

Most of the legal publishers have marketed their own CDs. Examples of CD databases include:

(a) CD-ROM Dalloz: *Dalloz* publishes in a CD-ROM the full text of its *Recueil* (since 1990), as well as the full text of its codes.

(b) Lexilaser, published by *Lamy*, is a full-text database of legislation and case law similar to *Jurisfrance* and *Juris-Data*.

(c) GPDOC, published by the *Gazette du Palais*, includes in its basic version the *Gazette*'s tables since 1987. A simple click on the table reference displayed on the screen and the relevant page of the review appears!

4.7.3 Internet

The main websites offering case law are those of the three highest courts in France:

www.conseil-constitutionnel.fr
www.conseil-etat.fr
www.courdecassation.fr

Although the website for the *Conseil Constitutionnel* gives all decisions since 1958, the year in which the *Conseil* was set up, the other two are less exhaustive, giving only a selection of leading cases.

It is of great interest to note the well presented visual display of the website for the French Ministry of Justice; apart from providing inside information on the French legal system and details on current law reform, it also provides direct links to the other main official French legal websites and has, therefore, become a very convenient point of entry for accessing legal material. The Ministry of Justice website is:

www.justice.gouv.fr

5

Law reform

Ce qu'a fait une loi, une autre pourra le défaire.

G. Ripert (1955) p. 318 no. 127.

Chapters 3 and 4 examined the manner in which courts, through the exercise of their functions, have been able to fill the gaps left by the law and, when necessary to update it, thereby in their own way contributing to the process of law reform. However, law reform achieved through adjudication is, by its nature, a piecemeal process. Law reform requires the certainty of primary legislation and, thus, needs to be the product of parliamentary output. The procedures involved in passing legislation having already been described (see Chapter 1.1.4 above), this chapter will only be concerned with the making of law reform proposals, and more particularly the sources from which they arise.

It is worth noting that although a full-time commission has been set up in France to deal with the codification of the law (see Chapter 2), no similar permanent institution exists for keeping the law under review and for making recommendations for its systematic reform. There is thus no French equivalent for the Law Commission or for standing committees, such as those existing in England, which concern themselves exclusively with the question of law reform, either generally or in a particular area. Professor Houin (1961), a former member of the Commission for the Reform of the Civil Code, attributed the lack of systematisation of the process of law reform in France to the fact that there was no permanent body in the country whose exclusive concern it was to undertake the task of investigating possible areas in need of reform. This, according to him, had the consequence of making law reform projects dependent on the goodwill of members of Parliament or of government ministers who, most of the time, acted under pressure from interest groups. This lack of systematisation in the law reform process accounts in part today for the continuing increase in general legislative output in the French legal system (see Chapter 1).

The fact that law reform initiative has been left entirely to government departments and members of Parliament is confirmed by the 1958 Constitution, art. 39: 'the Prime Minister and members of Parliament hold the initiative for the introduction of legislation'. Consequently, in practice, the majority of bills have their origin in government departments, and in particular the Ministry of Justice whose function it is to deal with the organisation of the civil and criminal justice system. They take the form of *projets de lois*, usually following the recommendations of some independent advisory commission or committee, appointed for this purpose by the Minister concerned. Nothing exists in the French legislative process similar to the Green and White papers formally setting out the government objectives and policy before a bill is introduced. However, in the course of law reform, French ministers deliver speeches or issue informal *documents d'orientation* outlining the government's objectives and policy in the specific area of law they intend to reform. Each year there is also a large number of private bills – called *propositions de lois* – which are introduced in Parliament. However, private bills are passed with difficulty, unless they benefit from government support. This is particularly true since the moves made in the 1958 Constitution to bring the legislative process more directly under the control of the government (see Chapter 1.1.4. (d) (ii) above). As a result, since then priority has been given to governmental proposals, thus considerably reducing the chances for the passage of private bills.

As already noted, law reform projects usually originate out of the recommendations made by ad hoc committees appointed by the government in order to fulfil ministerial commitments or to implement political parties' manifestos. However, law reform may also originate, although to a far much lesser degree, out of the annual reports of judicial or administrative bodies such as the Court of Cassation, *Conseil d'Etat* and, *Médiateur de la République*. Their reports, apart from providing a revealing account of their year's activities, also contain numerous suggestions for law reform, some of which are on occasion implemented by the government.

It has been suggested that committee recommendations and suggestions arising out of annual reports produced by advisory bodies are only the external visible part of a process whose origin may be traced back to a multiplicity of other sources; what French law professor and legal theorist Ripert (1955: p. 84 no 30), in his celebrated and ageless study on the legislative process, called *les forces créatrices du droit*. The chapter will begin with a reflection of Ripert's concept of *forces créatrices*, and will show how this still applies today in the context of the French legal system, before moving on, in a second and third part, to the actual role played by committees and annual reports in the process of law reform.

5.1 The *forces créatrices du droit*

In his book, Ripert (1955: p. 80 no. 28) speaks of a particular science called 'genetics of law'. According to him (1955: p. 80 no. 28) this new science makes possible a deeper analysis of the process of law reform. The actual passing of new legislation amounts only to its 'birth certificate'. Its 'lineage', i.e. the true motives for its adoption, still needs to be determined. In this respect, Ripert shows (1955: p. 82 no. 29) that law reforms can be traced back to 'opposite creative forces', and that the new law brought into being is in fact the result of a transactional equilibrium between these forces. It is, in practice, the final dominating influence amongst these competing forces that will determine the outcome of what individual laws turn out to be (1955: p. 81 no. 28).

At the beginning of his study Ripert (1955: 84–134) identifies and discusses the various forces that play a role in the process of law reform. These forces, he says, mirror social forces which interact in the democratic context. When these forces are in conflict with one other, as is often the case, only the strongest will be able to impose their will and, therefore, bring a new law. In Ripert's terms, these forces are made up principally of:

(a) The social classes (especially middle and working classes).

(b) The particular interests (pressure groups, corporations, trade unions).

(c) The political parties.

(d) The community of jurists.

These groups would be incomplete without adding to them further influential factors which, according to Ripert, are also of relevance although not to the same degree as those categorised above.

These factors are:

(e) Public opinion which, in Ripert's words (p. 97 no. 36) manifests itself through 'demonstrations, meetings, speeches, placards, articles in newspapers and also, private conversations'. In the formation of public opinion, Ripert notes the role played by the press by which means it is relatively easy to manipulate public opinion.

(f) The sheer determination of particular individuals.

(g) Ideology as particularly reflected in the public debates surrounding divorce, abortion, euthanasia, and human rights.

(h) Particular feelings such as fear and forgiveness.

(i) Particular circumstances or response to unexpected events.

Can Ripert's test that new legislation is only enacted when one or more of the forces cited above overcomes its rivals be applied to current law reform in France? The recent registered domestic partnership Loi of 15 November 1999, commonly known as PACS (cited at Chapter 1.1.5 above), would appear to provide a good illustration and test of what has been called the 'struggle for the law'. The origin of the PACS legislation can be traced back to various sources:

(a) Left-wing political parties' manifestos issued during the 1997 general elections.

(b) Particular circumstances: the AIDS tragedy which brought to the surface the unjust result created by the law that denied homosexual couples the right to take over rent-regulated housing upon the death of one of the partners in such a relationship.

(c) The pressure of pro-gay associations pressing for homosexual rights.

(d) The sheer determination of particular individuals, a notable example being J.P. Michel, a member of Parliament, who was at the origin of the bill and who, despite opposition in Parliament, repeatedly reintroduced the proposal in 1993, 1997 and 1999. Also, the then Minister of Justice, E. Guigou, was particularly supportive on the several occasions she addressed Parliament for what was only a private bill.

In the event these 'forces' prevailed over that part of public opinion representing the ideology of traditional family values and over the opinion of the wider community of jurists. Indeed, the law was passed despite large public demonstrations against it supported by the different religious authorities in France, a notable example being the huge demonstration, widely reported by the media, which took place in Paris on 31 January 1999. The fact that the majority of influential French scholars were also against the introduction of such a scheme was clearly reflected in the numerous disapproving articles and commentaries written on the new law in law reports.

Experience shows, in contrast with what Ripert suggests in his book, that some laws may originate from one source only. Such is the case of laws arising out of the sheer determination of one individual or, out of a shared sense of feeling or a set of particular circumstances. These may be determinant factors in their own right for creating a new law. By way of illustration, it is widely recognised that it was the personal involvement of the then Minister of Justice and active campaigner against the death penalty, R. Badinter, which was at the origin of its abolition by the Loi of 9 October 1981. Similarly, former President of the Republic Mitterrand was the originator of the amendments to the 1958 Constitution which took place in the 1990s. It was during a television interview given on 9 November 1992 that President Mitterrand announced his intention to propose a certain number of amendments to the 1958 Constitution which were to be examined later by the Vedel Committee (see Chapter 5.2 below). In the same vein, some laws are direct public responses to certain shared feelings expressed by the community at large, or indeed by the government itself. For example, laws intended to crackdown on crime, such as the Loi of 2 February 1981, conveniently referred to by the catchall phrase *Loi Sécurité et Liberté*, are very often the result of a general feeling of insecurity. The same with amnesty laws, which involve giving free pardons for certain types of offences, and which in France systematically follow presidential elections. Examples are the Lois of 4 August 1981 and 20 July 1988, which followed each of President Mitterrand's two elections to power, and the Law of 3 August 1995 following President Chirac's election. There are also laws which are made in view of particular circumstances and in response to unexpected events. An example is legislation against terrorism. The Loi of 9 September 1986 and the Loi of 22 July 1996, on terrorism, were both passed in response to waves of terrorist attacks. Other *lois de circonstances* include:

(i) The Loi of 31 December 1987 on incitement to suicide (arts 223-13 and 223-14 of the New Penal Code). This legislation, establishing a specific offence against those assisting suicide, was passed following the publication of a controversial book entitled *Suicide Mode-d'Emploi* whose sole aim was to provide advice on the different available means for committing suicide. Pressure was generated for the legislator to act immediately on behalf of young people who were perceived as being particularly at risk.

(ii) The Loi of 31 December 1991 establishing a special fund for the compensation of AIDS victims contaminated through blood transfusions. The 1991 Law was passed in order to provide an additional system of compensation, alongside damages awarded by the courts, for the large number of people – mostly haemophiliacs – who, owing to the negligence of the National Centre for Blood Transfusion, had been contaminated with the HIV-virus following blood transfusion.

5.2 Advisory commissions and committees

These committees play an important role in highlighting the need for reform when asked to review the operation of a specific area of law in the context of law reform proposals. However, these committees are not standing committees and act only within specific terms of reference and are dissolved upon submission of their report.

A good example of such a committee is the Vedel Committee. It was appointed in December 1992 by the then President of the Republic, F. Mitterand, as the *Comité Consultatif pour la Révision de la Constitution* to consider amendments to be made to the 1958 Constitution. Headed by G. Vedel, a respected academic and former member of the *Conseil Constitutionnel*, it was made up of 14 members including judges, academics, former government ministers and one member of Parliament. The committee submitted its report in February 1993, taking on board among its recommendations some of the changes the President of the Republic had himself proposed a few months earlier in a letter dated 30 November 1992 which had been respectively addressed to the heads of both houses of Parliament, as well as to the head of the *Conseil Constitutionnel*.

The committee's main recommendations were:

(a) a revision to the composition and powers of the *Conseil Supérieur de la Magistrature*, the judicial board responsible for the appointment of judges, with a view to strengthening the independence of the judiciary

(b) the extension of the referendum procedure to statutes which could affect fundamental freedoms

(c) the introduction of a new court to try members of the government suspected of criminal offences

(d) a new possible course of action, open to any citizen, for referring a statute to the *Conseil Constitutionnel* for its review.

Soon after submission of the Vedel Report, two draft bills for the revision of the Constitution were introduced in March 1993 to give effect to some of the recommendations made in the report. The first bill was aimed at strengthening the independence of the judiciary and at introducing stronger guarantees for citizens in relation to effective access to, and legal remedies for, the protection of their civil rights as well as to any claim they would wish to pursue against individual members of the government. The second bill dealt with the organisation of public powers with a view to a better distribution in the balance of powers between state institutions. This resulted in the series of constitutional amendments that took effect in the early 1990s, amongst which were the establishment in July 1993 of a new court, the *Cour de Justice de la République*, to take responsibility from then on for trying members of the government suspected of criminal offences.

More recently, in December 2000, the French Minister of Justice instructed P. Boucher, a high ranking judge in the *Conseil d'Etat*, to review and assess the French system of legal aid within the wider context of access to justice. A commission called *Commission de Réforme de l'Accès au Droit et à la Justice*, headed by P. Boucher and consisting of four members (two judges, one practising lawyer and one consultant in social affairs), was appointed. It submitted its report to the government in April 2001, after having heard a large and varied number of individuals and associations directly involved in the administration of justice – such as judges, practising lawyers, civil servants of the Ministry of Justice – but also including those less directly involved, such as insurance companies, consumer associations, trade unions and a broad range of lay organisations. This report, similar in content to the Woolf Report in England, was a follow-up to the 1996 Coulon report entitled *Réflexions et Propositions sur la Procédure Civile* in which J.M. Coulon, the then head of the Paris court of first instance (*Tribunal de Grande Instance*), made recommendations on various aspects of the French system of civil justice, some of which were later implemented in a Decree of 28 December 1998 modifying the Code of Civil Procedure.

Sometimes, it may also be of interest to note, ministers instruct individuals, expert in their field, to investigate and report on their findings in a certain area of law in need of reform. This was the case with the French legal sociologist I. Théry who, on 3 February 1998, was instructed by the Minister of Justice and the Minister of Employment and Solidarity to evaluate the changes which had taken place ·in the family and to propose possible legal responses to those changes. On 14 May 1998, I. Théry submitted her report entitled *Couple, Filiation et Parenté aujourd'hui* (Paris: Odile Jacob/La Documentation Française) which gave a thorough analysis of the problems facing the modern family in France with possible legally defined solutions to these problems. This report was soon to be followed by the setting up of a working group in August 1998, headed by family law professor F. Dekeuwer-Defossez (Box 5.1 shows the composition of the group), with a view to generating proposals for a comprehensive reform of family law. On 14 September 1998, F. Dekeuwer-Defossez submitted in her turn a report entitled *Rénover le Droit de la Famille: Propositions pour un Droit Adapté aux Réalités et Aspirations de Notre Temps'* which contained a whole series of recommendations aimed at forming the basis for a comprehensive reform of family law. In a *document d'orientation*, dated 4 April 2001, the then Minister of Justice called for a *débat-citoyen* which meant a greater involvement by the general community at large in the process of this reform. In this respect, the Minister proposed to arrange regional meetings where the public at large was to be

> **Box 5.1** Composition of the working group *'Droit de la Famille'*
>
> Madame **Françoise DEKEUWER-DEFOSSEZ**, Présidente, Professeur à l'Université Lille II,
> Madame **Jacqueline BEAUX-LAMOTTE**, Avocate au Barreau de Paris,
> Madame **Martine de BOISDEFFRE** Conseiller d'Etat Secrétaire général du Conseil d'Etat,
> Madame le Bâtonnier **Marie-Elisabeth BRETON** (en remplacement de M. Jean DENIS, empêché) Membre du Bureau de la Conférence Nationale des Bâtonniers,
> Madame **Yvonne FLOUR**, Professeur à l'Université de Paris I,
> Madame **Marie-Christine GEORGE**, Vice-Présidente du Tribunal de Grande Instance de Créteil ;
> Monsieur le Directeur des Affaires Civiles et du Sceau, **Francis CAVARROC**,
> Monsieur **Michel CLARIS**, Notaire,
> Monsieur **Hugues FULCHIRON**, Professeur à l'Université Jean Moulin, Lyon III,
> Monsieur **Patrick GUYOMARD**, Psychanalyste, Maître de conférence à l'Université Paris VIII,
> Monsieur **Pierre MURAT**, Professeur à l'Université Grenoble II,
> Monsieur **Pierre-Louis REMY**, Délégué interministériel à la Famille.

given an opportunity to discuss the proposals with lawyers and other professionals and interested parties.

5.3 Annual reports

5.3.1 The Court of Cassation's annual report

The requirement to publish an annual report was established by a Decree of 22 December 1967 (today arts R. 131-12 and R. 131-13 of the *Code de l'Organisation Judiciaire*) with a view to giving an opportunity to the Court of Cassation to report on its past year's work as well as to make proposals for law reform (carefully labelled *'suggestions de modifications legislatives et réglementaires'*). Box 5.2 provides a complete summary of the report's content. In one of his articles, Professor H. Mazeaud (1977) took a hard line against this direct participation of the highest court in the law reform process when he vigorously claimed that the role of the judiciary should be confined to applying the law and not to discussing its merits, thereby arrogating to itself part of the political function. Mazeaud's strongly expressed view later led his colleague J. Deprez (1978) to observe, with some justification, that the Court of Cassation was very well placed to assess and comment upon the shortcomings of laws it applies on a day-to-day basis, notably spotting conflicting or outdated texts, and texts whose strict application may lead to injustice. The judiciary, he added, being

---

Box 5.2 Court of Cassation annual report: Summary of contents

Part 1   Suggestions de modifications législatives et règlementaires (proposals for law reform)

Part 2   Etudes et Documents (series of studies carried out by judges of the Court of Cassation on specific topics and/or on a general thematic subject)

Part 3   La Jurisprudence de la Cour (provides a study of the most important cases decided over the past year)

Part 4   Les Avis de la Cour (report of some of the non-binding opinions handed down by the Court of Cassation to the lower courts over the past year)

Part 5   L'activité de la Cour (gives an account of the past year's work of the Court)

---

involved in the shaping of the law through its case law, could only have a positive influence on the process of law reform if someone were to take the trouble to listen to what it had to say. In fact, he concluded, the best way to reform the law in practical terms was through the joint efforts of judges and legislators acting in partnership, something, he said, that the annual report of the Court was trying to achieve.

The annual report for the year 2000 contains 11 proposals for reform. It is relevant to note that when, in a given instance, a proposal is not taken up, this is formally repeated in the following year's report. This is the case with suggestion number one, in the report for the year 2000, concerning the proposed amendment of art. 1648 of the Civil Code, a text already quoted in the context of *Collinet v Compagnie d'assurances Rhin et Moselle* (see Chapter 4.1.3, point 5 above) and whose vague wording in respect of the time-limit for commencing an action has led to a considerable number of conflicting decisions, with a consequent breach of legal certainty. The Court of Cassation took such elements into account when formulating its proposal for the reform of art. 1648 (see Box 5.3). This reform proposal, repeated from previous annual reports, shows, in response to H. Mazeaud's fear, that what the Court of Cassation does in its report is to set the agenda for proposed necessary legal reform, still leaving the execution decision process to the political function.

5.3.2 The *Conseil d'Etat's* public report

In its capacity as adviser to the government, each year the *Conseil d'Etat* issues suggestions for law reform through its *Section du Rapport et des Etudes*, a special division of the *Conseil* created in 1963 with responsibilities for preparing an annual report for submission to the President of the Republic. The report is divided into two distinct parts (470 pages in total for the 2001 report).

The first part provides an account of the past year's work of the *Conseil d'Etat*,

Box 5.3 An example of proposal for reform

*Suggestions de modifications législatives et règlementaires
(annual report of the Court of Cassation–year 2000)*

PREMIÈRE SUGGESTION :

Modification de l'article 1648 du Code civil

Cette suggestion a déjà été effectuée dans le rapport pour 1998

La durée et le point de départ du "bref délai", bien qu'abandonnés à l'appréciation souveraine des juges du fond, nourrissent un contentieux abondant qui invite la Cour de cassation à distinguer la garantie des vices cachés, le défaut de conformité et la responsabilité contractuelle de droit commun, voire l'erreur sur la chose vendue.

Il serait très souhaitable de substituer à cette notion la détermination d'un délai fixe comme le prévoient la Convention de Vienne du 11 avril 1980 sur les contrats de vente internationale des marchandises ainsi que les articles 1386-16 et 1386-17 nouveaux du Code civil issus de la loi du 19 mai 1998.

Ainsi, outre l'avantage de renforcer la prévisibilité et la sécurité juridique, seraient unifiés le régime des ventes internes et internationales ainsi que celui, voisin, des produits défectueux.

Cette réforme pourrait intervenir à l'occasion de la transposition de la directive CE n° 1999-44 du 25 mai 1999 sur certains aspects de la vente et des garanties des biens de consommation.

highlighting the difficulties encountered by litigants in the course of enforcement of the *Conseil*'s judgments by the administrative body concerned. In the first part of the report, the *Conseil* also engages in a discussion about research projects, called *études*, which the *Section du Rapport et des Etudes* carries out each year on the specific instructions of the Prime Minister. These studies are aimed at reviewing the operation of a particular area of law, at the same time proposing possible developments in practice and policy in the field under consideration. By way of illustration, the *Section* chose to study in 2000 the status of international norms within the French legal system as well as the legal status of state-recognised associations. When considering the extent to which these studies may be influential for the development of French law, the *Conseil*, in its 2001 report, remarks upon the difficulty of generally assessing this impact, the main reason being that, in the course of these studies, the *Section* does not recommend any amendment of specific code or statute provisions but rather, with a broad brush, provides a general critical analysis of the given area of law under consideration. However, the *Conseil* acknowledges that some of these studies have had a degree of influence on solutions later adopted by the legislature. For example, the review of the 1994 legislation on bio-ethics in its 1999 report prompted the legislator to introduce a new bill on bio-ethics intended to amend and supplement the existing 1994 legislation, in particular to forbid human cloning in procreation.

Part two of the report gives the *Conseil* a more direct opportunity to propose law reform on a thematic subject. For the year 2001, the subject chosen was the status and role of the various independent administrative bodies (*autorités administratives in-dépendantes*) existing in France, i.e. bodies acting on behalf of the State but without being under its direct authority (similar to quangos in England). These bodies, such as the *Commission nationale de l'informatique et des libertés* (commission for the protection of civil liberties in the area of data processing) or, the *Commission des Opérations de Bourse* (stock exchange regulating authority), each have a number of distinctive features in terms of their composition, function and powers. In this respect, the *Conseil* starts with a 'health' warning to the effect that any setting up of a common legal framework would fail if it were not adapted to each bodies' specific needs. The *Conseil* then spends considerable time (p. 364 of the report) on the issue of accountability and recommends that measures be taken to make these bodies more accountable to the government and to Parliament.

5.3.3 The *Médiateur de la République's* report

When, on the occasion of a complaint forwarded to the *Médiateur* (see Chapter 3.2.3 above), instances of failure in the working of an administrative body have been identified, the *Médiateur*, further to the particular solution proposed, can suggest to the administrative authority concerned various measures intended to improve or remedy the way it operates (art. 9 al. 2 of the Loi 3 January 1973). This power was strengthened in 1976 to include suggestions by the *Médiateur* for an amendment to or reconsideration of statutory texts whose strict application in this context might prove, in practice, to produce unjust results (art. 9 al. 3 of the 1973 Law). These suggestions for law reform form part of the *Médiateur*'s annual report to the President of the Republic and to Parliament, following an account, in the same report, of its past year's activities (art. 14 of the 1973 Law). By way of illustration, in the Report for 2000 (part I (2)), the *Médiateur* lists 20 recommendations for the year to come. Amongst them is recommendation 00-R1, concerned with the situation of transsexuals who, during the transitional period between their undergoing gender reassignment surgery and the moment in time when the courts grant them a new civil status, are faced with a discrepancy between the information provided by their obligatory identity documents and their physical appearance. The *Médiateur* suggests that, in order to improve and regularise the situation of these individuals, they should be allowed, during this critical period of time, to use art. 60 of the Civil Code, a provision enabling individuals to have their first name rectified on their birth certificate and identity documents when they can show a legitimate interest in doing so. The *Médiateur*, as part of this recommendation, formally requests that the Minister of Justice issues a circular addressed to the courts instructing judges in this respect.

An original feature of the *Médiateur*'s power to issue reform proposals is the possibility given to his office to follow through on the proposals which have been made. If it appears that these proposals have not been implemented, the *Médiateur* by sending a formal letter can make an official enquiry about them from the ministry or department concerned and, if this is unsuccessful, call for the setting up of an inter-departmental committee with a view to being formally advised on the latest developments concerning these proposals and, by using this forum, to further debate on these issues. In this respect, the annual report conveniently provides a list of past recommendations which have been implemented together with a list of those which have not.

Finally, it may be noted that in the carrying out of his functions, the *Médiateur* is assisted by a team of *délégués départementaux*, spread out across the country, through whose agency, at a local level, primary responsibility is exercised in handling the complaints which are then forwarded to the *Médiateur*. This team of *délégués* is also entitled, as is the *Médiateur* himself, to formulate proposals for law reform, some of which may be taken up in the *Médiateur*'s report.

Chapter references

DÉPREZ, J., 'A propos du Rapport Annuel de la Cour de Cassation. Sois Juge et Tais-Toi (Réflexions sur le Role du Juge dans la Cité)', *Revue Trimestrielle de Droit Civil*, 1978, pp. 503–534.

HOUIN, R., 'De Lege Ferenda' in *Mélanges en l'Honneur de Paul Roubier*, Vol. 1, Paris: Dalloz-Sirey, 1961, pp. 273–294.

MAZEAUD, H., 'L'Enfant Adultérin et la Super-Rétroactivité', D.1977, Chr.1.

RIPERT, G., *Les Forces Créatrices du Droit*, Paris: LGDJ, 1955.

ZANDER, M., *The Law-Making Process*, (Chapter 9: The Process of Law Reform), 5 edn, London: Butterworths, 1999, pp. 404–453.

The annual reports of the Court of Cassation, *Conseil d'Etat*, and, *Médiateur de la République*, are available on the respective *Rapport* page of each of these bodies' websites at, respectively:

www.courdecassation.fr

www.conseil-etat.fr

www.mediateur-de-la-republique.fr

PART II

THE METHOD OF DECIDING CASES

The previous chapters have shown how the nature of French law derives largely from what is considered to be a proper source of law and from the way legal rules are arranged, formulated and interpreted. A further characteristic feature of the French legal system is the reasoning process adopted in a court decision, coupled with the way these decisions are expressed and written.

When confronted for the first time with the difficult task of reading and analysing cases, foreign lawyers, are very often baffled, if not frustrated, by the formal and rigid form of reasoning employed by French judges and the highly technical and laconic style used in their judgments. The aim of the following chapters is to facilitate their task by providing them with some guidelines on how to decipher court decisions.

A good grasp of the language and patterns of reasoning used in judicial decisions is of particular importance to law students who, as part of their training, are required to comment upon the meaning and implications of court decisions. Chapters 7 and 8, dealing respectively with judicial reasoning and judicial style, will serve as an introduction to the basic techniques of judgment analysis, known in French law as *commentaire d'arrêt*, for which a method will be provided in the last chapter of this book entitled 'Legal Exercises'.

Chapter 9 also highlights the crucial role played by academic writers in the understanding of court decisions, especially through their analytical notes published in law reports.

Thus, Part II of the book consists of four chapters: Chapter 6, Judges; Chapter 7, Judicial reasoning; Chapter 8, Judicial style; and Chapter 9, Case notes.

6

Judges

Il n'y a pas de grande et de petite justice. Il ne doit pas y avoir de grands et de petits juges. Il y a seulement des citoyens qui ont le droit de faire valoir leurs droits devant un juge impartial, compétent, loyal, attentif.

> Elisabeth Guigou, Minister of Justice, *Ecole Nationale de la Magistrature*,
> 3 February 1998.

A number of factors determine the judicial modes of thought and argument that will be addressed here. Amongst them are the particular concept of the law in France and the authority vested in judicial decision making that have been considered in Part I. To these must be added the fact that behind every court judgment is the individual who has delivered it and whose mind has been shaped by years of learning, training and practice. This introductory chapter to Part II looks briefly at the way judges are recruited and trained in France and how and to what degree this is reflected in their way of reasoning and style of argument.

6.1 General considerations

In every jurisdiction, the ways in which judges are recruited and trained is the subject of ongoing debate and new developments. In the case of France itself, a number of reforms have been introduced in the recent past, and others are expected in the near future, all with a view to improving the recruitment and professional skills of judges.

Legal history and comparative studies show that there is no single 'ideal' or 'obvious' procedure for judicial appointments and training. The fact that a system of training needs to be put in place is generally agreed, although duration and content may differ greatly from one jurisdiction to another. Opinion is divided, however, over the method of recruitment, particularly regarding whether judges should be recruited on the basis of their academic qualifications, their professional experience, or by way of election. Generally the method of recruitment adopted is based on historical tradition or arises out of the functions judges are expected to perform in a given legal system and at a given time. As an example, it was with a view to subordinating the judiciary to the legislature and to end the increasing power enjoyed by the old royal courts (whose member judges held their positions through heredity or through a system of sales of office) that, in 1790, the French revolutionaries decided to introduce a system of elected judges.

Today, the debate surrounding the selection and training of judges has been revived with the emergence of a new institutional environment focusing on the preservation of democracy and human rights. Some have argued that, if the 'new' judge is to be the guardian of individual rights and freedoms, then members of the judiciary should be elected to office by an elective college representative of those to whom this protection is afforded. The participants at a multilateral meeting on the training of judges in Europe, which was held in 1995 under the auspices of the Council of Europe, emphasised the need for an adequate method of selecting and training judges able to give them not only theoretical and practical knowledge, but also the professional skills required by their function in the context of a democratic society, based on the rule of law and the protection of human rights.

It is in this light that the present chapter now outlines the requirements for admission to the profession of judge in France and the method adopted for training judges in this country. This outline is confined to professional judges (in France, commercial and employment cases are adjudicated at first instance by lay-judges).

6.2 Recruitment

Unlike English judges who are selected from the ranks of successful barristers, the French judiciary is a career judiciary. Recruitment is conducted by competitive entrance examination to the *Ecole Nationale de la Magistrature* (ENM) where successful candidates are trained to become judges over a period of 31 months. This procedure is described below. The general method by which candidates for the French judiciary are chosen on the basis of their academic qualification and aptitude rather than on the merits of their professional achievement will be briefly contrasted with the English approach in a subsequent discussion.

6.2.1 Entrance examinations to the ENM

There were until recently three types of entrance examinations to which has been recently added, by a *Loi organique* of 25 June 2001, a fourth examination whose purpose is to widen the possibilities for recruitment:

(a) the external entrance examination open to students aged 27 or under who hold a four-year university degree

(b) the internal entrance examination open to civil servants who have served for at least four years and who are under 40

(c) a third examination is open to persons having spent at least 8 years in legal or professional practice without age limit and without specific degree requirements

(d) the fourth examination is open to persons aged 35 or under, holding a four-year degree and who have accumulated a minimum of ten years working professional experience in any branch of administrative, legal, economic, or social sector of employment.

The external examination (a) is the source of recruitment for the largest number of judges who make up the French judiciary, consisting in large part of young and highly qualified men and women. This system based on competitive examination emphasises formal and academic recruitment criteria. Only the brightest candidates are admitted to follow the training course provided by the ENM. It is also interesting to note that, since the 1980s, there has been an increasing tendency towards the feminisation of the judicial profession, and today almost 50 per cent of its members are women. Figures published by the Minister of Justice for the year 2000 show that of the 6,882 French judges, 3,469 are men and 3,413 are women.

Entrance examinations to the ENM consist of written papers, oral tests and, worthy of a particular mention, an interview with the examining board. The content and form of these tests have been developed with a view to evaluating the candidates' legal, analytical, critical and communication skills as well as their interest in topical issues. The following list of past exam papers illustrates this latter aspect:

(a) *la fonction du procès dans les sociétés contemporaines* (general knowledge paper, 1995)

(b) *quelle place pour le contrat dans le droit de la famille?* (Civil law paper, 1993)

(c) *vers une société sans prison?* (Criminal law paper, 1998)

(d) *la primauté de la constitution vous parait elle assurée de façon satisfaisante dans la France d'aujourd'hui?* (Public and European law, 2000).

Apart from recruitment through entrance examinations, direct recruitment to the judiciary is possible but remains the exception, representing no more than around 10 per cent of the total number of vacant posts. Only those candidates whose academic qualifications and professional experience make them particularly suitable for judicial duties (e.g. advocates or legal advisers from the private sector) can be, and are, recruited to the judiciary directly. However, in recent years legislation has been introduced (notably a Loi *organique* of 24 February 1998) aimed at widening the procedure for direct recruitment in order to help remedy the current shortage of judges in view of the increasing workload of cases being litigated.

6.2.2 Academic qualification v experience

The French system of recruitment, principally by means of competitive examination, contrasts sharply with the way English judges are recruited. Indeed, the central criterion for appointment in the English legal system is experience in advocacy. In his Hamlyn lecture Lord Mackay (1994: 3) justifies this emphasis placed on advocacy by the 'practical necessity that those who preside over the court should be familiar with its working and be able to give authority to rulings as cases proceed without undue delay or hesitations on matters of evidence and procedure'. However, many, such as D. Pannick, QC in particular (1987: 51–52), have challenged the English method of selecting judges. The thrust of Pannick's argument is that the function carried out by advocates and judges requires different skills and should therefore be kept separate. He says:

The jobs of barrister and judge self-evidently require different skills. To have the ability to argue a proposition is not necessarily to have the qualities required fairly to decide the same issue according to law.
[and]
By recruiting the judiciary almost exclusively from amongst barristers our legal system wrongly implies that because someone is a successful advocate he will therefore make a similar success of being a judge and that no one can be a good judge who has not been an eminent barrister

It is true, as Lord Mackay suggests above, that some of the qualities required of judges, such as a sound knowledge of the substance and procedure of the law and the capacity to analyse complex questions of law, are usually, though not exclusively, to be found with people having experience of advocacy. However, Pannick may have a legitimate cause for concern when he argues further on that advocates, whose professional life consists of taking sides in cases and for whom selection criteria for judicial office reflect a particular uniform set of social values, might not become fair and impartial judges aware of the realities of life faced by the majority of people who come to court. It follows that they might not be able to decide cases fairly and to evaluate the wider social implications of their decisions. In France, these concerns would appear less acute than in England due, firstly, to the system of recruitment by competitive entrance examination which guarantees equal opportunity to a wider section of the population, and secondly, as will be seen below, to the nature of the training received by prospective judges which focuses, in great detail, on an awareness of wider social, economic and racial issues.

6.3 Training

The training of French judges is formal in the sense that it follows a specific programme of studies, broken down into successive stages. As will be seen, this training is both theoretical and practical. Furthermore, the way this training is carried out and its content have a direct influence on judicial practice.

6.3.1 Initial and further training

In a report presented at the multilateral meeting organised by the Council of Europe (see Chapter 6.1 above), M. Vignau, Director of initial training at the ENM (1995: 41) clearly stated the objectives of the ENM training course for prospective judges as follows:

(a) To provide students with methodology and a high level of professional know-how, designed to ensure that justice is reliably administered.

(b) To make students aware of and able to analyse the human, economic and social framework of the law.

(c) To encourage students to analyse judicial functions, the basic principles of judges' action, their status and ethics.

These set goals, referred to by M. Vignau in her report, are today implemented through a seven-month study period at the ENM where tuition is provided in the form of lectures, seminars and also *direction d'études*. In *directions d'études*, prospective judges, working in small groups under the guidance and supervision of a lecturer or a practitioner, are initiated into the judicial process and into the method of working particular to each type of court using practical examples and actual case files. Apart from the development of professional skills, the training also focuses on the acquisition of a 'judicial culture' achieved through the study of particular 'themes' related to the role, status and ethics of judges as well as to judicial reasoning. Within the study of each 'theme' students are introduced to law related subjects such as economics, sociology, psychology, psychiatry and forensic medicine. The stated objective here is that, in addition to technical skills, the training of future judges should include the wider environment in which courts operate. Apart from being multidisciplinary, the training provided at the ENM is also cast wide within the different branches of law. This is because French judges are expected to decide all types of legal disputes. In the course of a single day a French judge may be called upon to decide on questions relating to contract, tort, family or criminal law and is therefore expected to have competence in all these areas of law.

The study period at the ENM is supplemented by a three-month training vacation period which takes place at a host institution such as a governmental body or a company. There is a further training period of 14 months in court where trainees, under the supervision of a senior judge, are given the opportunity to carry out tasks related to the judicial function, such as taking part in proceedings and the drafting of decisions.

The ENM also arranges refresher courses for French judges which take the form of a national training programme intended to update existing judges' legal knowledge. Every judge is entitled to a minimum period of five days annually for further training. A programme of wide-ranging lectures and seminars is proposed each year. For the year 2001 this programme included, in particular, introductory courses in Common law systems, EU institutions and legislation, as well as exchange programmes with other European jurisdictions, and with Canada and the United States.

6.3.2 Influence of recruitment and training on judicial practice

Because of their experience in advocacy, English judges have a more pragmatic approach to legal issues. This is clearly reflected in the way they write their judgments, avoiding technical concepts and language, and articulating policy arguments when necessary, all in a very discursive manner. English judgments clearly show the way a judge's mind has worked out and how he has arrived at a particular decision. Just as advocates try to persuade the court to decide in favour of their side of the case, so English judges try to persuade the legal profession and the public at large that the solution chosen is correct. As will be seen in the chapters which follow, this contrasts sharply with the dryness of French judicial decisions where, as in B. Markesinis' (1994) remark 'French judges are trained to keep their thoughts to themselves'. This arises partly from the fact that the French judiciary is educated and trained as a unit, a fact further witnessed by the collegial form of French courts (see Chapter 8.3.2 below). Moreover, the fact that a majority of French judges enter the judiciary straight from their course of studies explains to a great extent why they approach the law primarily through their theoretical and academic education. They are thus mainly preoccupied with fitting actual problems into the framework offered by the codes as they have been taught to do at university. As R. David (1972) rightly states 'the French judge, within the family of lawyers, feels closer to the law professor, who was his teacher, than to the advocate'.

Chapter references

BODIGUEL, J.L., 'Qui Sont les Magistrats Français? Esquisse d'une Sociologie', *Revue Pouvoirs*, 1981, Vol. 16, pp. 31–42.

LORD MACKAY OF CLASHFERN, *The Administration of Justice*, London: Stevens and Sons/Sweet and Maxwell, 1994.

MARKESINIS, B. S., 'A Matter of Style', *The Law Quarterly Review*, 1994, Vol. 110, pp. 607–628.

PANNICK, D., *Judges*, Oxford University Press, 1987.

The Training of Judges and Public Prosecutors in Europe, Strasbourg: Council of Europe Publishing, 1996.

VAN CAENEGEM, R.C., *Judges, Legislators and Professors*, Cambridge University Press, 1987.

7

Judicial reasoning

C'est vraiment une chose admirable que la logique de nos magistrats, leur aptitude à relier, avec une maîtrise consommée, à de vieux articles du Code civil des solutions de jurisprudence qui disent exactement le contraire.

Villey, M., *Seize Essais de Philosophie de Droit*, Paris: Dalloz, 1969, p. 269.

7.1 General considerations

Examining judicial reasoning in France entails looking at the structure of a typical judgment. French judgments are usually portrayed as logical deductions drawn from pre-existing premises. This form of reasoning, whereby French courts justify their decisions by subsuming a case under a legal rule, is commonly referred to in French legal literature as the *syllogisme judiciaire*. As will be examined further in the next chapter, the formal and logical structure of French judgments is further accentuated by the fact that they are very short and consist of a single statement with no expression of dissenting opinion (Chapter 8.3 below). This contrasts sharply with the lengthy decisions of the Common law courts where each judge gives an individual judgment using different patterns of reasoning, arguments and examples. The difference in decision structure between the French and the Common law courts is summarised as follows by G. Samuel (1998: 172):

In contrast to the structure of decisions in the *Cour de Cassation*, the common law courts rarely take as their starting point an abstract rule which then has to be applied to the facts before them. Instead, they start out from the facts and the arguments of counsel and arrive at a solution through a reasoning process that tends to focus on the particularities of the actual institutions in play in the case before them.

The form of reasoning employed by French courts constitutes one of the most distinctive features of the legal system and is very often mirrored in the way lawyers construct and present their argument. Experience has shown that views articulated by scholars, or counsel's submissions to courts and even law students' answers to problems, all adopt to a considerable degree the deductive method practised by the courts. Indeed, the overall tendency is to shape arguments as a series of stringently logical steps almost always beginning with a statement of the statutory law and aimed at showing that the end point is the culmination of this chain of consistent logical steps. It is, therefore, imperative for those engaging in the study or in the practice of French law to be able, through a study of judicial reasoning, to meet the common expectations of what constitutes a good, or at least an acceptable, type of legal argument.

The style of argument displayed in French judgments certainly exhibits, as is often suggested, the virtues of traditional formal logic to which French lawyers subscribe with great pride. The French Cartesian propensity for conceptual thinking, whereby particulars are subsumed under universals by an act of categorisation, explains why the deductive method, when applied in a legal context, is considered in France to be best able to settle legal issues conclusively. Emphasis on deduction in judicial decisions is also common in other Civil law systems, such as Germany and Italy, where the prevailing tendency in judicial opinions, as in France, is to present the final ruling as the necessary outcome of a logical set of arguments structured in a syllogistic form. It has been further suggested that syllogistic logic is particularly suited to the philosophical cast of mind of civil lawyers who, for centuries, have been exposed to the abstract process of reasoning prevalent in Continental law schools. Common law in contrast, organised and developed mainly as a by-product of litigation, seems more concerned with securing decisions that make good practical sense, rather than exhibiting the virtues of logic. This is usually accounted for by the frame of mind of Common lawyers, often described as a frame of mind which habitually looks at things in the concrete, not in the abstract, and which places its confidence in experience rather than in abstractions. Lord Justice Cooper (1950) highlighted the difference of approach between Common law and Civil law in his famous address delivered to Edinburgh University:

The civilian naturally reasons from principles to instances, the common lawyer from instances to principles. The civilian puts his faith in syllogisms, the common lawyer in precedents; the first silently asking himself as each new problem arises, 'What should we do this time?' and the second asking aloud in the same situation, 'What did we do last time?'

More significant, when attempting to explain the form of reasoning adopted by French courts, is the primacy of statutory law and the passive function ascribed to the judiciary (see also the role played in this respect by legal education in Chapter 10.2.1 and 10.2.2 below). These factors have contributed, not only in France but also in other civil law systems, to a fairly rigid conception of adjudication. As Zweigert and Kötz (1998: 264) have pointed out:

Continental judges, in Italy and France rather more than in Germany, are still imbued with the old positivistic idea that deciding a case involves nothing more than applying a particular given rule of law to the facts in issue by means of an act of categorisation; indeed, they often entertain the further supposition that ideally the rules of law to be applied are statutory texts.

In the following passage Zweigert and Kötz further emphasise this tradition of judicial decision making particularly reflected in the style and form of reasoning employed by judges in the highest courts:

Above all, judgments of supreme courts of the Continent still sometimes reflect the traditions of the authoritarian state of a hundred years ago: judgments should primarily be impersonal acts of state which parade the majesty of the law in front of citizens in awe of authority; therefore they must not let it emerge that judges reach their decisions through a hesitant and doubtful balancing of the pros and cons of concrete solutions of the problem thrown up by the case rather than by sheer intellect and cold logic.

In France, the long established assumptions, still deeply rooted in the French legal mind, that only the legislature can make the law (see Chapter 4) and that codes provide a self-contained and internally consistent body of legislation, have greatly contributed to the deductive model of legal reasoning which prevails in the French judicial method. In such a system, codes are deemed to provide the axioms and postulates from which conclusions are drawn. From this it follows that judicial decisions cannot, overtly at least, be the outcome of what the judge feels to be the best solution. They are primarily the result of applying a rule of law to an actual situation. At the end of the nineteenth century, a certain judge Magnaud challenged this tradition by refusing to adhere in his decisions to the purely deductive model of reasoning. One of his most famous decisions was *Min. Public* v *Demoiselle Ménard* (1898) D.P.1899, 2, 329, in which a poor woman was prosecuted for having stolen a loaf of bread because she was hungry. Although the facts were established, Judge Magnaud nevertheless decided that, given the circumstances, the defendant was not guilty of theft on the grounds that it was 'within the power and duty of judges to construe humanely the inflexible prescriptions of the law'. However, the 'Magnaud phenomenon' has remained an isolated one amongst the French judiciary. French judges usually take the view that the rigid and logical form of the syllogism provides them with an ideal form of reasoning, minimising their contributions to the law making process. Also the legal duty imposed on them to publish reasons for their decisions implies that they have to indicate the legislative enactment serving as a basis for their decision and say how this decision relates to the law they are invoking. This requirement goes back to the 1790 legislation, art. 15 of which provided that judicial decisions must 'express the reasons that were decisive for the judge'. It was reintroduced later in art. 455 of the New Code of Civil Procedure (see Chapter 8.2.1 below) and has been reinforced by the power given to the Court of Cassation to quash any decision given without sufficient reasons or with reasons which are mutually contradictory.

The fact that judicial reasoning can only be cast in a strictly syllogistic form has been strongly questioned for not conveying the reality of legal reasoning – which is never strictly deductive – and for simply being unable to solve all the problems raised in a legal dispute. The speculation as to whether syllogistic logic can on its own satisfactorily account for judicial reasoning arises in the wider debate on the extent to which legal decisions are the outcome of logical processes rather than judges using their own discretion or expressing their own personal views. This question has important implications in legal theory, especially when it comes to determining the nature of legal analysis often presented as 'scientific' and 'objective'. Also, it raises issues proper to constitutional law in the sense that it questions the nature and scope of the judicial function. Holmes, J, *The Common Law*, p. 1, is very often presented as the source of the long-running controversy as to the respective weights to be attributed to syllogistic logic or to judicial discretion in the decision making process:

The actual life of the law has not been logic: it has been experience. The felt necessities of the times, the prevalent moral and political theories, the intuitions of public policy, avowed or unconscious, even the prejudices which judges share with their fellow men, have had a good deal more to do than the syllogism in determining the rules by which men should be governed

In France where judicial opinions are generally reduced to the skeleton of a syllogism, Holmes, J's assertion is particularly relevant. However, despite the predominance of logical processes in judicial opinions and the official doctrine, supported by a core of fundamental rules, that the judge's role is primarily to apply legislative provisions to given factual situations, no lawyer in France today would seriously maintain the view that judicial decisions are only determined by the formal, not to say mechanistic, operation of a syllogism, irrespective of the consequences for particular factual situations. This view is considered by the majority of French scholars to belong to a nineteenth century conception of the legal process which assumed that all legal questions may be decided by applying rules which are definite, unchanging and whose application is thoroughly predictable. In France, as elsewhere, legal rules are too diverse and often unclear, if not contradictory. They need, therefore, to be identified, interpreted and formulated in a precise manner. Facts also have to be proved and categorised. All these operations which are inherent to the judicial process involve a certain amount of choice on the part of judges. And even though they have to exercise their discretion within the limits imposed by constitutional and procedural rules, there is still room left for selecting and directing the law towards the achievement of a just and desirable result. This objective is made significantly easier by the fact that code provisions and statutes are written in general terms. This leaves judges with broad scope for interpretation and considerable leeway in the choices they make. Thus, any suggestion that the French judicial process rests on a mode of reasoning that is solely deductive or syllogistic is illusory. However, this does not mean, as is often claimed, that syllogistic logic does not play a role other than being an expository decoration in the judicial process. Syllogistic logic serves a certain number of functions inherent to adjudication, such as the functions of rationality and justification to which we will return in this chapter.

What follows first explains and illustrates the judicial syllogism and looks at the functions it fulfils. The chapter then examines the limitations of syllogistic logic.

7.2 The judicial syllogism

7.2.1 Definition and illustration

French opinions are usually very brief and are couched in the form of the Aristotelian syllogism in which a conclusion is drawn from a pair of two premises – the major premise and the minor premise, as illustrated by the following classic example:

> All men are mortal (major premise)
>
> Socrates is a man (minor premise)
>
> Therefore, Socrates is mortal (conclusion)

This example shows that the logical form of the syllogism rests on a process of inferring from two propositions, considered as true premises, a further proposition, the conclusion, the truth of which is believed to follow from the previous two. Syllogistic reasoning also rests on an organisation of classes – here, the class of mortals and the class of men – fitting into each other and moving from the general to the particular. Using the same example of Socrates, this organisation can be illustrated as follows:

> Since men belong to the class of mortals
>
> Then Socrates, who belongs to the class of men
>
> Also belongs to the class of mortals.

In the eighteenth century, the Swiss mathematician Leonhardt Euler (1707–1783) used a diagram with three interlocking circles in order to test the validity of syllogistic inferences. Taking the Socrates example, each of the following circles represents a class with a particular membership (see Fig. 7.1).

Syllogistic inferences of this kind appear clearly in French judicial decisions where a legal principle or rule operates as the major premise of the syllogism, a short statement of the relevant facts as the minor premise, the conclusion consisting of a subsumption of the facts within the principle or rule. The case of *Goutaillier v Epoux Jacob* (1974) Bull. civ. III, no. 330, offers a simple illustration of the syllogistic form of reasoning employed in French judgments. In this case the vendor of a house in the country had not revealed to the purchasers the existence of a plan to set up a pig farm nearby. The purchasers claimed the repayment of the sum they had already paid on account, relying on art. 1116 of the Civil Code which provides that any dishonest dealing – called *dol* – on the part of one of the parties to a contract, in the absence of which the other party would not have entered into the contract, is a ground for nullity of an agreement. The issue here was whether the vendor's deliberate failure to disclose the plan to set up a pig farm near the house could be categorised as a *dol* within the meaning of art. 1116. Deciding on this issue, the Court of Cassation used the following syllogistic construction:

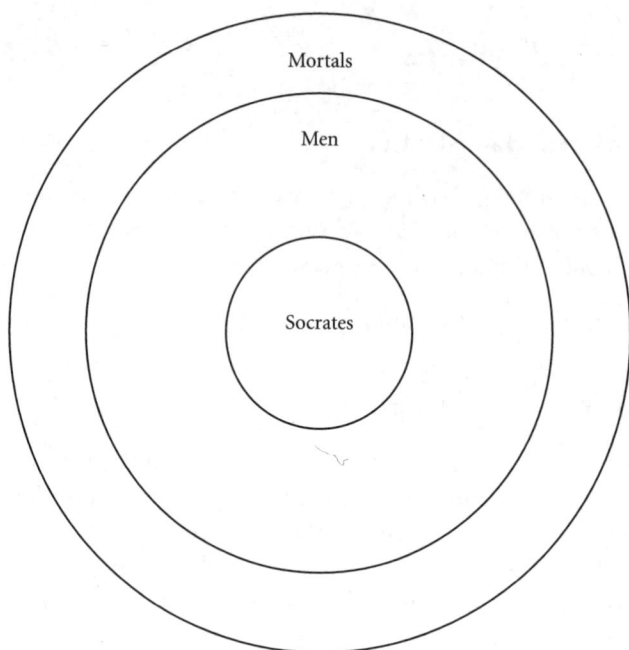

Fig. 7.1 Syllogistic reasoning: Euler's diagram

Intentional failure to disclose a fact which, if known by the other party, would have dissuaded the latter from entering into a contract, amounts to a *dol* [*major premise*]

The vendor of a house has intentionally failed to disclose to the purchasers a plan to set up a pig farm nearby which if known to them, would have resulted in their being unwilling to enter into a contract [*minor premise*]

Therefore, the vendor's failure to disclose this fact is a *dol* (and the sum paid on account by the purchasers must be reimbursed by the seller) [*conclusion*]

Using Euler's diagram the syllogistic reasoning of the Court of Cassation would be as in Fig. 7.2.

Overall, the prevailing practice of French courts, in particular the Court of Cassation, is to deliver short decisions where syllogisms are cast in the form of a single sentence without any attempt to justify each step of the reasoning. Thus, a typical judgment moves logically from the applicable statutory provisions, followed by an outline of the relevant facts, to a final part that constitutes an inescapable conclusion. The following divorce case provides a good illustration of this practice. In X v MmeY (1997), D. 1997, 296, a husband had produced as evidence his wife's secret diary and a series of confidential letters addressed by her to a third party. The Court of Appeal refused to rely on these various documents as evidence against the wife on the grounds that this would infringe her rights of privacy. The Court of Cassation quashed the decision of the Court of Appeal relying on arts 259 and 259-1 of the Civil Code and deciding that in accordance with these provisions facts in divorce cases may

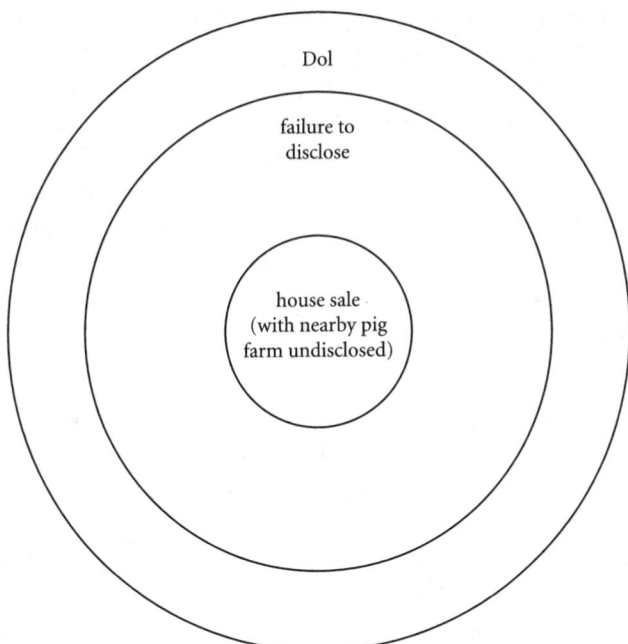

Fig. 7.2 Application of Euler's diagram to the Court of Cassation reasoning

be proven by any means, including any kind of documents, provided these documents have not been obtained by fraud or violence. For the Court of Cassation it did not appear from the findings of the appellate judges that the confidential letters produced had been obtained, as defined by the Civil Code arts 259 and 259-1, by fraud or violence; only these particular circumstances would have enabled the Court of Appeal not to rely on these documents in reaching its decision. The Court of Cassation judgment took the following form:

Vu les articles 259 et 259-1 du code civil; Attendu qu'en matière de divorce la preuve se fait par tous moyens; que le juge ne peut écarter des débats tous documents dont un conjoint entend faire usage que s'ils ont été obtenus par violence ou fraude; [*major premise*]

Attendu que pour écarter des débats des lettres adressées par Mme Y à des tiers ainsi que son journal intime et son carnet de bord et prononcer le divorce aux torts partagés des époux, l'arrêt attaqué énonce que la production de ces documents qui n'appartiennent qu'à elle porte atteinte à sa vie privée; [*minor premise*]

qu'en statuant ainsi sans constater que M.X s'était procuré ces documents par fraude ou violence, la cour d'appel a privé sa décision de base légale au regard des textes susvisés; [*conclusion*]

In this case, therefore, after simply referring to the applicable code provisions, followed by an outline of the relevant facts, the Court arrives at the final part of its judgment which constitutes an irrefutable and inescapable solution. There is indeed no effective justification here, such as arguments of interpretation, illustrating why the Court applied to the case the code provisions invoked instead of applying the reasoning of the court of appeal based on the argument of privacy rights. The decision is delivered as if there were no other possible alternative solution and irrespective of the consequences it may have for the actual situation (for a further discussion of this case see Chapter 7.3.1 below). A large body of French judgments published in law reports follows this model. However, this model has a few important variations that are outlined below.

7.2.2 Variations

(a) One is where, unlike the above divorce decision, the Court of Cassation dismisses the appeal. In this type of decision, called *arrêt de rejet* (see further on this notion, Chapter 11.3.2 – Legal Exercises, under '*commentaire d'arrêt*'), the syllogism usually appears after the statement of facts and the summary of the arguments by counsel. For example, in *Société d'assurances La Cité* v *Héro* (1988), D. 1988, 513, an employer (*Société La Cité*) had been held vicariously liable under art. 1384 al. 5 of the Civil Code, for dishonest dealing engaged in by one of his employees (Héro). The Court of Cassation dismissed the employer's appeal on the grounds that he did not show that the employee's act 'did not take place in the course of his employment, without authorisation and for purposes outside the scope of that employment'. The judgement was structured as follows:

Attendu que [*statement of the facts*];

Attendu que [*summary of the submissions and arguments made by the appellant*];

Mais attendu que le commettant ne s'exonère de sa responsabilité que si son préposé a agi hors des fonctions auxquelles il était employé, sans autorisation, et à des fins étrangères à ses attributions [*major premise of the syllogism*];

Et attendu que l'arrêt relève [*follows the statement of the relevant findings of the lower court which constitutes the minor premise*];

Que de ces énonciations, d'où il résulte que M. Héro, en détournant des fonds qui lui avaient été remis dans l'exercice de ses fonctions, ne s'était pas placé hors de celles-ci, la cour d'appel a exactement déduit que la Société La Cité ne s'exonérait pas de sa responsabilité civile [*conclusion*];

It must be pointed out, however, that this syllogistic form of *arrêt de rejet* is rare. Usually, in this kind of decision, the reasoning of the court is handed down in a brief formal refutation of the arguments presented by the appellant.

(b) Another is when the major premise, instead of being a statutory provision, is a general principle of law (on this notion see Chapter 3.2.3 above). For instance, in matters of restitution, judges may resort to the principle *nul ne peut s'enrichir aux dépends d'autrui* which prohibits someone from enriching him or herself at another's expense. Another example is in criminal cases where judges very often refer to the principle of *l'autorité au civil de la chose jugée au pénal*. Under this principle, when the victim of a crime sues a wrongdoer for compensation in the civil courts after a criminal decision has been reached in respect of the same facts, the civil judge cannot give a decision which would contradict the earlier criminal ruling.

(c) There is also the case in which the relevant statute or code provision is not expressly stated. Apart from the frequent cases in which an article of a code is merely cited by number, there can be an implicit reference to the rule applied which has then to be inferred from the propositions enunciated by the courts or even from the solution itself. Again, this usually occurs in an *arrêt de rejet*, i.e. when the Court of Cassation dismisses the appeal. This can be accounted for by the fact that, in accordance with procedural rules (Art. 1020 of the New Code of Civil Procedure), the Court of Cassation is under a duty to quote the relevant statutory provisions – called for this purpose the *visa* – only in *arrêts de cassation*, i.e. when it quashes the decision of a lower court. More generally, there are some cases where no new point of law is raised and where the decision of the court simply confirms a particular interpretation of a rule found in a series of other similar cases. Because these cases have limited value as precedents, the court does not feel a need to set out clearly the principle of law it is applying and, for brevity, only states the particular factual circumstances of the case when handing down its decision. A recent decision by the Court of Cassation on privacy rights offers a suitable illustration. In *Mme Li Shu Xian* v *Editions Laffont* (1995), Bull. civ. I, no. 356, the Court of Cassation rejected the appeal made by the widow of the last Chinese emperor, Pu Yi. The appellant had brought an action against the author (M. Behr) of a biography of her late husband on the grounds that, in disclosing certain aspects of Pu Yi's private life, the defendant had actually infringed his right to privacy. However, the Court of Cassation relied on the findings of the lower judges establishing that in his own autobiography Pu Yi had already disclosed the facts published in the book. The Court further noted that the re-disclosure of these facts by the defendant had not been made, as suggested by the appellant, with the intention to harm, but, simply to relate Pu Yi's life in an objective way without distorting the truth. Thus, following a brief statement of the facts and a short summary of the arguments presented by the appellant, the Court justified its decision as follows:

Mais attendu que la cour d'appel a retenu, par motifs propres et adoptés du jugement, que Pu Yi lui-même avait, dans ses écrits autobiographiques, fait état de certains aspects de sa vie intime que M. Behr avait repris dans son ouvrage sans manquer au respect dû à la vérité, compte tenu des éléments objectifs sur lesquels il s'était appuyé; que la cour d'appel a ainsi, par un arrêt motivé, légalement justifié sa décision sur ce point:
Par ces motifs:
Rejette le pourvoi.

The right to respect for one's private life, which was the point at issue in this case, is protected by art. 9 of the Civil Code. However, in dismissing the appeal, the Court of Cassation does not refer explicitly to this rule or to any interpretation or limitation of this rule but would appear to have drawn its conclusion merely from the findings of the lower judges. However, it would be wrong to assume, because the standard syllogism does not stand out clearly – the major premise not being apparent – that the decision lacks grounds. The proposition of law on which the decision is based may be inferred from the facts, coupled with the conclusions drawn from these facts by the Court. Thus, the syllogism may be easily pieced together as follows:

Art. 9 of the Civil Code allows for the disclosure of facts previously published unless this is intended to distort the truth [*major premise*]

The defendant has disclosed facts previously revealed by the plaintiff in an autobiography, in an objective way and without distorting the truth [*minor premise*]

Therefore, the defendant has not committed a breach of art. 9 [*conclusion*]

It is important to point out that the reformulation of the syllogism in such a situation rests on the amount of information found in the judgment. Also it assumes, to a greater degree than in other instances, a good knowledge of French substantive law, particularly the way in which the relevant rule has been constructed and applied in earlier cases, without which the major premise cannot be reformulated.

(d) Finally, although lower courts adhere to the pattern offered by the syllogism, they seem less rigid in their approach than the Court of Cassation. Usually, lower courts deliver a longer and more elaborate justification. This may be accounted for by the fact that the function of lower courts is to establish facts or review them in light of the weight of evidence, whereas the highest court deals mainly with issues of law, confining itself to ascertaining whether the law has been correctly applied. Moreover, following the recommendations issued by the *Commission de modernisation du langage judiciaire* (see next chapter), the practice of the lower courts has been to write judgments in a less formal and technical language and to structure them in a way which does not always stick to the more rigid logical patterns of reasoning of the Court of Cassation.

7.2.3 The functions of the judicial syllogism

As observed in the introduction to this chapter, the judicial syllogism serves a number of essential functions which are briefly outlined here. These are:

(a) *Rationality* – the syllogism has often been described as the hallmark of rationality. Indeed, unlike the other traditional modes of reasoning, syllogistic logic presents a cogent form of argument with its set of premises and its exposition of logical links, and provides an alternative to what would otherwise look like an arbitrary decision.

(b) *Certainty* – the syllogism facilitates the building up of a logically consistent system of propositions which enhance consistency and predictability and lead to a greater degree of certainty within the legal system.

(c) *Justification* – since French judges are required to state the grounds for their decisions (see Chapter 7.1 above), they must expound them in an open manner. Once again, the syllogism provides the courts with an ideal mechanism for justifying what they do. To the party losing a case it shows in a most objective and straightforward way that the judgment has been given in conformity with the law and is nothing other than a straightforward deduction from the principles of this law. Similarly, the syllogism with its function of justification allows the Court of Cassation to which a case has been referred to exercise control over the correct application of the rule of law by the lower courts. This exercise of control is crucial in France where the system of courts is far less centralised than in England (see Chapter 4.2.1.1 above). Indeed, this contributes towards consistency in French judicial decision making, the Court of Cassation's role, here, being to ensure that the law is correctly and uniformly applied throughout the court system.

(d) *Guidance for the resolution of further cases* – the syllogism provides a working guide for the judges, the litigants and their legal advisers. Earlier, in Chapter 4, we saw that there are a variety of factors that determine how much persuasive value a case has as a precedent (see Chapter 4.2 above). In particular, case law becomes increasingly authoritative when the interpretation or principle serving as the major premise in a case is confirmed and applied in a series of other cases (*jurisprudence constante*, see Chapter 4.2.2 above). Thus, the syllogism, in setting forth grounds for the decision reached, provides a rule for dealing with similar cases in the future.

7.3 The limits of syllogistic reasoning

As already pointed out, despite the strict adherence of French courts to the syllogistic form of reasoning, any attempt to reduce the judicial process to a mechanical application of given premises immediately fails. Indeed, the process of reaching a decision is not as straightforward as the syllogism suggests. As will be examined here, it carries with it a certain number of operations made necessary by the specific nature of law and legal analysis, which are inherent to adjudication and for which the syllogism is of no help at all. Furthermore, in that the main task of a court is the resolution of a legal dispute, this implies that in deciding a case the judge takes one view in preference to another, after having considered the arguments presented by each side. In fact, the major and minor premises, far from being fixed antecedent propositions, only gradually emerge from the judges' analysis of the concrete factual situation and from the arguments presented by each of the parties to a case in support of their respective claims. In a celebrated essay on the relationship between law and logic, John Dewey (1924: 23) emphasises this point:

As a matter of fact, men do not begin thinking with premises. They begin with some complicated and confused case, apparently admitting of alternative modes of treatment and solution. Premises only gradually emerge from analysis of the total situation. The problem is not to draw a conclusion from given premises; that can be best done by a piece of inanimate machinery by fingering a keyboard. The problem is to 'find' statements of general principle and of particular fact, which are worthy to serve as premises

This suggests that arguments in law are not exactly about logical deductions but, rather, are concerned with the premises upon which those deductions are based. Thus, the essential task of the judge is to find the 'correct' premises. It is this process of 'finding' appropriate premises that will now be examined through the interrelated questions of assessing the facts and determining the law applicable to a particular case. As will be seen, the process of finding premises cannot be carried out solely by using deductive reasoning; it depends on a less clearly defined recourse to induction, analogy, persuasion and judicial discretion. The major difficulty in French law is that judgments do not account for this process; they merely set out its results. This explains why it is that the true reasons for a decision will only be fully understood by reading the analytical notes to reported cases (see Chapter 9) or the *Avocat Général's* opinion (*conclusions*) to the Court of Cassation, provided these are printed along with the judgment (see Chapter 8.3.1 below).

7.3.1 The search for the major premise

The syllogism cannot offer guidance to the judge when it comes to identifying or establishing the appropriate legal rule or principle serving the function of the major premise, for it can only show that a conclusion is deduced from fixed and ready-made propositions. Yet, before serving as a major premise, legal rules are reformulated with a view to giving effect to the meaning, extensions and limitations that judges wish to attach to them. Indeed, the major premise in French judgments is never the exact formulation of the actual relevant code or statute provision but rather the meaning attached to it by the court. For example, in the 1997 divorce case *X* v *Mme Y* (discussed at 7.2.1 above), the establishment of the major premise was arrived at, not from the actual wording of arts 259 and 259-1 of the Civil Code referred to in the *visa*, but from the interpretation of these two provisions. Indeed, the first of these texts reads as follows: 'The facts alleged in divorce cases either by the petitioner or by the respondent can be proved by any means of proof, including admission'. Immediately after, art. 259-1 provides: 'one of the spouses cannot produce in court as written evidence letters addressed to the other spouse by a third party when these letters have been obtained by fraud or violence'. Interpreting these two provisions the Court of Cassation lays down the major premise as 'In divorce cases the judge cannot exclude documentary evidence unless it has been obtained by fraud or violence'. However, art. 259-1 does not specify or even suggest that fraud and violence are the only circumstances in which letters can be excluded as evidence. Thus, the Court considerably reduces the scope for excluding evidence which, for some reason, cannot be permitted or relied upon in these or in similar circumstances. According to this ruling, evidence obtained in breach of civil liberties – being not technically 'fraud' or 'violence' – would, thus, be admissible in court. This example demonstrates that the wording of the major premise in French judicial decisions is not achieved by the use of tracing paper in copying the code provisions. Instead it results from a more complex process which has a great deal to do with judges' approach to rules in a particular system of law.

In respect of the major premise, there are two further points to be made:

(a) The first one is that in France, just as elsewhere, the legal system is characterised by a large number of competing, conflicting and overlapping rules, once described by the French legal philosopher Villey as a *panier de crabes qui s'entredévorent* (always at each other's throats). As a consequence, judges are frequently faced with legal situations in which two or more rules are equally applicable or, though equally applicable, are incompatible. The decision as to which rule takes precedence will not depend on the use of logical deductions, but rather on interpretative choices as well as on the weighing up against each other of conflicting interests or, more generally, on policy considerations. The criminal case of *Pélegrin* (1977), D. 1978, 42, is a classic example of a situation of conflicting rules. Here, the Court of Cassation put an end to a long lasting conflict between civil and criminal law rules in situations where a purchaser had in good faith acquired movable property from a non-owner. Whilst under art. 2279 of the Civil Code the true owner had no remedy against this purchaser who could, as a result, keep the property acquired, under the then art. 460 of the Criminal Code, this purchaser once having become aware of having obtained the property from a non-owner had no choice other than returning it on pain of being prosecuted as a receiver of stolen goods. So, under one rule (2279) the purchaser had become the owner, under the other (460) he became a receiver of stolen goods. In *Pélegrin*, the Court of Cassation decided to apply art. 2279. What is important here to note is that the decision as to which of the two rules – art. 2279 or art. 460 – should serve the function of major premise in such a situation did not proceed from deductive reasoning but rather from a realistic balancing of the competing interests of owners and third party purchasers. This example highlights the limitation underlying syllogistic logic in that, even in a system favouring logical processes, law cannot exclusively lie in definite rules with the promise of a certain outcome.

(b) The second point is that, as experience shows, it is extremely unlikely that judges will find an enacted rule or principle that corresponds exactly to a given set of facts. Legal rules, especially in a codified system as in France, do not provide for concrete facts, they only refer to categories of facts in a very abstract way. This frequently forces French judges to look for code provisions governing a class of situations capable of encompassing situations brought before them which have not been specially 'catered for'. In these circumstances, judges are very often faced with a choice between competing provisions, or even between competing interpretations of the same provision. The exercise of this choice will very often be dependent upon the specific nature of the case or upon comparisons judges can make with similar situations identified in earlier cases as situations falling within the scope of the rule selected. A particular choice between alternative rules may also be dictated by practical or policy-based arguments. For example, in *Proc.Gén. C. Cass.* v *Madame X* (cited at Chapter 4.2.4 above), judges had to decide, in the absence at the time of any specific provisions governing this type of agreements, under which particular category of agreements provided for by the law surrogate agreements fell. The Court of Appeal of Paris decided that, because of the similarities they had with authorised organ donation, surrogate agreements had to be categorised in the same way. Indeed, for the appellate judges, 'womb leasing' in surrogate motherhood was no different in essence from the donation of an organ. The Court of Cassation reversed the judgment of the Court of Appeal applying to the case art. 1128 of the Civil Code which prohibits such things, as the human body, which are held to be *hors du commerce*, from being the subject-matter of an agreement. Thus, there was a choice, in this case, between two competing sets of rules: the statutory provisions allowing organ donation in certain circumstances and the Civil Code provisions prohibiting legal transactions involving the human body. Although, in its usual style, the Court of Cassation says nothing about the reasons which have determined its choice, one can speculate that policy considerations and value judgements concerning the practice of surrogacy were paramount in the solution adopted. On the other hand, the Court of Appeal came to its conclusion by openly drawing comparisons with known examples of organ donation using a type of reasoning from analogy. Based on the Latin maxim *ubi eadem ratio, ibi idem jus*, analogy in France is as much a device for interpreting statutes (see Chapter 3.3.1 above) as it is a mode of reasoning.

7.3.2 Fact finding and problems of categorisation

It follows from what has been said above that, assuming legal rules can be found, the application of these rules to a particular case will depend, provided that the existence of the facts alleged have been established and their relevance to the issues of the case determined, on the characterisation of these facts as ones which fit within the class governed by one of those rules. This latter process, called *qualification des faits*, is crucial in the reasoning process of French judges. It is provided for by art. 12 of the New Code of Civil Procedure which states:

le juge tranche le litige conformément aux règles de droit qui lui sont applicables. Il doit donner ou restituer leur exacte qualification aux faits et actes litigieux sans s'arrêter à la dénomination que les parties en auraient proposée.

(judges decide on a dispute in accordance with the relevant rules of law. They must characterise the facts without necessarily relying on the assertions made in this respect by the parties to the case).

Qualification can be defined as a process whereby judges compare the 'raw' facts of a given case or, *faits bruts*, with a legal rule and decide on the proper inference to be drawn from this comparison. A simple example will help to understand how *qualification* operates. Under art. 242 of the Civil Code, divorce can be granted on grounds of serious and repeated violation of the duties and obligations deriving from marital status when this violation makes life together unbearable. One spouse has applied for divorce on the grounds that the other is always absent from home engaged in political activities. The 'raw' facts stated by this spouse need to be *'qualifiés'* prior to the application of art. 242. This means that the court may, after analysing and discussing the nature of these facts, decide to categorise them as a serious and repeated violation of marriage duties and obligations making life together unbearable. However, the court may decide otherwise, in which case no divorce will be granted on these grounds. This illustrates how *qualification* confronts judges with a choice. This is further demonstrated in cases where more than one *qualification* is arguable (as in *Proc. Gén, C. Cass* at Chapter 7.3.1(b) above). In such a situation, before giving their decision, judges have to weigh against each other the arguments in support of each of the possible *qualifications*. This involves considering the relevant code provisions or statutes capable of being matched up with each of the other proposed *qualifications*. From this process follows what Ghestin and Goubeaux (1983: 40) call a *'va-et-vient du fait au droit'* in which judges move backwards and forwards between facts and rules in order to decide the outcome of the case. The process of *qualification* thus involves a fair amount of judicial freedom of action, not to say creation. As such it cannot offer the certainty of a purely deductive system.

French scholar Ivainer (1986), in what has become a classic work on the subject, has demonstrated that the process of *qualification* is, in fact, primarily a process of evaluation. According to Ivainer, in the context of the *qualification* process, judges first determine the relevant facts (*faits pertinents*) and establish their existence (*jugement d'existence*), and secondly make value judgements on these facts (*jugement de valeur*). They then transform these value judgements into a number of specific parameters (*paramètres*) to which they apply assessment coefficients (*coefficients de pondération*). To illustrate this, and in order to test the value of his argument, Ivainer gives an example taken from a Court of Cassation's judgment *Société Immobilière et Commerciale de Banville v Dame Laroye* (1967), Bull. soc., no. 239. Here, an employee L had been dismissed without notice by her employer S for having been repeatedly late arriving for work. The main issue was whether the employee's conduct could be classified as a 'serious fault' justifying under the law a summary dismissal. In order to decide on this issue, the judges selected and established the existence of a number of *faits pertinents* under the following headings:

(i) the number of years of employment

(ii) the number of occasions when L was late for work during the relevant period of time

(iii) examples of any other misconduct on the part of L during this period

(iv) instances of good behaviour on the part of L

(v) reasons claimed by L for being late, such as heavy traffic

(vi) the fact that some animosity already existed between L and S

(vii) the disturbance caused by L's late arrival at work to the smooth running of the business.

The judges then made a value judgement by allocating assessment coefficients to each of the selected items above. In particular, in the lower court, the judges considered that the traffic difficulties suffered by L were paramount, when compared with all the other *faits*. Consequently, they refused to categorise L's late arrival as a 'serious fault' and decided that the dismissal was unfair. However, the Court of Cassation took the opposite view, categorising L's conduct as a 'serious fault'. The Court reached its decision by classifying the disturbance caused to the business by L's late arrival as being of greater significance than the traffic difficulties suffered by her. This example suggests that *qualification*, as argued by Ivainer, is nothing more than an evaluative process whereby facts are construed by judges with a view to supporting the legal argument they have chosen to favour. Some have gone so far as to suggest that judges decide the outcome of the case first and then make every effort to work back to a *qualification* of facts which can justify their decision. This method of operating has been labelled *syllogisme ascendant* or *syllogisme régressif* in French because, contrary to the standard syllogism, the conclusion comes first, before the establishment of the major and minor premises.

Apart from showing the limits of syllogistic logic, this discussion surrounding *qualification* also demonstrates that it is misleading to assume, as is very often heard, that facts do not matter in French judicial procedure, this argument being supported by the fact that they are usually only briefly stated in court decisions. On the contrary, *qualification* is a prerequisite for the application of a rule of law to a case, in the absence of which the syllogism cannot operate. The importance accorded to the facts is further reflected in the Cour de Cassation's power to consider and review *qualification*, this being categorised in French civil procedure as a question of law, not a question of fact. This may be contrasted with the process of assessing the material nature of facts, which, unlike *qualification*, is an issue of fact to be decided by the lower courts only.

7.3.3 The role of persuasion in decision making

A further limit to syllogistic logic in the judicial process is the role played by persuasion. The function of a judicial decision being primarily to resolve a legal dispute, the court must, therefore, choose between two rival versions. It is this controversy between the parties, supported on each side by arguments aimed at convincing the judge, that will finally determine the court's reasons for its decision. The syllogism by its nature does not address this fundamental aspect of the judicial function. This is so because it uses fixed premises and makes the conclusion derived from them logically necessary and unquestionable. Indeed, with syllogistic reasoning it is not possible to prove the pros and cons of a proposition unless the system is to be incoherent and unworkable. The Belgian philosopher Perelman has highlighted these fundamental defects of the syllogism in his New Rhetoric theory. This theory of legal reasoning is rooted in the old Greek tradition of rhetoric and dialectic which emphasises the non-compelling nature of the arguments used to support a thesis. Its central idea is that it is in relation to an audience that these arguments are pursued. According to Perelman, these arguments are never conclusive, as in a mathematical system of reasoning illustrated by the judicial syllogism. They seek rather to persuade the audience that the reasons given are better than those advanced by the adverse party. Applied in the legal context such a theory explains why, before a court, it is possible to plead both for and against. According to Perelman (1963: 101), 'the judge who takes a decision after hearing both parties does not behave like a machine, but like a person whose power of evaluation, free but not arbitrary, is more often than not decisive for the outcome of the argument'. Consequently, the decision of the judge reveals a preference for one of the theses presented by the parties. In order to make it work, the judge will so construe the facts in such a way as to support the legal argument he has chosen to favour. This further demonstrates that the judicial process does not rest on the syllogism alone.

Chapter references

ANCEL, J.P., 'La Rédaction de la Décision de justice en France', *Revue Internationale de Droit Comparé*, 1998, Vol. 3, pp. 840–852.

COOPER, T.M., The Common and the Civil Law', *Harvard Law Review*, 1950, Vol. 63, pp. 468–475.

DEWEY, J., 'Logical Method and Law', *The Cornell Law Quarterly*, 1924, Vol. 10, pp. 17–27.

GHESTIN, J., and GOUBEAUX, G., *Traité de Droit Civil: Introduction Générale*, 2nd edn, Paris, LGDJ, 1983.

IVAINER, T., 'L'interprétation des Faits en Droit', JCP 1986, I, 3235.

MACCORMICK, D. N., *Legal Reasoning and Legal Theory*, Oxford: Clarendon Press, 1978.

MACCORMICK, D. N., and SUMMERS, R. S., *Interpreting Statutes*, Dartmouth, 1991, pp. 461–510.

PERELMAN, C., *The Idea of Justice and the Problem of Argument*, Routledge and Kegan Paul, 1963.

PERELMAN, C., *Logique Juridique-Nouvelle Rhétorique*, 3rd edn, Paris: Dalloz, 1999.

SAMUEL, G., 'The Impact of European Integration on Private Law', *Legal Studies*, Vol. 18, no. 2, 1998, pp. 167–176.

SINCLAIR, K., 'Legal Reasoning: in Search of an Adequate Theory of Argument', *California Law Review*, 1971, Vol. 59, pp. 821–858.

VILLEY, M., *Seize Essais de Philosophie du droit*, Paris: Dalloz, 1969.

ZWEIGERT, K., and KÖTZ H., *An Introduction to Comparative Law*, 3rd edn, Oxford, 1998.

8

Judicial style

Les hommes de loi aiment à enserrer leur écriture dans le carcan des attendus, sinon des considérants, tout comme ils se drapent, avec dignité, dans leur ample robe noire.
Almairac, G., 'A Temps Nouveaux, Formes Nouvelles', JCP 1975, I, 2689.

Part I of this book has already dealt with the style and techniques of legislative drafting in French Law. This chapter is concerned only with the form, structure and language of French judicial decisions, as well as with the style of justification characteristic of the French judiciary. While lawyers from other jurisdictions often praise French statutes and code provisions for their absence of complexity and their clear language, they tend to be more critical about the manner in which judicial decisions are written and expressed in France. In this respect, the following list of adjectives, used repeatedly in legal writing to describe French opinions, is indicative of the way French judicial style is usually perceived by foreign observers:

Peculiar

Terse

Cryptic

Monolithic

Laconic

Highly technical

Formalistic

Spartan

Brief

Depersonalised

Assertive

Legalistic.

One must say that, for those not used to French court decisions, some of their stylistic features are striking. French judgments, especially those of the highest courts, apart from being remarkably brief, have a peculiar logical and grammatical construction. The language employed is highly technical and is chosen meticulously. They do not contain any kind of policy or interpretative discussion. In spite of being handed down by a college of judges, no provision is made for dissenting opinions. A number of French jurists have traditionally regarded these qualities as virtues, not as defects. In a celebrated and authoritative work on the style of French judgments, Judge P. Mimin (1978) commends the forms traditionally associated with the French judicial style for their elegance and what, according to him, has become 'a style full of prestige'. Working through a series of do's and don'ts, Mimin encourages judges to be concise, clear and to stick to the traditional single-sentence grammatical structure of French judgments. 'Just as at the Sorbonne', he says, 'Law Courts must ensure that grammar is respected in judicial decisions'. These words earn Mimin the honour of being compared with the famous French seventeenth century grammarian Vaugelas (1585–1650) who, in his *Remarques sur la Langue Francaise* (1647), advises his readers on the *bon usage* of French grammar and language. In his book, Mimin also castigates, sometimes vehemently, judges' attempts at inserting into their decisions policy arguments, personal views, alternative approaches, or what he calls 'humanitarian nonsense'.

However, a number of French scholars, judges and practitioners have distanced themselves from Mimin's views, voicing concern about the traditional forms and style of expression in French judgments. It has been argued that, since judicial opinions are primarily addressed to the litigants, they should firstly be written and shaped in a more accessible way, and they should secondly give more detail about the judges' reasons for their decisions. The first point, relating to the drafting and the structure of judicial decisions, has been addressed with the setting up, in 1973, of a *Commission de Modernisation du Langage Judiciaire*. This commission issued a number of recommendations, examined further on in this chapter, which were taken up again in two 1977 ministerial circulars addressed to the courts: one the presentation of judgments and the other on judicial vocabulary. However, on the issue concerned with the lack of elaborate and substantive judicial justification, not much has been done to remedy the paucity of detail in French opinions. This may be attributed to political and institutional factors which have been decisive in the attitudes that the French have taken towards law and the judicial function. These factors, examined earlier in this book, have contributed not only to shaping the mode of reasoning adopted by French judge (discussed in Chapter 7), but also to defining the manner in which judges justify their decisions.

The aim of the present chapter is to familiarise readers with the manner in which French judicial decisions are drafted and structured. In these respects, it will examine to what extent French courts have followed the recommendations of the *Commission de Modernisation du Language Judiciaire*. A special emphasis has been placed here on the terminology used in judgments to which the first part of the chapter is devoted. At this stage, the reader's attention will be drawn to the main areas of difficulty with respect to the meaning of some of the most common technical terms and expressions used in French judgments, including Latin words and phrases still in common use. Then, the second part will explain and illustrate the basic form and structure of a typical French judgment. The final part of the chapter deals with the principal characteristics of the French judicial style of justification, and more particularly, the complete absence of policy arguments and of dissenting opinion.

8.1 Legal terminology

As with every legal system, the jargon employed in French judicial decisions confronts the uninitiated person with a real difficulty. Law is a kind of 'foreign' language and to be part of and communicate within the community of lawyers demands the correct use of their language. This difficulty is exacerbated in the case of English speaking law students and practitioners who, apart from having to overcome the difficulty arising from legal terminology, may also have to improve their linguistic competence in the everyday language. For these students and lawyers, comprehension of judicial decisions full of complex and often ambiguous technical terms and expressions, is made even more difficult by the very particular style of writing and the lack of any substantive discussion of arguments in these texts.

The first subheading will consider to what extent law dictionaries provide a suitable source of aid in establishing the meaning of French technical words and expressions found in judicial decisions. The process of ascribing a correct meaning to a word, may, however, require more thought and evaluation than may be gained by the simple act of looking up the meaning of a word in a dictionary. A more helpful way of dealing with problems of meaning is to define specific areas of difficulty and propose a number of possible answers. This will be considered under a second subheading. The third subheading looks at the recommendations made by the *Commission de Modernisation du Language Judiciaire* in its attempt to make legal French more 'jargon-free'.

8.1.1 Using dictionaries

There are a few multilingual and bilingual technical dictionaries aimed at an English speaking audience. However, these are not always reliable and must, therefore, be used with caution. One reservation in using these dictionaries is that as with any dictionary, they mostly offer a number of alternative translations, which means that, unless users are familiar with their subject, they cannot choose which one of these translations best fits the question in hand. Also, the authors of these specialist dictionaries do not necessarily combine linguistic competence with the technical knowledge of all the different legal systems they are dealing with. The result is that the translations offered are by no means always accurate and error free.

Moreover, there is a more fundamental difficulty common to every system of law which is that there are legal terms that simply cannot be translated into another language as this language has no exact equivalent concept or institution. For example, the doctrine of consideration has no exact equivalent in French law and, although the word 'consideration' has a linguistic equivalent in ordinary French, in the legal context it means a very different thing altogether and cannot be translated directly into legal French. In similar fashion the French legal notion of *erreur*, in contract, cannot accurately be translated as 'mistake' in legal English even if this may, on the face of it, appear convenient. It is true that there is some common ground between *erreur* and 'mistake' in that both refer to a defect of consent making contracts void both in French and in English law. However, they are not identical concepts. Case law shows that *erreur* has a much wider and more flexible meaning than 'mistake' and, consequently, would not provide an accurate translation for this latter term, and vice versa. In fact, legal terms with no exact equivalent in another language need to be explained at some length, an area in which multilingual and bilingual legal dictionaries are lacking. Viewed from this standpoint, monolingual law dictionaries are far more helpful because they provide the definitions and explanations that are missing in the former ones. The most authoritative and widely used French law dictionaries are:

(i) Guillien, R., and Vincent, J., *Lexique de Termes Juridiques*, 12th edn, Paris: Dalloz, 1999. This is a concise dictionary covering around 4,000 legal terms. It is also regularly updated to cover the latest changes in the French legal system. For example, its latest edition includes such new entries as *bioéthique* – the ethics of biomedical research, and *PACS* – the abbreviated form of *Pacte Civil de Solidarité* which is the registered domestic partnership introduced by the Law of 15 November 1999. It also features a useful system of cross-references whereby after each entry the relevant code provision is cited.

(ii) Cornu, G., *Vocabulaire Juridique*, 1st edn Quadrige, Paris: PUF, 2000. This larger and more exhaustive work is a widely respected dictionary which provides comprehensive coverage for over 10,000 legal terms, also with references to code provisions. One of the key features of *Vocabulaire Juridique*, is that terms are entered in their general and secondary meanings which are in turn subdivided into complex forms called *sous-mots* ('sub words'). As an illustration, the word *règlement* is entered (pp. 740–41) in its general meaning as: *espèce de règle, disposition de portée générale* (a type of rule of general application); this meaning is then followed by a secondary meaning which is: *texte de portée générale émanant de l'autorité exécutive* (legal text of general application issued by the government); *règlement* is then subdivided into *sous-mots* amongst which are: *règlement intérieur* (internal regulations applying to a particular organisation, assembly or council), *règlement autonome* (decrees issued by the government in its legislative capacity – art. 37 Constitution) and *règlement d'administration publique* (decrees issued by the government in execution of parliamentary statutes).

Apart from law dictionaries, ordinary bilingual dictionaries such as *Collins.Robert's French and English Dictionary* or *Harrap's New Standard French and English Dictionary* may also be consulted as they contain translations of many legal terms which, paradoxically, are very often more reliable than those offered in the bilingual specialist dictionaries.

Finally, a few books devoted to French law have placed a particular emphasis on the legal language and can be useful sources for explanation and translation. Amongst them are:

(i) Weston, M., *An English Reader's Guide to the French Legal System*, 2nd edn, Oxford: Berg Publishers Limited, 1993. This book provides general guidelines for the translation of French legal texts and offers an English translation of key terms in selected areas of French Law.

(ii) Steiner, E., and Ditner, D., *French For Lawyers*, London: Hodder and Stoughton, 1997. This is a course book focusing on French legal terminology within the context of French legal documents. The main text in each chapter gives an outline of a particular area of French Law and is complemented by a series of exercises aimed at reviewing essential vocabulary and at drawing attention to possible areas of confusion between French and English terms.

8.1.2 Defining areas of difficulty

The scale of the difficulty that occurs when establishing the meaning of legal terms varies depending on the type of word involved. In this respect, legal words can be classified into the three following main categories:

(a) Category A: words used in the legal language only

(b) Category B: words having an ordinary meaning and a legal meaning

(c) Category C: words in the legal language having more than one meaning.

Each category is now considered in turn.

8.1.2.1 Words used in legal language only

In this category are to be found a few technical terms which have entered into common usage in everyday language and thus do not need to be explained at length. This is the case for terms like *contrat* (contract), *testament* (will) or *tribunal* (court). The vast majority of legal terms, however, require greater explanation and initiation into their meaning. Here, however, two major problems arise. One is the lack of synonyms, a difficulty common to any technical language. Legal terms have a precise meaning used to describe a particular concept or institution. Consequently, they cannot easily be replaced. If this were the case, however, it would lead only to approximation which, in a subject like law, must be avoided. This is why the *Commission de Modernisation du Langage Judiciaire* recommended in its report on judicial vocabulary that it was neither possible nor desirable to eliminate technical terms. Beginners are, therefore, advised to use these terms with their correct meanings as early as possible. Regular attendance at lectures and tutorials, where technical terms are defined and explained in context, and regular use of a good law dictionary, are both recommended to ensure a thorough initiation to legal terminology. The second problem in connection with legal terms is that their meaning can only be fully understood if apprentice lawyers are already familiar with the subject-matter in hand. These lawyers are presented with a circular difficulty here. On the one hand, they cannot fully understand the meaning of a technical term without some experience of the subject, but on the other hand, a good grasp of a subject presupposes that the meanings of the relevant terms are known. Although the use of a law dictionary may help here, nothing apart from the actual practice of law will help overcome this difficulty. Notwithstanding the difficulty arising from the lack of accessibility to their meaning, technical terms offer a significant advantage, namely that of 'time saving'. By way of illustration, the French legal term *chirographaire* is used to describe an unsecured creditor. If this word were to be removed from the legal language it would have to be replaced by the following full sentence: '*le créancier ordinaire dont la créance ne bénéficie d'aucune sûreté spéciale*'. Thus, instead of one word, 12 words would have to be employed in its place. Legal terms are, therefore, concise ways of expressing what otherwise would require a lengthy explanation each time they were used. Their absence would lead to impossibly long and convoluted legal texts.

8.1.2.2 Words having an ordinary meaning and a legal meaning

This category of words constitutes a major area of confusion, especially when a word of this kind is employed in a legal context, not in its legal meaning, but in its ordinary meaning. This can happen with a term in common usage such as *auteur* which, in a judicial decision, can be used, either in its ordinary meaning of writer, composer or painter or in its legal meaning which, depending on the context, may mean:

(a) the father or mother of a child (in family and tort law)

(b) a person who has transferred a right to another person (in contract or ownership)

(c) a perpetrator of a crime (in criminal law).

Treacherous words like *auteur* are correctly labelled in French *faux-amis* or 'false-friends', literally translated. Indeed, when presented with such a word the novice might presume to be on familiar ground whereas technically, in fact, the word may have a completely different meaning in context. Here, a close examination of the textual context may assist in determining which of the ordinary or legal meanings is intended. Dictionaries with examples of the headword in use in actual sentences and quotations to show applied usage are of particular value in this area, as they considerably reduce the risk of error and consequent misuse.

8.1.2.3 Words in the legal language with more than one meaning

A third level of difficulty arises from polysemy, meaning here the characteristic of legal words having more than one meaning. A significant number of French legal terms have many meanings and it is sometimes difficult, even for an experienced person, to know which of these meanings is intended. In the simplest case legal terms may have one general and one special meaning. For example, the word *loi* in its general meaning refers to enacted rules as opposed to customary rules, whereas in its special meaning it refers to parliamentary statute as opposed to governmental regulations. However, in the most extreme case, there are terms which, apart from one or two general meanings, have a multiplicity of specific meanings when used with an adjective or a noun complement. A typical example is the term *acte*. In Cornu's *Vocabulaire Juridique*, *acte* has three basic meanings and 70 other different meanings when used with a noun or an adjective such as, for example, *acte authentique* (deed) or *acte de commerce* (commercial agreement). Ascribing the correct meaning to such complex words may prove a difficult task, especially when the adjective or noun complement is missing in the text. Alongside the problem of polysemy, there are two further difficulties that inexperienced users of legal French may face. Firstly, there is the frequent case of legal acts, persons or situations having different designations depending on the circumstances involved. For example, depending on the court in which a case is heard, a judicial decision in France may be called either a *jugement* (lower court), an *arrêt* (Court of Cassation), an *ordonnance* (non collegial court), a *décision* (*Conseil Constitutionnel* or *Conseil d'Etat*) or a *sentence* (industrial tribunal or private arbitration). The same applies to the party against whom a court action is brought who is, either a *défendeur* (lower court), an *intimé* (court of appeal), a *prévenu* (criminal court for minor or less serious offences) or an *accusé* (Court of Assizes in cases of serious offences). A second common source of difficulty which has practical significance for foreign lawyers is when a French legal term is similar or identical to a word in their own language but different in meaning. This occurs frequently with English and French terms, very often leading to mistranslation. A classic illustration is the word 'jurisprudence', spelled the same in French and in English, but meaning something totally different in both languages. In French, '*jurisprudence*' refers to case law whereas, in English, it refers to the philosophy of law. More difficult is the situation where there is an overlap of meaning between two identical terms. This is the case with the French word *cour* which, like the English word 'court', refers to a specific court such as the *Cour d'Appel*, or the *Cour de Cassation*, but which, unlike English, cannot be used to describe law courts in general. In this latter case, the precise translation in French of 'law courts' would be *juridictions*, not *cours*. The French word *juridiction* is also a term that causes difficulty. Apart from referring to a law court in general, it also means, as in English, the limits or territory within which any particular power may be exercised, or the actual power and right to exercise authority. These particular examples show that similarities in words between languages represent a fearsome area of potential confusion and must be dealt with carefully by those engaged in the study of more than one legal system.

8.1.3 Legal jargon and access to legal documents

In its report on judicial vocabulary, the *Commission de Modernisation du Langage Judiciaire* identified five main areas needing improvements with a view to making the judicial language 'more clear, more modern and more accessible'. These are:

(a) Latin phrases and maxims

(b) archaic forms of language and outdated phrases

(c) discourteous expressions

(d) useless or empty phrases

(e) ambiguous words.

Each of these sections are now considered in turn, using the examples and illustrations given by the Commission in its reports as a basis for proposed changes.

8.1.3.1 Latin phrases and maxims

The importance of Roman law as a source of French law is demonstrated by the continuing frequent use of Latin by French lawyers. From very early times in French legal history many rules or principles have been formulated in Latin very often in the form of maxims. Latin maxims are usually conveniently referred to in judgments or scholarly works by quoting only the first two or three words. By way of example one may take the rule *infans conceptus pro nato habetur quoties de commodis ejus agitur*. This rule, which allows children to claim rights arising out of situations which took place at a time when they were as yet unborn, is simply known as *infans conceptus*. Latin phrases are also used in French law to describe a particular concept or situation. Thus the *de cujus* refers to the deceased in succession law; the *pretium doloris*, in tort law, is a particular category of damages for pain and suffering caused to a victim by physical injuries; *res nullius*, in property law, is an object without an owner. Latin maxims and phrases have been compiled in France in two comprehensive and complementary volumes, which are: Roland, H., and Boyer, L., *Locutions Latines du Droit Francais*, 4th edn, Paris: Litec, 1998 and, by the same authors, *Adages du Droit Francais*, 4th edn, Paris: Litec, 1999. These two books are particularly useful in that they provide not only a translation for each maxim or phrase but also ample explanations including historical background.

As already mentioned, the use of Latin in law produces the advantage of allowing the formulation of a well-known rule or concept in an abbreviated form. It also fills gaps in French legal terminology. For example, in contract law, the words *contrat* and *acte* are both used equally well to describe both the agreement and the written document. This linguistic ambiguity leads to confusion, especially amongst students when asked to distinguish between (a) the rules that make an agreement enforceable as a binding contract and (b) formal and evidential requirements. To remedy this situation, for the agreement itself, French jurists use the Latin equivalent *negotium* and for its written counterpart, the term *instrumentum*.

Despite these practical advantages for lawyers, the use of maxims or doctrines dressed up in Latin do not make them readily comprehensible for those whose benefit they are supposed to exist, that is to say, the parties in a case. This is why, in its report, the *Commission de Modernisation du Langage Judiciaire* recommends that Latin should no longer be used when writing judgments, as is the case already with codes and other statutory instruments where Latin is avoided in the formulation of legal rules. As useful illustrations, the *Commission* gives a list of commonly used Latin phrases and maxims, with their proposed translation, from which the following examples are taken:

Accessorium sequitur principale   L'accessoire suit le principal
(*adjuncts to a principal thing are governed by the same rules as those applying to the principal*)

Actori incumbit probatio   La preuve incombe au demandeur
(*the burden of proof rests with the plaintiff*)

Fraus omnia corrumpit   La fraude vicie tout
(*fraud invalidates everything*)

Nulla poena sine lege   Pas de peine sans loi
(*no punishment without a pre-existing law*)

Intuitu personae   En consideration de la personne
(*in consideration of the person*)

However, despite the *Commission*'s recommendations, this attempt to translate all Latin expressions into French has partly failed owing to the jurists' attachment to expressions and maxims that have become part of the legal language in its original form.

8.1.3.2 Archaic forms of language and outdated phrases

In order to keep up with the development of the French language and with new terminology, the *Commission* has also proposed updating the following outmoded expressions commonly used in French judgments. Thus:

Le sieur X has been updated as *M. X* (abbreviated form for *Monsieur X*).

La dame Y as *Mme Y* (*Madame Y*).

La demoiselle Z as *Mlle Z* (*Mademoiselle Z*).

Also:

Il échet has become *il échoit, il convient* or *il incombe* (it is incumbent upon, it falls to someone to do something).

Ouï M. X en son rapport has become *après avoir entendu M. X dans son rapport* (having heard M. X in his report).

In the same vein, the *Commission* has advocated avoidance of the following outdated terms also in constant use in court decisions: *ledit* (the said), *le susdit* (the aforesaid), *le susnommé* (the above named), *dont s'agit* (in question), *de céans* (here or this one).

Courts have been eager to remove these obsolete terms from their decisions. In this respect, the readers of French law reports will notice differences in language between decisions published before and after the 1977 Commission's recommendations.

8.1.3.3 Discourteous expressions

Some may find it hard to believe that judges can ever be discourteous in their decisions. However, it is under this heading that the *Commission* has listed some expressions which, with the passage of time, now sound 'awkward or offensive, if not indeed traumatic', in the Commission's words. This was the case with expressions describing the parties to a case as *le nommé X* (the man named X), *la fille Y* (girl Y), or *la femme Z* (woman Z). These have now been replaced with the more civilised *M. X*, *Mlle Y* or *Mme Z* which, since 1977, have been used in court decisions.

8.1.3.4 Useless or empty phrases

Following the Commission's suggestions, a few vacuous phrases have been shortened in order to facilitate the reading of decisions by non-lawyers. For example: *Ordonnons que les pièces de la procédure seront transmises à M. le procureur de la République pour être pour lui requis ce qu'il appartiendra* has been replaced by the more accessible: *ordonnons la transmission des pièces de la procédure à M. le procureur de la République* (request the forwarding of the file to the public prosecutor). Similarly, *dit que le jugement sortira son plein et entier effet pour être exécuté selon ses forme et teneur* has become: *ordonne l'exécution du jugement* (the court orders the enforcement of its judgment).

8.1.3.5 Ambiguous words

Under this heading, the Commission has selected some frequently used legal terms, whose meaning might not be immediately apparent to those coming across them in a judgment. For example, calling the parties by the technical term describing the position they hold in the case, i.e., *défendeur* or *appelant*, may not be very clear to them. The Commission recommended that the parties should be called instead by their proper names. Also, it recommended that ambiguous words such as *louer* (which in French means both 'to let' and 'to rent'), should be avoided and replaced by either *donner à bail* (meaning 'to let') or *prendre à bail* (meaning 'to rent').

8.2 Form and structure

With respect to the form and structure of French judgments, Mimin (1978: 186) makes a useful distinction between procedural, grammatical and logical aspects. Only the first two aspects will be considered in this chapter since the logical form and structure of judicial decisions has already been dealt with under judicial reasoning in the previous chapter.

8.2.1 Procedural aspects

The procedural rules governing the form and content of French judgments are laid down in arts 454 and 455 of the New Code of Civil Procedure. Firstly, all judgments must specify the court in which the case is heard, the names of the judges, the date of the judgment, the names and addresses of the parties involved and the names of counsel appearing in the case. The judgment must also indicate at its beginning the relevant statutory provisions on which the decision is based, or *visa* (see Chapter 7.2.2 (c) above). Next comes a summary of the claims and arguments of the parties, followed by the reasons for the decision, called *motifs*, and, the actual ruling of the court, known as the *dispositif*. The *motifs* are a somewhat detailed statement of the reasons justifying the decision. As has been seen earlier (7.2), *motifs* are set out in the text of the decision in a syllogistic form. The *dispositif* is the final clause of the decision in which the court states its position on the points at issue. *Res judicata* applies, in principle, only to the *dispositif*, although it has been extended by the courts to the *motifs* that necessarily support the *dispositif*. The *dispositif* is usually easily identifiable as it is invariably prefaced in every judgment by the expression *Par ces motifs* (on these grounds). Each point at issue decided upon in the *dispositif* is called *chef de la décision*. The formal presentation of *chefs de la décision* varies according to the nature of the court in which the case is heard. In civil and criminal courts they consist of a series of short sentences, each prefaced by a verb in the indicative form such as *dit, juge que, déclare, condamne, reçoit en sa demande*. Here are some examples of *dispositifs* found in judgments published in law reports:

(i) In a criminal court: *Par ces motifs, déclare A. coupable des faits qui lui sont reprochés; condamne A. à deux mois d'emprisonnement avec sursis.*

(ii) In a Court of appeal: *Par ces motifs, reçoit l'appel jugé régulier en la forme, réforme le jugement déféré en toutes ses dispositions, prononce l'adoption de l'enfant S.*

(iii) In the Court of Cassation: *Par ces motifs, casse, renvoie devant la Cour d'Appel de Paris.*

In administrative courts, the *dispositif* consists of 'articles' similar in style to statute or decree articles. Here is an example:

Article 1er – Les interventions de X et Y sont admises.

Article 2 – Les décisions du 30 juillet et 20 septembre 1998 du Ministre de la Santé sont annulées.

The use of the article format in administrative courts can be explained by the fact that administrative proceedings are mainly concerned with the annulment of decisions made by administrative bodies which do not conform to the French principle of *légalité* to which state and public bodies must comply. In giving their decisions in this way the administrative courts emphasise the authority of their ruling by formulating and presenting them in a quasi-legislative style.

The above description of the structure of French judgments should be supplemented with the information provided in Chapter 11.3 dealing with case study where the format in which judicial decisions are presented in law reports is considered.

8.2.2 Grammatical aspects

Grammatically, French judgments are cast in the form of a single sentence with one or several main clauses and various subordinate clauses. Each of these clauses is prefaced by the phrase *attendu que*. However, some courts of appeal, as well as the administrative courts, use the phrase *considérant que* instead.

French *Avocat General* Lindon (1968: 23) once praised the elegant perfection of the *attendu* phrase in judicial decisions:

The phrase *attendu que* does not, in fact, constitute a rigid vice, but on the contrary a flexible corset whose strictures are actually its main virtue. With respect to the judicial prose writer it plays a similar Alexandrine role as in poetry. Just as the greatest poets, under the constraint of writing within a framework of twelve-foot rhyming verses, have thus managed to achieve perfection in the expression of their thoughts and in the elegance of their forms, so with judges, who must give reasons for their decisions in the form of *attendus*, thereby succeeding in incorporating logic and order into the presentation of their ideas.

Despite this laudatory statement, the use of *attendus* has given rise to much criticism amongst practitioners, scholars and governmental bodies concerned with the need for clarity in judicial language. It is in this context that the *Commision de Modernisation du Language Judiciaire* recommended in its report on the presentation of judgments that all *attendus* should be removed from the part of the decision dealing with the statement of facts including the statement of claim (referred to, for this purpose, as 'the descriptive part'), to be only maintained in the part where the court expounds its reasoning. According to the *Commission*, this new presentation would have the advantage of making the decision more accessible to litigants, especially those acting alone without the assistance of a lawyer, by distinguishing between what is claimed and what is held. Indeed, the *Commission* pointed out that the systematic use of *attendus* had the effect of blurring this fundamental distinction by giving the losing party the impression that the court accepted its claim but nevertheless dismissed it. The *Commission* further suggested breaking up the text of the decision with headings and subheadings in order to improve its clarity. The illustrations provided show that, while the Court of Cassation has continued to structure its decisions according to the old model (Box 8.1), most of the lower courts have opted for the presentation advocated by the *Commission* (Box 8. 2). Some courts have gone further by removing completely the use of *attendus* from their judgments with a view to making them more user-friendly for laymen (Box 8. 3).

Box 8.1 Traditional style of presentation: Court of Cassation decision

COUR DE CASSATION

2e CIV.

•

4 mars 1998

RESPONSABILITÉ CIVILE * Responsabilité du fait des choses * Garde * Immeuble * Explosion criminelle * Matériau projeté.

Une femme n'est pas la gardienne des gravats qui ont endommagé un immeuble voisin provenant de l'explosion de son habitation que son mari séparé de corps a fait sauter par explosifs.

(Société d'assurance moderne des agriculteurs et autre c/ GMF et autres) • ARRÊT

LA COUR – Sur le deuxième moyen : – Vu l'article 1384, alinéa 1er, du code civil ; Attendu, selon l'arrêt attaqué (CA Colmar, 16 févr. 1996), que M. H... a fait sauter, par explosifs, la maison de sa femme dont il était séparé de corps ; que cette explosion ayant endommagé l'habitation voisine des époux Sieffert, ceux-ci et leur assureur, la Garantie mutuelle des fonctionnaires (GMF), ont assigné en réparation M. H..., Mme H... et leur assureur, la Société d'assurance moderne des agriculteurs (SAMDA) ; – Attendu que, pour condamner in solidum les époux H... et la SAMDA à payer diverses sommes tant à la GMF, subrogée dans les droits des époux Sieffert, qu'aux époux Sieffert eux-mêmes, l'arrêt énonce que les matériaux en provenance de l'immeuble ayant joué un rôle actif et causal dans la réalisation du dommage, la responsabilité de Mme H... doit être retenue comme gardienne de cet immeuble ; qu'en statuant ainsi, tout en relevant que le jardin et l'habitation des époux Sieffert avaient été endommagés par des gravats provenant du souffle de l'explosion de l'immeuble H..., ce dont il résultait que Mme H... n'était pas la gardienne des matériaux ainsi projetés, la cour d'appel, qui n'a pas tiré les conséquences légales de ses constatations, a violé le texte susvisé ;

Par ces motifs, et sans qu'il y ait lieu d'examiner les autres griefs du pourvoi, casse et [...] renvoie devant la Cour d'appel de Metz...

CASS. 2e CIV., 4 mars 1998 • 96-14.119 • *MM. Chevreau, f.f. prés. et rapp. – Monnet, av. gén. – Mes Parmentier et Blanc, av.* • *Cassation de CA Colmar, 16 févr. 1996*
[2e ch. civ. A].

Source: Civ. 2, 4 mars 1998, Recueil Dalloz, 1999, p. 217

Box 8.2 New style of presentation: Lower court decision

COUR D'APPEL DE PAU

2ᵉ CH.

•

28 octobre 1996

> **APPEL CIVIL** ∗ Recevabilité ∗ Filiation naturelle ∗ Recherche de paternité ∗ Action en justice ∗ Recevabilité ∗ Examen des sangs ∗ Expertise génétique ∗ Irrecevabilité de l'appel.

Le jugement entrepris a, d'une part, dit que l'action en recherche de paternité naturelle exercée par la mère était soumise aux dispositions de l'art. 340 c. civ. dans sa rédaction de la loi n° 93-22 du 8 janv. 1993, d'autre part, avant dire droit sur le bien-fondé de l'établissement judiciaire de la paternité naturelle, tous droits et moyens réservés, ordonné un examen d'identification génétique ;

Si les premiers juges ont considéré que les éléments fournis par la mère rendaient vrai-semblable la paternité de l'appelant et ont déclaré l'action en recherche de paternité recevable, ils n'ont nullement tranché le principal ;

En effet, si le tribunal s'est prononcé sur l'admissibilité de la preuve, il n'a pas préjugé du bien-fondé de l'action ;

Le jugement attaqué ne peut en conséquence être frappé d'appel indépendamment du jugement sur le fond.

(X... c/ Mlle Y...) • ARRÊT

Prétentions et moyens des parties : Par conclusions du 27 mars 1995 Monsieur X... soulève dans un premier temps l'irrégularité de l'exploit introductif d'instance [...].

De plus et à titre subsidiaire, Monsieur X... souligne que malgré sa rédaction assez libérale le nouvel article 340 du code civil suppose pour son application que les juges se réfèrent aux anciens cinq cas d'ouverture supprimés par la loi du 8 janvier 1993 pour juger de la recevabilité d'une action en recherche de paternité naturelle. En conséquence, Monsieur X... précise que les pièces versées aux débats par l'intimée ne sont aucunement constitutives de présomptions ou indices graves. – L'appelant conclut à la nullité de l'assignation et à l'irrecevabilité de l'action introduite par Mademoiselle Y... Il demande que cette dernière soit condamnée aux dépens de première instance et d'appel.

Par conclusions du 12 septembre 1995, Mademoiselle Y... soulève tout d'abord l'irrecevabilité de l'appel formé par Monsieur X... car le jugement du Tribunal de grande instance de Tarbes n'ayant ordonné qu'une mesure d'instruction, il ne pouvait pas faire l'objet d'un appel immédiat selon les articles 544 et 545 du nouveau code de procédure civile, à moins qu'il ait été fait usage des dispositions de l'article 272 du nouveau code de procédure civile, ce qui n'a pas été le cas.

Box 8.2 *Contd.*

Enfin, Mademoiselle Y... répond que la nouvelle rédaction de l'article 340 du code civil a été faite dans un esprit évidemment plus libéral que l'ancienne et qu'en conséquence les pièces qu'elle rapporte sont constitutives de présomptions et indices graves tels que les entend l'article susvisé. En conséquence, Mademoiselle Y... conclut à l'irrecevabilité de l'appel et demande de condamner Monsieur X... à lui payer 7 000 F sur le fondement de l'article 700 du nouveau code de procédure civile ainsi qu'à supporter les entiers dépens.

Par conclusions complémentaires et responsives du 2 avril 1996, Monsieur X... souligne que la recevabilité d'une action en recherche de paternité naturelle et le bien-fondé de cette dernière sont deux questions intimement liées et que donc le jugement du tribunal de grande instance est un jugement mixte dont il peut être fait appel.

....

Le ministère public conclut à l'irrecevabilité de l'appel du jugement avant dire droit prononcé par le Tribunal de grande instance de Tarbes. La clôture de la procédure a été prononcée par ordonnance en date du 28 mai 1996.

LA COUR (*extraits*) – Attendu que l'examen de la recevabilité de l'appel impose de rechercher quelle est la nature du jugement prononcé par le Tribunal de grande instance de Tarbes ; que l'article 544, alinéa 1, du nouveau code de procédure civile dispose que les jugements qui tranchent dans leur dispositif une partie du principal et ordonnent une mesure provisoire peuvent être immédiatement frappés d'appel comme les jugements qui tranchent tout le principal ;

Attendu qu'en l'espèce le jugement entrepris a dit que l'action en recherche de paternité naturelle exercée par Mademoiselle Y... était soumise aux dispositions de l'article 340 du code civil dans sa rédaction issue de la loi du 8 janvier 1993 ; avant dire droit sur le bien-fondé de l'établissement judiciaire de la paternité naturelle, tous droits et moyens réservés, a ordonné un examen d'identification génétique ; que si les premiers juges ont considéré que les éléments fournis par Mademoiselle Y... rendaient vraisemblable la paternité de Monsieur X... et ont déclaré l'action en recherche de paternité recevable, ils n'ont nullement tranché le principal ; qu'en effet si le tribunal s'est prononcé sur l'admissibilité de la preuve, il n'a pas préjugé du bien-fondé de l'action ; que le jugement attaqué ne peut en conséquence être frappé d'appel indépendamment du jugement sur le fond ; qu'il s'ensuit que l'appel interjeté par M. X... est irrecevable ; qu'il n'y a donc pas lieu d'examiner les moyens soutenus par l'appelant ;

Attendu que Mlle Y... bénéficiaire de l'aide juridictionnelle totale ne justifie pas de débours particuliers exposés en cause d'appel ; qu'il n'y a pas lieu de lui allouer une quelconque indemnité sur le fondement de l'article 700 du nouveau code de procédure civile ; que M. X... supportera les dépens d'appel.

Par ces motifs, vu les articles 544 et 545 du nouveau code de procédure civile, déclare irrecevable l'appel formé par M. X... contre le jugement du Tribunal de grande instance

Box 8.2 *Contd.*

de Tarbes en date du 27 juin 1994 ; dit n'y avoir lieu à application des dispositions de
l'article 700 du nouveau code de procédure civile...

*CA PAU, 2e ch., 28 oct. 1996 • MM. Pujo-Sausset, prés. – Caujolle et Mme Riboulleau,
conseillers. – Me Galinon et SCP Longin, avoués. – Mes Cami et Rolfo (tous deux au barreau
de Tarbes), av. • Irrecevabilité de l'appel contre TGI Tarbes, 27 juin 1994.*

Source: CA Pau, 28 octobre 1996, *Recueil Dalloz*, 1998, p. 281

8.3 Style of justification

This part of the chapter examines the manner in which French judges express the
grounds for their decisions. Among the civil law systems, France is said to be the
country where judges display in their decisions the most cryptic and formalised style
of justification. Judgments are usually very short. On average, the Court of Cassation
will deliver a 30-line ruling, a lower court a single typewritten page. This constitutes a
marked difference from the much longer decisions of English judges. As an illustration, it took exactly 30 lines for the Court of Cassation, in *Vilela v Weil* (1997), D.
1998, 111, to decide on the claim by a homosexual man that he was entitled to succeed
to a tenancy in the name of his deceased partner; whereas, by way of contrast, the
House of Lords gave a lengthy judgment of 42 pages on a similar claim in *Fitzpatrick v
Sterling Housing Association Ltd* (1999) WLR 1115-1157. Accounting for the brevity
of French judicial decisions it may be pointed out that, unlike English judicial practice, policy arguments and dissenting opinions do not form part of court decisions.
These characteristics, held in common with other civil law systems, are examined
below.

8.3.1 Absence of policy arguments

French judges are known to reach their decisions relying only on 'legal' arguments
(*arguments juridiques*), as opposed to policy arguments (*arguments d'opportunité*).
Arguments juridiques means that they justify their decisions solely by showing how the
solution they have adopted fits within the prescriptions of the law, and this is the case
even when code provisions and principles do not provide a clear answer to the case
before them. Policy arguments are usually regarded in France as arguments falling
within the domain of the legislative arena. Indeed, according to the prevailing view, it
is rules of law that decide cases, policy being for the legislature. To what extent this is
actually true will be examined further below. Officially, however, policy arguments
naturally come into being in France only during the course of the parliamentary
debates surrounding the introduction of a new law. These arguments are usually

Box 8.3 Example of a judgment without *attendu*

Tribunal de grande instance de Lille, ord. réf. 20 avr. 1999

Louis Carpentier, propriétaire d'un fonds de commerce de bijouterie-joaillerie qui était exploité en location-gérance par la Societé Bijouterie centrale Carpentier, a cédé le fonds de commerce par acte de vente du 20 janvier 1989 à cette société dont le gérant est Jean-Paul Hérbaut. Suivant assignation du 25 janvier 1999, Louis Carpentier, qui prétend que la lettre « L » ou le prénom « Louis » n'ont jamais fait partie des éléments du fonds de commerce cédé, reproche l'utilisation abusive qui en serait faite par la Société Bijouterie centrale Carpentier et sollicite en conséquence d'interdire sous astreinte l'utilisation de la lettre « L » ou du prénom « Louis » sur tous les éléments permettant d'identifier la bijouterie (publicités, affiches, présentoirs, vitrines) et de condamner la société à une indemnité provisionnelle de 10 000 francs outre la somme de 2000 francs en application de l'art. 700 NCPC.

La Société Bijouterie centrale Carpentier soulève l'incompétence du juge des référés en raison de l'absence d'urgence et d'une contestation sérieuse ; subsidiairement, elle conclut au débouté et demande de condamner Louis Carpentier au paiement d'une somme de 4000 francs au titre de l'art. 700.

LE TRIBUNAL – Sur l'exception d'incompétence : Il est demandé au juge des référés de faire cesser l'utilisation abusive d'un prénom par une bijouterie-joaillerie, or, quand il y a lieu de faire échec à un trouble manifestement illicite, l'application de l'article 809 alinéa 1 NCPC n'est pas subordonnée à la preuve de l'urgence de la mesure concernée, en outre, l'existence d'une contestation sérieuse n'empêche pas le juge des référés de prendre les mesures propres à mettre un terme à un trouble manifestement illicite, sur le fondement du même article, dès lors, il convient de rejeter l'exception d'incompétence ;

Sur le trouble manifestement illicite : Dans l'acte de vente en date du 20 janvier 1989, la désignation du fonds de commerce cédé est la suivante : « un fonds de commerce de joaillerie, orfèvrerie, horlogerie, exploité à Tourcoing, 4 & 5, Grand Place, – numéro d'identification au répertoire nationale des entreprises (SIREN) 885 775 213 00014 – numéro d'inscription au registre du commerce de Tourcoing 57 à 521 et comprenant : a) l'enseigne, le nom commercial, la clientèle, l'achalandage et l'installation y attachés. b) le droit au bail des locaux d'exploitation tels que ledit fonds existe et que la partie acquéreur déclare bien connaître pour l'avoir visité étudié et estimé à sa propre valeur » ;

Par ailleurs, concomitamment à la vente du fonds de commerce, a été signé le 15 janvier 1989 un bail commercial entre Louis Carpentier et la société Bijouterie centrale Carpentier portant sur l'immeuble sis à Tourcoing, 4 et 5 Grand Place ; le contrat de bail précisait « le preneur prendra les lieux dans l'état où ils se trouveront au jour de l'entrée en jouissance » ;

Box 8.3 *Contd.*

Il ressort de ces pièces que ni l'enseigne, ni le nom commercial ne sont définis avec précision et qu'aucune réserve les concernant n'a été émise par le demandeur ; Dès lors, il ne peut être reproché au défendeur d'avoir laissé figurer sur la partie haute de la façade de son commerce l'inscription « Bijouterie centrale L. Carpentier » qui existait antérieurement à la cession du fonds de commerce (constat de Maître Pichon, huissier de justice, en date du 9 janvier 1996), en revanche, la dénomination sociale mentionnée au registre du commerce est « Bijouterie centrale Carpentier » sans aucune initiale, ni aucun prénom, pourtant, le nom qui figure sur les documents et publicités diffuses par la société Bijouterie centrale Carpentier à sa clientèle n'est pas celui qui se trouve sur le registre du commerce puisque l'initiale « L » est systématiquement ajoutée sur ces pièces ;

Comme la personne morale ne peut exercer sous un autre nom que celui qui résulte de son inscription au registre du commerce, il convient de constater l'illicéité de l'utilisation de la lettre « L » par la société dans ses relations avec les tiers, occasionnant un trouble manifeste à Louis Carpentier qui peut légitimement vouloir d'une part qu'aucune confusion n'existe dans l'esprit du public – puisqu'il n'exerce plus l'activité de joaillier – et, d'autre part, que l'initiale de son prénom soit protégée ;

En conséquence, il convient de mettre un terme à ce trouble en faisant défense à la Bijouterie centrale Carpentier d'utiliser la lettre « L » ou le prénom « Louis » et en la condamnant à une indemnité provisionnelle, enfin, il est inéquitable de laisser à la charge du demandeur le montant des frais irrépétibles qu'il a dû exposer ; le défendeur qui succombe ne pourra pas prétendre à une indemnisation à ce titre ;

Par ces motifs, rejette l'exception d'incompétence, fait défense à la société Bijouterie centrale Carpentier d'utiliser la lettre « L » ou le prénom « Louis » dans ses relations avec les tiers, condamne la société Bijouterie centrale Carpentier sous astreinte de 500 francs par jour de retard dans le mois à compter de la signification de l'ordonnance à intervenir, à faire disparaître la lettre « L » ou le prénom « Louis » des éléments suivants permettant d'identifier la bijouterie : documents publicitaires, affiches, en-têtes, cachets, papier à lettre, déboute Louis Carpentier pour le surplus de sa demande, condamne la SA Carpentier à payer au requérant la somme provisionnelle de 1 franc à valoir sur les dommages et intérêts ainsi qu'à la somme de 2 000 francs en application de l'article 700 NCPC, la condamne aux dépens...

Demandeur : Carpentier – *Défendeur* : Bijouterie centrale Carpentier (Sté) – *Composition de la juridiction* : M. Barrois, premier vice-prés. – Mes P. Labbée, Vandenburie, av.
Source: TGI Lille, 20 avril 1999, *Recueil Dalloz*, 2000, p. 435

formalised in an *exposé des motifs* drafted by the proponents of a new bill with a view to its proposed adoption by Parliament. By way of illustration, see the text of the *exposé des motifs* on the Loi 2001-588 of 4 July 2001 amending French abortion law at Appendix 2 to this chapter. Once the new law has been passed, *exposés des motifs* become part of the *travaux préparatoires* and are usually published in the *Journal Officiel* (see Chapter 3.3.2.1 above).

The absence of policy arguments in French judicial decisions, not even accompanied, as happens in Germany for example, by the detailed consideration of academic writings or previous case law, has created a situation where it has been left to commentators to ascertain the meaning of judicial decisions. French jurists have from there developed a method of reading judicial decisions based partly on textual interpretation, but also on legal, political, social and economic theory. This hermeneutic approach to judicial decisions is particularly reflected in the practice of written commentary on reported cases given by academics or practitioners, as will be examined in the following chapter.

This lack of substantive justification in French judicial decisions was, at one time, the subject of an academic debate between eminent French scholars and judges, a debate which seems to have dried up today. In their thorough study of judicial argumentation in France, A. Tunc (1974), a distinguished scholar, and A. Touffait, a high-ranking judge, called for a more explicit justification of judicial decisions, especially in the highest courts. In support of their view, Tunc and Touffait put forward the following two main arguments:

(a) it would make judicial decisions more accessible to the parties in a case and would help jurists to better understand their meaning and appreciate their implications

(b) it would clarify the meaning and scope of the statutory provisions, rules and principles established by the judges.

Tunc and Touffait additionally suggested that:

(c) the use of policy arguments – as well as the admission of dissenting opinions – in French judgments would generally enhance the judicial function in France

(d) it would also allow the law to adapt to social realities and would promote law reform.

Despite the strength of their argument, Tunc and Touffait's suggestions met with more scepticism than enthusiasm.

It was first pointed out that there are a number of inevitable practical and procedural constraints contributing to the lack of substantive argument in French decisions, and in those of the Court of Cassation in particular. One of these is a heavy caseload. The Court of Cassation is swamped with an increasing number of cases referred to it each year, which means that if it wishes to get through its work-load it cannot be too thorough in deciding legal issues and is even less able to evaluate the social consequences of its decisions. In 2000, the Court of Cassation was presented with 30,345 new appeals, whilst it ruled on 30,108 others. It is hardly surprising, therefore, that this court has developed a speedy way of justifying its decisions, especially in a system where each judgment has to be in written form. More generally, what contributes further to the lack of lengthy justification in French judgments, is the fact that French judges must also have regard to a certain number of strict rules of procedure when deciding cases. In particular, although it has to consider all the arguments put forward by the parties, a French court cannot, on its own initiative, raise issues that would have the effect of modifying the plaintiff's claim, either by awarding what was not demanded in the pleadings, or by going beyond what was demanded. If this were to happen the decision would be characterised as being *ultra petita* (art. 464 of the New Code of Civil Procedure). Therefore, judges, in keeping with what is claimed, considerably reduce the length of their judgments.

In response to Tunc and Touffait's arguments it has been further argued that policy considerations are not completely banned from the practice of French courts, particularly the lower courts. Courts of first instance and courts of appeal sometimes overtly raise social and institutional policy concerns based on public welfare, equity or morality when deciding cases. A well-known early example is *Doerr* v *Keller* (1855), D. 1856, 9, where the owner of a property built a false chimney on his roof with the sole purpose of depriving his neighbour of access to light. The Court of Appeal of Colmar ordered the demolition of the chimney justifying its ruling as follows:

Whereas though in principle the right of ownership is in a certain sense absolute and entitles the owner to use and dispose of the thing owned, nevertheless the exercise of this right, as of every other, must have as a constraint the satisfaction of a serious and legitimate interest; and, principles of morality and fairness call for a sanction in response to an action performed out of malice, motivated by an evil passion, not justified by any personal advantage, and causing serious damage to another.

This decision is based on the doctrine of abuse of right in the context of ownership, a doctrine already mentioned which has no statutory basis in French law and is a complete creation of the courts. It appears clearly from the terms of the judgment that moral considerations and arguments of fairness provide the basis for this doctrine whereby the right of ownership should not be exercised maliciously with the sole intention of inflicting harm on another. The doctrine of abuse of right has never been disregarded or overruled since the case of *Doerr* and is still employed in court decisions. Another illustration of policy arguments being contained in court judgments is the more recent famous case *Ville de Genève et Fondation Abegg* v *Consorts Margail* (1984), D 1985, 208, concerning wall paintings discovered in a church situated in the village of Casenoves in southern France. These paintings, after being removed from the wall, were misappropriated by an antique dealer who later sold them in part to the museum of Geneva, and in part to a private Swiss charitable trust. The Court of Appeal had to decide whether these paintings should be treated as *immeubles par destination*, a legal construct whereby the movable adjuncts (here, the paintings) to an immovable property (here, the church) are artificially considered as being component parts of that property and thus governed by the same rules. If this were to be the case here, then the return of the paintings would have to be a question falling within the jurisdiction of the French courts. However, one of the points at issue here was that the relevant code provision, art. 524 of the Civil Code, only provided under the heading *immobilisation par destination* for the case of movable things that are part of an agricultural, industrial or commercial enterprise with no mention of artistic works. Interpreting art. 524, the Court of Appeal ruled that this provision should be extended to artistic items such as paintings, giving the following justification:

The legal protection afforded to agricultural, industrial and, later on, commercial enterprises through the concept of *immeubles par destination* is expressed in broad terms with no exclusion and can therefore be extended to sites of historical or artistic value; legal protection in this latter case is further justified in view of the fact that these sites have increasingly become the objects of misappropriation and despoilment, if not outright plunder.

Although the Court of Cassation quashed the decision a few years later on the grounds of misinterpretation of art. 524, it is important to note that the Court of Appeal, in expounding the reasons for its decision in this case, went beyond a strict reliance on rules and principles established by code provisions, invoking sentiments of national cultural pride.

It is worth repeating that the above two illustrations come from the lower courts where more time and textual space is usually spent on justification. Policy arguments are practically never found in Court of Cassation judgments. However, it may happen that the highest court gives a hint as to the policy considerations behind its decisions, as in *Madame X v Société Transport Agglomération Elbeuvienne* (1995), D 1996, p. 69 (case reproduced as *Arrêt* 1 (in Box 11.2) Here, a person left in a vegetative state following an accident was nevertheless awarded damages for pain and suffering on the grounds that, being in a vegetative state did not preclude any human being from the existing right to obtain full compensation, including damages for pain and suffering. The use of the words 'human being' in the text of its decision suggests that the Court of Cassation gave consideration to the rights of individuals and the treatment they should be accorded, thus not restricting itself, as may have been expected, to its usual legalistic approach in assessing loss.

In further disagreement with Tunc and Touffait's argument it was pointed out that the lack of explicit reference to policy in the Court of Cassation decisions did not necessarily mean that the Court does not consider the social or practical consequences its decisions may have. Behind the façade of formal justification lies a 'secret garden' internal to the Court where judges confer with each other, freely expressing their opinions about how they would resolve a case in the light of existing legal rules and taking account of social factors. In a thorough study of the way judgments are worked out in the Court of Cassation, former Court of Cassation judge E. Frank (1983) shows that what the highest court openly publishes when delivering its judgments is only the 'tip of the iceberg'. Indeed, what Judge Frank's survey demonstrates, which is still valid today, is that the decisions produced by the Court of Cassation are only the end result of a more complex process in which judges, after going through case documents and evidence, take part in discussions consisting largely of case analysis and policy arguments. This process, as described by Judge Frank, is only a preliminary phase to the hearing and subsequent deliberations in a case. It is outlined as follows, starting, firstly, with the appointment of a *conseiller rapporteur* from amongst the panel of judges in charge of the case. The function of the *conseiller rapporteur* is to review the lower court record, identify the issues and, finally, recommend a solution. The recommendations of the *conseiller rapporteur* are contained in a *rapport* where, after explaining the facts and the history of the case, the *conseiller* presents to the Court a personal opinion based mainly on a detailed analysis of relevant past decisions as well as on policy considerations. The second stage of the process involves the *avocat général*, a member of the judiciary, already referred to in previous chapters, whose function in the Court of Cassation is to argue on behalf of society's interests in ensuring that the law is applied correctly. Like the *conseiller rapporteur*, the *avocat général* examines and analyses relevant judicial precedents, and in the light of these makes recommendations on how the case should be resolved in a document called *conclusions*. In the *conclusions* the *avocat général* frequently presents a line of reasoning based on social, economic or institutional considerations, in this respect going further than the *conseiller rapporteur* by not hesitating, when appropriate, to call for a change in established precedent, in this way preparing the ground for legislative reform. Unlike the *conseiller rapporteur*, the *avocat général*, not being a member of the panel hearing the appeal, feels freer to suggest such modifications to the Court. By way of illustration are the celebrated *conclusions* of *Procureur Général* Matter in *Pélissier du Besset* (1927), D.P. 1928, 1, 25 and in *Jand'heur* v *Galeries Belfortaises* (1930), (cited at Chapter 4.2.4). *Rapports* and *conclusions* are primarily regarded as internal Court of Cassation documents, which explains why they are not routinely published in law reports and are, therefore, difficult to access. In this connection, the interested reader will find the study on 'French judicial portraits' by Lasser (1995) very useful. In his well- researched essay the author gives a detailed analysis of the content and style of *rapport* and *conclusions* with typical published examples which, for this purpose, have been translated into English. The ultimate stage of the process described by Judge Frank is the *conférence* where judges meet and confer prior to the hearing of the case. The *conférence*, unlike the two previous stages, has no statutory basis but nevertheless constitutes a significant aspect of the day-to-day practice of the Court of Cassation. It is there that, after reviewing the lower court decision, the written arguments of the opposing parties, the report of the *conseiller rapporteur*, and the *conclusions* of the *avocat général*, judges finalise the grounds for their decision relying mainly on the drafts produced by the *conseiller rapporteur*. In the context thus described, the actual hearing of the appeal is only a formality where all the participants in the case outline their views, emphasising the particular points at issue, when appropriate. Following this, during the deliberations that take place, each judge voices his or her opinion in turn, the issues are summarised by the chairman of the panel and the voting proceeds.

From the foregoing it can be seen that the real issue in respect of policy arguments is not whether these arguments are used in judicial decision making, but rather whether they should appear in the actual text of the judgment. This raises the wider issue, which goes beyond the scope of this book, as to whether and to what extent in any particular system of law, the judiciary should publicly espouse political opinions, a question which has, for years, been debated in Common law systems where policy arguments frequently appear in judicial decisions.

8.3.2 Absence of dissenting opinions

Another particularity of French judicial decisions, held in common with other civil law systems, is that, unlike English law, dissenting opinions do not form part of the published decision of the court. The absence of dissenting opinions in French judgments is a direct consequence of the collegial form of the courts. Collegiality is a central feature of the French court system and still remains as such despite several unsuccessful attempts at replacing collegiate courts by single judge courts, especially at first instance level. Collegiality means two things. First, it means that, unless otherwise stated, cases are tried by a group of at least three judges. Second, it implies that the judgment pronounced is the 'judgment of the court', not the opinion of each individual judge. From this follows the fact that the names of the judges who heard the case do not appear in the text of the judgment, but are mentioned only on the front page under the heading '*composition du tribunal/de la cour*'. If the judgment is published in a law report, judges' names are written in small type following the decision (see case samples provided in Box 11.2). Absence of dissenting opinion is further accounted for by the fact that court deliberations are kept secret and the results of the voting in a court, including any dissent, are never made public. This contrasts sharply with the Common law tradition of judges stating their individual opinion in open court. The French tradition of secrecy has its origin in a series of royal ordinances issued in the reigns of Philippe VI and Charles VII. The rule of secrecy was abandoned shortly after the 1789 Revolution when public deliberations were prescribed, first for criminal trials, then for all court proceedings. Secrecy was reintroduced in 1795, since when the tradition has remained unbroken. It now has a statutory basis in art. 448 of the New Code of Civil Procedure and art. 355 of the Code of Criminal Procedure. The rule of secrecy is meticulously enforced by the Court of Cassation in that it ensures that only the judges who have heard the case attend the deliberations, excluding from the room any other members of the court, in particular the clerk of the court (in French the *greffier*). The rule of secrecy, in so far as it does not allow the expression of dissent in judicial decisions, is however not free from criticism. Indeed, the publication of dissenting opinion may present advantages, amongst which are:

(i) Dissenting opinion provides arguments that may lead subsequent judges to take the view that the precedent should be modified or overruled. As Cardozo, J claimed in one of his 1925 Yale Lectures on Law and Literature: 'the dissenter speaks to the future'.

(ii) It prevents a false formal unanimity amongst judges at the expense of strong conflicting views.

(iii) It forces judges to take their responsibilities seriously and justify the position they are adopting to their colleagues, to the parties in the case and to the public at large.

(iv) It forces judges to prove their worth by giving them the opportunity to show their independence by dissenting.

(v) It allows a public control of the courts, which is otherwise weakened if dissenting opinions are hidden.

(vi) The publication of dissenting opinion speaks to liberal democratic values, as it allows people to consider both sides of the story.

However, despite these considerable advantages, absence of published dissenting opinions has been justified in civil law countries by four main arguments:

(i) Dissent detracts from the force of the judgment. Indeed, the appearance of dissent in the decision may undermine the court's authority, whereas its absence suggests that the decision has been taken unanimously.

(ii) In the same vein, dissent further weakens the legitimacy of the courts because the decision is perceived not as an expression of legal truth but as the mere private opinion of the majority of the court.

(iii) Moreover, when a decision is given by a group of judges on behalf of the court it has the advantage of preserving the anonymity of the votes. In this way, judges do not become easy targets for criticism and are not left open to the personal resentment by any of the parties in a case.

(iv) Finally, published dissent is useless since, in any case, it can be easily deduced from the arguments developed by counsel, which are usually outlined in the judgment. In the context of the French legal system, opposing arguments may also be found in the *rapport* of the *conseiller rapporteur* and in the *conclusions* of the *avocat général* (see Chapter 8.3.1 above).

A further point to bear in mind is that the right of judges to express individual opinions does not necessarily clarify the sense of a judicial decision. In his analysis on the House of Lords decisions, Professor Jolowicz (1979) has pointed out how a multiplicity of speeches in the House of Lords may lead to uncertainty. Indeed, even when the majority of the court agrees on the solution to be adopted, the formulation of this agreement in the format of individual judgments creates uncertainty as to what extent judges have also agreed on the reasoning and principles leading to this solution. In a system of binding precedent this uncertainty may lead to what has been called a 'failure of judicial technique' (Cross and Harris, 1991: 93), because in such circumstances the principle on which the House of Lords has acted is unascertainable. The absence in English law of any legal requirement, as in French law, for deliberations preceding voting adds to this lack of clarification. Deliberations contribute to clarifying issues in two ways. First, they throw light on issues which might not have been foreseen by one of the members of the panel. Second, they allow judges to better appreciate in advance of decision taking to what extent they agree or disagree on the points at issue. A third beneficial effect of deliberations, also worthy of mention, is that they make decision making more impartial. Impartiality can be better achieved through prior deliberations because they allow judges to check upon each other, thus putting a brake on reactions based on social and intellectual backgrounds and values which are likely to give rise to biased views.

Chapter references

CROSS, R., and HARRIS, J.W., *Precedent in English Law*, 4th edn, Oxford: Clarendon Press, 1991.

FRANK, E., 'L'élaboration des Décisions de la Cour de Cassation ou la Partie Immergée de l'Iceberg', D.1983, Chr.119.

GOUTAL, J. L., 'Characteristics of Judicial Style, in France, Britain and in the USA', *The American Journal of Comparative Law*, 1976, Vol. 24, pp. 43–72.

JOLOWICZ, J.A., 'Les Décisions de la Chambres des Lords', *Revue Internationale de Droit Comparé*, 1979, Vol. 31, pp. 521–537.

LASSER, M., 'Judicial (Self-) Portraits: Judicial Discourse in the French Legal System', *The Yale Law Journal*, 1995, Vol. 104, pp. 1325–1410.

LINDON, R., *Le Style et l'Eloquence Judiciaire*, Paris: Albin Michel, 1968.

LINDON, R., 'La Motivation des Arrêts de la Cour de Cassation', JCP1975, I, 2681.

MIMIN, P., *Le Style des Jugements*, 4th edn, Paris: Librairies Techniques, 1978.

NADELMAN, K. H., 'The Judicial Dissent', *The American Journal of Comparative Law*, 1959, Vol. 8, pp. 415–432.

RUDDEN, B., 'Courts and Codes in England, France and Soviet Russia', *Tulane Law Review*, 1974, Vol. 48, pp. 1010–1028.

TOUFFAIT, A., and MALLET, L., 'La Mort des Attendus', D.1968, Chr.123.

TUNC, A., and TOUFFAIT, A., 'Pour une Motivation plus Explicite des Décisions de Justice, notamment de celles de la Cour de Cassation', *Revue Trimestrielle de Droit Civil*, 1974, pp. 487–508.

WELAMSON, L., 'La Motivation des décisions des Cours Judiciaires Suprêmes', *Revue Internationale de Droit Comparé*, 1979, Vol. 31, pp. 509–19.

Appendix 1 to Chapters Seven and Eight

Portrait of a new judge

Two years ago, the Court of Tarascon gave a most unusual judgment in *Etat Français* v *Pinoncely* (1998), D. 2000, 128. Tarascon, a small town in Southern France, became famous in the nineteenth century through French novelist Alphonse Daudet's famous trilogy *Tartarin de Tarascon* in which the main character, Tartarin, entertains his contemporaries with his colourful manners and loquacious speech. One may ask whether the judge of Tarascon will become as famous as Tartarin and make a similar impression on the judicial history of French law? However, seen from another perspective, it may be that this judgment will not be held to have been an indication of change in the method of reasoning and style of French judges, but will simply be viewed as the consequence of the unusual factual circumstances of this particular case.

The facts were as follows. In 1993, Pierre Pinoncely, a self-styled artist, visited an exhibition of the works of Marcel Duchamp (1887–1968), an artist known for making works of art out of everyday objects, classed as ready-made. On entering the museum of Nîmes, where the works were displayed, Pinoncely approached one of Duchamp's most famous works entitled 'Fountain', a work in the form of a public urinal, and urinated onto it, following which he took a hammer and smashed it up. Sued in tort by the State for the destruction of a work of art, his defence was that by his act he had completed the artistic function for which this work had been created, namely urinating. In so doing, and completing its purpose, the work, he argued, no longer had artistic significance and, thus, his act of breaking it, whatever else it may have been, was not the destruction of a work of art.

At the beginning of its judgment, the court explicitly referred to the method usually employed by French judges of applying an appropriate syllogism to the case when giving a decision. Thus, according to the court:

Any act causing damage to somebody obliges the one by whose fault it has occurred to make reparation (art. 1382 of the Civil Code). The very act of entering a museum with a hammer, to urinate on one of the works displayed, and then use this hammer in order to destroy the work, falls within the framework of the rules governing civil liability. There has been a deliberate act of destruction here which constitutes the fault that caused the damage on which the plaintiff's claim is based.

However, the court then declined to apply the syllogism it had formulated in the first place, choosing instead to adopt a reasoning that reflected an approach based more on discourse and persuasion. The court said:

However, the syllogism runs the risk of being thought simplistic, of giving substance to the assumption that the judicial institution is closed to an avant-garde artistic approach. The primary function of the judicial decision being that it should be understood by those to whom it is addressed, the court has the duty here to reconcile legalistic and artistic viewpoints. The debates and abundant literature generated by this case show that there is a risk of the judgment being misunderstood if the court justifies itself simply by applying to the case the provisions of the code, without any discussion of the context in which the facts have taken place.

The defendant was eventually found liable and was ordered to pay compensation for the damage caused. The grounds given for the decision may be summarised as follows: the defendant cannot, without contradicting himself, allege on the one hand that his own act of destruction was 'artistic' and say on the other hand that the destruction of Duchamp's work is not the destruction of a work of art. Therefore, he must pay for the damage caused.

What is significant in this judgment is not only the refusal to apply a strict syllogism, but also the manner in which the court expounds the reasoning justifying the decision it has reached. A real effort is being made here, on the part of the judges, to openly justify each step in the reasoning process identifying the possible alternative choices and stating and discussing the conflicting arguments. In this respect the judgment is informative, in the sense that it not only reveals all the meanderings of the judge's reasoning, but also provides interested readers with ample quotations from Marcel Duchamp's writings as well as extracts from the writings of other contemporary art specialists. A further unusual feature of this judgment is that it is written in a literary prose style in which technical concepts and language are avoided. The language is also unusually rich and expressive, sometimes even pompous, as may be noted in the following extracts which have been left in the French language for more authenticity:

Ainsi, le raisonnement juridique se trouve-t-il confronté à une double mystification.
(. . .)
Pinoncely prétend s'affranchir de tout examen des conséquences patrimoniales de son acte dès lors qu'il se drape dans ce statut protecteur à nul autre pareil.
(. . .)
Il est permis de penser que, par sa requête, le ministre de la Culture, loin de se comporter en mercanti inaccessible à l'évolution de l'art contemporain, entend que soit évalué le contenu artistique du geste de Pinoncély.

Because of its original features, the Tarascon judgment will certainly find its place in the history of the style of French judicial decision making. However, whether it will become an influential landmark in judicial method is another story.

Appendix 2 to Chapter 8

Exposé des motifs on the loi 2001-588 of 4 July 2001 amending French abortion law

Projet de loi relatif à l'interruption volontaire de grossesse et à la contraception

Exposé des motifs

Il se pratique encore en France plus de 200 000 interruptions volontaires de grossesse (IVG) chaque année. Près de 10 000 adolescentes sont confrontées à une grossesse non désirée dont 7000 ont recours à une IVG. 5000 femmes partent dans les pays voisins parce qu'elles sont déterminées à interrompre leur grossesse mais qu'elles sont au delà du délai légal autorisé pour recourir à une IVG.

En termes de santé publique, ces chiffres sont alarmants. Ils ne peuvent qu'inciter à réagir. Ils ont conduit le Gouvernement à diligenter des travaux plus approfondis sur les difficultés d'accès à l'IVG en France et les insuffisances de la contraception. A partir de leurs conclusions, une politique volontariste a été mise en place. Des mesures ont été prises dès 1999, destinées à améliorer l'accès à l'IVG dans les hôpitaux publics, notamment en renforçant la présence et la continuité du service public et en ouvrant largement l'accès aux nouvelles techniques d'IVG aujourd'hui disponibles comme l'IVG médicamenteuse. Parallèlement, une vaste campagne d'information sur la contraception a été lancée, prenant pour cible privilégiée les populations les plus vulnérables: les jeunes, les femmes en difficulté d'insertion sociale ou économique, les populations françaises d'outre-mer.

Cependant, un an plus tard, et après avoir pris le temps de la réflexion et de la concertation, le Gouvernement entend renforcer ce plan en prenant les mesures législatives susceptibles de faciliter l'accès à la contraception d'une part, à l'interruption volontaire de grossesse d'autre part.

Si la loi n° 67-1176 du 28 décembre 1967 relative à la régulation des naissances, dite «loi Neuwirth» et la loi n° 75-17 du 17 janvier 1975 relative à l'interruption volontaire de la grossesse, dite «loi Veil», ont été en leur temps des acquisitions fondamentales pour la vie des femmes au quotidien, elles ne sont plus aujourd'hui, près de trente ans plus tard, totalement adaptées ni à la réalité sociale ni à la réalité médicale de notre pays. Elles méritent d'être actualisées et modernisées.

En ce qui concerne l'IVG, certaines des femmes qui voudraient y recourir ne peuvent y avoir accès, du fait des termes actuels de la loi, alors même qu'elles sont parmi celles qui sont le plus en difficulté face à l'événement qu'elles ont à affronter, du fait de leur jeune âge ou d'une situation sociale particuliérement dé favorisée.

C'est pourquoi le Gouvernement souhaite, par le présent projet de loi, ouvrir le droit d'accès à l'interruption volontaire de grossesse au-delà des dispositions que prévoit aujourd'hui la loi, notamment en allongeant de dix à douze semaines de grossesse le délai légal de recours à cette intervention et en aménageant le droit d'accès des mineures à l'interruption volontaire de grossesse.

L'allongement de dix à douze semaines du délai légal de recours à l'interruption volontaire de grossesse devrait permettre de réduire de près de 80 % le nombre de femmes qui sont contraintes de partir à l'étranger pour interrompre leur grossesse parce qu'elles sont hors délai.

Avant de proposer cette modification législative, le Gouvernement a souhaité véri-fier qu'il n'existait aucune contre-indication technique à cet allongement. L'avis de l'agence nationale d'accréditation et d'évaluation en santé (ANAES) sur ce sujet est clair: il n'y a pas d'obstacle ni en termes médicaux ni en termes de sécurité sanitaire, à ce que ce délai d'accès à l'IVG puisse être porté à douze semaines, à l'instar de ce qui se fait chez la plupart de nos voisins européens.

Quant à l'aménagement du droit d'accès des mineures à l'interruption volontaire de grossesse, il est destiné à tenir compte des difficultés de celles qui sont dans l'impossibilité de recueillir le consentement parental, ou qui sont confrontées à une incompréhension familiale telle qu'elles southaitent garder le secret.

Il n'est pas question de revenir sur le principe de l'autorisation parentale, qui demeure la règle. Mais il apparaît souhaitable que la décision d'IVG puisse être prise à la demande de la seule mineure pour les cas où cela s'avère vraiment indispensable. Pour autant, et afin de ne pas la laisser seule face à cette décision, le projet de nouvelle rédaction législative prévoit que la mineure désigne alors une personne majeure de son choix, susceptible de l'accompagner tout au long de cette période à l'évidence difficile, et souvent douloureuse.

La loi du 28 décembre 1967 relative à la régulation des naissances mérite elle aussi d'être actualisée, afin notamment de faciliter l'accès à la contraception et à l'ensemble des nouveaux contraceptifs: en effet, mener une politique active en faveur de la con-traception est la meilleure manière de prévenir les grossesses non désirées et les interruptions volontaires de grossesse qui en sont la conséquence.

Le Gouvernement entend pour cela proposer des modifications législatives visant en particulier à permettre l'accès des mineures à ces médicaments, même si elles désirent garder le secret, et visant à lever les interdictions d'information sur la contraception, mesures contraires à toute politique de prévention et d'éducation pour la santé.

Il s'agit de faire progresser à nouveau, près de trente ans plus tard, le droit des femmes à disposer de leur corps et à maîtriser leur fécondité. Pour cela, il faut rendre la loi cohérente avec l'évolution de la société et des besoins des femmes – de toutes les femmes, y compris les plus fragiles; et il faut leur faciliter l'accès aux progrès réalisés dans le domaine des contraceptifs et des nouvelles techniques d'IVG, en particulier médicamenteuses.

9

Case notes

The analytical note is a great invention. It is hard to imagine what French Law would be without it.

Dawson, J.,P., *The Oracles of the Law*, The University of Michigan Law School, 1968, p. 398.

The part of this book describing the method employed by French courts when deciding cases cannot be concluded without saying a few words about the importance of case notes as an aid to interpreting and evaluating judicial decisions in France. It has been stated earlier (at Chapters 7.3 and 8.3.1 above) that the lack of sufficient justification in French judgments resulted in the need for the commentaries on cases written by French scholars. These commentaries, known as *notes d'arrêts*, started to appear in law reports during the nineteenth century and today have become one of the most characteristic and noteworthy elements of French legal writing. This significance of *notes d'arrêts* can, in particular, be observed in the way that law is taught in French law schools, where reading and analysing cases involves equally the reported judgment and the note which immediately follows it. In fact, one can say that the judgment, once published in a law report, forms a single entity with the note that follows it, and from which it becomes inseparable. The significance of case notes, the form they take and the functions they perform, need to be further examined here. However, in order to fully understand how French legal scholars were able to accomplish their task of clarifying court decisions, one has to be aware of the status and role assigned to academic writing – referred to as *doctrine* – in France.

9.1 Status and role of doctrine

9.1.1 General points

The influence French legal writers have exerted on the development of French law is widely recognised. The drafters of the Civil Code in 1804 were largely inspired by the systematic writings of such authors as Domat and Pothier. Later, the writings of Aubry and Rau, H. Capitant, G. Ripert and L. Josserand had a considerable impact on the case law of the first part of the twentieth century. In recent years, J. Carbonnier, a renowned scholar, has been the main architect of contemporary family law reforms. Today, although academic writings are not a source of law and are generally not cited in court cases or in court decisions, they are still used by judges and counsel when preparing for court hearings and judgments. The high esteem in which academic lawyers have traditionally been held in the French legal system contrasts sharply with a long tradition of ignorance suffered by the academic community in England. This difference of attitude towards academic lawyers can be accounted for by the fact that law in England became a proper subject for study much later than in the other European jurisdictions (see Chapter 10.2 below). Also, the fact that judicial decisions in France are only a secondary source of law has made it easier for legal scholars to rise to the status that they hold today without fear of being accused of overshadowing the judiciary.

Commenting on academic writing in France, A. Tunc (1976: 470–71) describes its role as being twofold:

Doctrinal writings comment on statutory law and judicial decisions in order to clarify them, to give them a systematic view without which there would be no law. Of equal importance, however, is the purpose of guiding the courts and, more broadly, the lawgivers. In fact, *doctrine* could easily assign to itself a prophetic function.

This dual aspect to the role of *doctrine* – clarification and guidance – is clearly reflected in the current working method of French scholars and in the ways in which they approach legal questions. They do not merely study the law as it is, but feel that it is also part of their function to consider the law as it should be. Both of these aspects are commonly referred to in the two Latin phrases *de lege lata* (the law as it is) and *de lege ferenda* (the law as it should be) as illustrated below. As will be further shown, this twofold role of *doctrine*, can be traced back to two benchmark periods in the history of legal literature, periods of equal importance in the shaping of French *doctrine*: the period of *doctrine classique* and the period of *doctrine moderne*.

9.1.2 *De lege lata, de lege ferenda*

Foreign lawyers consulting French law treatises, student textbooks and articles published in legal journals, or attending lectures delivered by French law teachers will notice they all start by stating and expounding in a systematic way the law as found in statutes and codes and as interpreted by the courts. They then proceed to point out the deficiencies or gaps in the law, proposing remedies and solutions both for the legislature and for the courts. A typical recent illustration of this approach may be found in an article written by Professor R. Cabrillac in the *Recueil Dalloz* (1999), Chr. 71, concerning the then proposed French legislation on registered domestic partnerships (now Loi of 15 November 1999, cited at Chapter 1.1.5 above). In his thorough study, the author examines the question of property rights of homosexual partners addressed in the then proposed law from two points of view:

(i) First, the author reviews the statutory and case law then currently in force on this issue (introduced by the author in his text by the phrase '*de lege lata*'). He says:

De lege lata, la prise en compte des circonstances d'espèces par les juges du fond, par exemple pour étendre aux concubins homosexuels la continuation du bail en cas de décès du locataire sur le fondement de l'art. 14 de la loi du 6 juillet 1989, ou admettre l'indemnisation d'un concubin en cas de décès accidentel de son compagnon, peut atténuer la rigueur des règles existantes.

(ii) Then Professor Cabrillac considers the possible changes to be made in the law in order to enhance the property rights of homosexual partners (prefaced this time in the text by the phrase '*de lege ferenda*'):

De lege ferenda, si l'adoption d'un statut ne semble pas une solution satisfaisante, les propositions du rapport Théry constituent peut-être une piste séduisante. Des modifications ponctuelles de la législation sont également envisageables, dans le droit au bail, par une modification de l'art. 14 de la loi du 6 juillet 1989, ou, en matière fiscale, par un assouplissement des droits de transmission à titre gratuit entre concubins, y compris de même sexe.

9.1.3 *Doctrine classique*

This period refers to the legal literature published in the course of the nineteenth century. During that time French legal writers would spend most of their time and effort in trying to clarify the body of rules emerging from the newly enacted codes, paying little attention to judicial decisions. It was the then prevailing postulate, based on a strong doctrine of separation of powers, that the law making function belonged exclusively to the legislature, and the consequent censure on judges that would have followed any deviation from code or statutory provisions which, taken together, explain why legal writers in this period chose to focus mainly on the study of enacted law. Under the influence of the *Ecole de l'Exégèse*, exegesis became the favoured method for explaining and interpreting the law. Exegetical method being a method characterised by a strict adherence to the texts of the codes, no attempt would be made at that time to confront these texts with practical realities. Legal scholarship would thus mainly consist of studying the articles of the codes one by one, attempting to ascertain the intention of the legislator and, where necessary, employing logical reasoning in order to clarify the meaning of code provisions and to draw from their wording general principles that the interpreter could extend later to similar situations. The *Ecole de l'Exégèse* was to dominate legal thought in France until very late in the nineteenth century. We owe to this school of thought several comprehensive commentaries on the Civil Code written by leading law professors of the time such as Demolombre or Laurent, and even by such high-ranking judges as Troplong. Exegetical method has not completely disappeared from the working method of French jurists as seen in Chapter 3 on statutory interpretation (see Chapter 3.2.2 above). However, it has been supplemented by a more contextual approach to legal rules, which has led to the development of case notes in the period of *doctrine moderne*.

9.1.4 *Doctrine moderne*

It was under the influence of authors such as Saleilles and Gény (see Chapter 3.2.4.3 above), who pointed out, in their writings, the defects of the exegetical method, that scholarly works of the twentieth century showed more interest in sources other than codes and statutes, and judicial decisions in particular. Also, the fact that a considerable time span had elapsed since the codes were enacted, and the significant economic changes that France had undergone by the end of the nineteenth century, prompted the emergence of a doctrine which would value judicial practice as much as legislation. As early as 1830 law reports, which included the famous *Sirey* and *Dalloz*, had already started to insert occasional annotations to reported cases. By the 1850s these annotations had become more frequent and expansive. Labbé was the first scholar to initiate a new genre in legal writing, the *note d'arrêt*. His famous *notes* were published between 1859 and 1894 in the *Sirey* law reports. With more attention paid to contemporary needs in society, legal writers would use the newly developed case notes as a forum for expressing their views about the policies of the legislature and the courts, taking into account not only social and economic factors, but also employing the teachings of history, sociology and comparative law to this end. Thus, the 'prophetic function' of *doctrine* referred to earlier by Tunc, actually took root in these case notes and quickly grew, expanding to the whole field of legal writing.

Since the time of Labbé, the *note d'arrêt* has developed into what has become a specific genre of legal literature in which writers, called for this purpose the *arrêtistes*, have each contributed to this whole, yet still creating their own individual distinctive style. Amongst the most celebrated *arrêtistes* who have devoted much time and effort to the methodical analysis of reported cases are René Savatier who wrote hundreds of notes in the *Recueil Dalloz* between 1920 and 1979 on private law topics ranging from contract and torts to family and medical law. In the area of public law, starting in 1889, date of the famous *Cadot* decision, and for the following 40 years, Maurice Hauriou annotated all the leading cases which have contributed to the development of administrative law in France. Today the *notes d'arrêts* are written not only by law professors but also by judges and practitioners. It has also become more 'democratic' within the academic profession, in the sense that writing case notes is not exclusively reserved for the most distinguished academic lawyers. Younger scholars have also tested their skills in this popular exercise of legal writing.

Although case notes are not peculiar to France, since similar notes are regularly published in the law reports of other jurisdictions, the French *notes d'arrêts* have a much greater impact on legal research, teaching and the practice of French law than elsewhere. This is due to the particular form they take, and also to the specific functions they perform.

9.2 **Form and functions of** *notes d'arrêts*

9.2.1 Form of *notes d'arrêts*

Notes d'arrêts take the form of extended footnotes to reported cases in private law reports. They are usually structured as traditional French essays in two parts, each part being in turn divided into subparagraphs (see Chapter 11.2 below). This essay structure can be illustrated by a recent note written by Professor C. Atias in the case of *Le Collinet* v *Compagnie d'assurances Rhin et Moselle* (cited at Chapter 4.1.3, point (5)). Professor Atias' commentary on the decision in this case adopted the following structure:

I-La neutralité de la jurisprudence ou la jurisprudence sous la loi
  A-Formation de la jurisprudence
  B-Le corps de la jurisprudence
II-L'immunité de la jurisprudence ou la jurisprudence au-dessus de la loi
  A-La 'notion' de jurisprudence
  B-La portée de la jurisprudence

Not all *notes d'arrêts* follow this strict model of presentation. In fact, notes are very often shorter and less formal. This is to a great extent dependent on the importance of the issues raised by the case, the format of the law report, and also on the style adopted by the commentator. For example, J. Massip, a judge in the Court of Cassation and regular commentator in the *Dalloz* law report on judicial decisions in family law, adopts a very concise style with no apparent formal structure, without this in any way undermining the force of his analysis (see by way of illustration his note under the decision given by the Court of Cassation in *Mme X* v *Y* (1995), D.1996, 111). On the other hand, certain notes, such as those written by the famous *arrêtiste* René Savatier, are powerfully structured, all arguments being developed gradually into paragraphs and subparagraphs (see, for example, his note under *Dame Walter* v *Dame Roque* (1974), D. 1974, 629, concerning a paternity suit brought by one of the children of Picasso following the death of the famous painter). Whatever their stylistic features, *notes d'arrêts* are generally considered to be pieces of academic writing, which make them as much a source of information as a model of legal argument. This accounts for the heavy reliance placed on them by law teachers, researchers, practitioners and students in their day-to-day work. As we will see below, their popularity is further accounted for by certain essential functions they perform.

9.2.2 Functions of *notes d'arrêts*

These are principally two in number:

  (a) clarifying the meaning of judicial decisions
  (b) shaping precedent.

9.2.2.1 Clarification

Case notes clarify the meaning of judicial decisions in the sense that they look in detail at the specific issues of the case and expand on the facts and the reasons for the decisions (the *motifs*, see Chapter 8.2.1 above), either expressed or unstated. Despite the lack of justification characteristic of French judgments, clarification is still feasible because case annotators usually have access to the court's file through a personal connection with, or as a result of having worked closely with, one of the lawyers or judges involved in the case. *Notes d'arrêts* also look at the language employed in judgments and help readers to deduce, from the terms and expressions used by the courts, a number of particular, and sometimes very important, conclusions. To take a simple example, when the Court of Cassation states, as it very often does in one of its judgments: '*les juges du fond ont pu décider que*' (the lower court could decide that), this doesn't mean merely, as the term *pu* (could) suggests, that it was within the power of the lower court to decide as it did; it indicates something further which adds an additional perspective: that the lower court has decided rightly, in accordance with the law and that this is fully approved by the Court of Cassation. Correctly interpreting the language used by the courts is crucial when it comes to understanding the true import of a case. J. Voulet (1970), a judge in the Court of Cassation, has devoted a study to this topic, which has become a classic text for those seeking a key for interpreting the Court of Cassation judgments. This study represents a good complement to case notes when attempting to understand the true meaning and value of judicial decisions.

9.2.2.2 Shaping precedent

According to Sauvel (1955), the *arrêtistes* 'explain today's case law and prepare tomorrow's case law'. Indeed, case annotators try to reconcile the particular outcome of the case in hand with those of earlier cases and to show the true impact of a given decision on future cases. They spot the inconsistencies or any incoherence between cases. More generally, they critically assess the pros and cons of alternative solutions, as well as the actual solution eventually adopted by the court. Finally, where appropriate, they propose their own solutions. All these different points of legal analysis have an influence on the continuing development of case law. This ongoing dynamic relationship between academic writing and judicial decisions in France can be better understood by taking account of the particular historically defined status of the judiciary in France. It has been said in Chapter 4 that French judicial decisions are not considered binding as 'authorities' in the English sense. Consequently, they do not enjoy the same prestige as judicial decisions do in England. It follows that French judges do not perceive scholarly suggestions or even criticism as undermining the authority of their decisions, and are therefore, it may be suggested, more willing than their English counterparts to consider them with an open mind. The fact that French judges, as much as academics, annotate decisions given by their colleagues, is further evidence of the fact that *notes d'arrêts* are not perceived by the judiciary as an 'attack' on their manner of adjudicating cases but are rather part of an ongoing constructive exercise in the development of French case law. Meynal (1904) in his thorough study on the *arrêtistes* already stressed, one century ago, how the *notes d'arrêts* had become decisive in bridging the gap between *L'Ecole*, i.e. academic theory and *Le Palais*, i.e. judicial practice.

Chapter references

ATIAS, C., 'La Mission de la Doctrine Universitaire en Droit Privé', JCP 1980, I, 2999.

CARBONNIER, J., 'Notes sur les Notes d'Arrêts', D. 1970, Chr.137.

MEYNIAL, E., 'Les Recueils d'Arrêts et les Arrêtistes', *Le Code Civil 1804–1904-Livre du Centenaire*, Vol. 1, Paris: Rousseau, 1904, pp. 173–204.

SAUVEL, V., 'Histoires des Jugements Motivés', Rev. dr. publ. 1955, pp. 5–53.

TUNC, A., 'Methodology of the Civil Law in France', *Tulane Law Review*, Vol. 50, 1976, pp. 459–473.

VOULET, J., 'L'Interprétation des Arrêts de la Cour de Cassation', JCP 1970, I, 2305.

PART III
LEGAL EDUCATION

Parts I and II of this book have shown how the way law is made and applied in France has been decisive in defining the nature of the legal system and in shaping the mind of French jurists. Part III will consider the way law is taught in French law schools and will examine how legal education contributes, in its own way, by adding particular colour to the character of the legal system. This link between legal education and the nature of a legal system has been emphasised by J. Dainow (1967: 428) in his study devoted to a comparison between the civil law and the common law systems:

There is naturally a direct reciprocal influence between the nature of a legal system and the pattern of legal education. The nature of the former promotes the method of the latter, which in turn perpetuates the original character of the system. The program of law studies and the method of legal education establish and fix the fundamental understanding and the mode of thought which condition the individual for his entire professional career.

It would appear from Dainow's statement that there is no universal mode of legal thinking, since it is dependent on the nature of the particular legal system being considered, more specifically on the way lawyers in such a system have been taught to think. This certainly has consequences for those students studying law on an exchange programme and for multi-national firms whose lawyers may wish to practise in a jurisdiction in which they have not received their legal education. In both circumstances, learning the rules will not be sufficient; for they will have to adapt as well to different expectations with respect to patterns of thought, without falling back into their own mode of thinking. This is particularly difficult in view of the fact that lawyers use particular patterns of thought without necessarily being aware that, in doing so, their mind-set has been shaped out of their own legal culture and, more particularly, out of the environment in which they studied. In this respect, it is regrettable that comparative legal studies on legal thinking and teaching method in both civil and common law systems are lacking whereas, given the current European legal context, they should rather be encouraged and developed. The paucity of literature on each other's way of thinking may have its roots in feelings of resentment shared by many legal scholars on each side, feelings which, paradoxically, have been sharpened as they have been brought to the surface by the continuing legal development and operation of the European Communities. In this respect, the influence that the civil law tradition and mode of thinking have had on current European institutions and law have been perceived, not unreasonably, by many Common lawyers as a threat to their own legal tradition. In their turn, some civil lawyers take great pride in their tradition of 'learned law' as opposed to a Common law which, according to the predominant view, does not display the level of rationality that they feel is achieved by their own system.

Chapter 10, which follows, examines in a comparative perspective, the method of teaching used in French law schools as well as the way in which it impacts on French lawyers' approach to the law. Whereas Chapter 10 focuses on the setting and the structure within which law is taught, Chapter 11 provides a method for answering the typical legal exercises used in French law schools to sharpen and hone French law students' legal skills.

10

Method of teaching

Il y a un usage, des lois, des coutumes: où est le temps, et le temps assez long, que l'on emploie à les digérer et à s'en instruire?

La Bruyère, Les Caractères, Chapter XIV, 48.

This chapter describes the methods of teaching adopted in French law schools, their dominant role in shaping French lawyers' mode of thought and the ways in which they differ from the system of legal education in England. Owing to the significance of environmental factors in this area, the chapter will provide readers with a brief outline of the cultural and historical context. By way of introduction, the chapter starts with the salient features of French legal education.

10.1 Salient features of French legal education

Foreign academics visiting French law schools or foreign law students spending part of their time of study in France are struck by at least three aspects of French legal education:

(a) students are taught in very large groups

(b) the structure and content of the law degree espouses that of a liberal education not directed to any particular profession

(c) a strong emphasis is placed on the teaching of abstract concepts and on methodology.

These features specific to French legal education are now considered in turn.

10.1.1 Size

Whereas a large law department in England consists of approximately 1,000 students, in France, this figure represents roughly the first year intake of a small law school. In larger law departments, such as the law faculties of the University of Paris, nearly 3,000 students are recruited annually at first year level. Such a number, which is by no means specific to law studies, goes a long way to accounting for the difficulties encountered in the administrative management of the course degrees, the general lack of space, and the anonymity of French universities. It also has a considerable impact on teaching method, especially with regard to the relationship between students and teachers. In particular, it makes interaction between teachers and students difficult, and makes it very hard to generate student participation. Differences in numbers between French and English law schools is due to the fact that, in France, entry to university is not selective. However, it has to be pointed out that the number of French law students drops considerably after the first year of studies owing to the high failure rate amongst first year students. Cynics view this failure rate as an alternative to formal selection, a so-called '*sélection par l'échec*', the advantage being for those subscribing to this view, that this form of selection does not interfere with the French policy of an equal right to higher education open for all.

10.1.2 Liberal education

A second noticeable feature of French legal education is that it stands as an independent liberal education, not tied to any specific vocation. Indeed, whereas in English law schools the academic stage is still perceived as a preliminary for the vocational courses leading to legal practice, in a French law faculty, in accordance with the liberal tradition of French universities, this stage is aimed at promoting an intellectual environment with a view to broadening the student's mind not only within the relevant discipline, but in conjunction with other ones as well.

This tradition is reflected in the structure of the law degree as well as in its content.

10.1.2.1 Structure of the law degree

Currently the French law degree is a four-year degree course whose total duration is divided up into distinct stages with distinct corresponding qualifications (see Fig. 10.1). This has the effect of extending the range of possible careers leading on from legal education, beyond the narrow choice of becoming a practising lawyer. Thus, on completion of the first two or three years of studies, students who obtain either a *DEUG* (*diplôme d'études universitaires générales*, after two years) or, a *Licence* (after three years), can then move into such occupations as banking, public administration, insurance, tax authority administration, or estate agencies. Very often, prior to joining the institution or the training college of their choice, students will have to sit a competitive entrance examination (this, for example, is the case with the *Banque de France* with respect to a banking career or, the *Ecole Nationale des Assurances*, in the field of insurance and, the *Ecole Nationale des Greffes* which leads to a career as a court clerk). However, students looking for entry to the judiciary or the legal profession must finish their second stage of studies (second cycle) with a *Maitrise*, thus completing their four-year law degree course and, in addition, take a competitive examination for entry to the professional stage of training organised either by the *ENM*, for judges, or by the *CRFP* (*centre régional de formation professionnelle*), for advocates. It is noteworthy that preparation for both *ENM* and *CRFP* entrance examinations is left to the law schools themselves. More specifically, it is the *Instituts d'Etudes Judiciaires* (IEJ), attached to each law faculty, which provide the one-year preparation for these examinations (usually in conjunction with the final *Maîtrise* year of the law degree). The presence of these IEJs in French law schools has the effect of bridging the gap between the law schools and the legal profession, thereby countering, at least in part, the criticism very often raised of lack of partnership between the academic lawyer and the practitioner. There is also a third cycle of studies which leads either to a *DEA* (*diplôme d'études approfondies*) or to a *DESS* (*diplôme d'études supérieures spécialisées*). Whilst the former is more academic, usually leading to a doctorate and to an academic career, the latter is more specialised and is a one-year preparation for professional life as an in-house lawyer in a large firm, a training period in such a firm generally forming part of the course.

However, the whole structure of the law degree is about to change into Licence (3 years), Master (5 years) and Doctorate (8 years) in harmony with other European countries.

10.1.2.2 Content of the law degree

The French law curriculum encompasses a wide range of subjects including, as early as the first year, other disciplines associated with law, such as economics, sociology, and legal history. With respect to subjects taught, it must be noted that French law schools are not under the same pressure as their English counterparts to follow the requirements of the legal profession when setting the law curriculum. The law

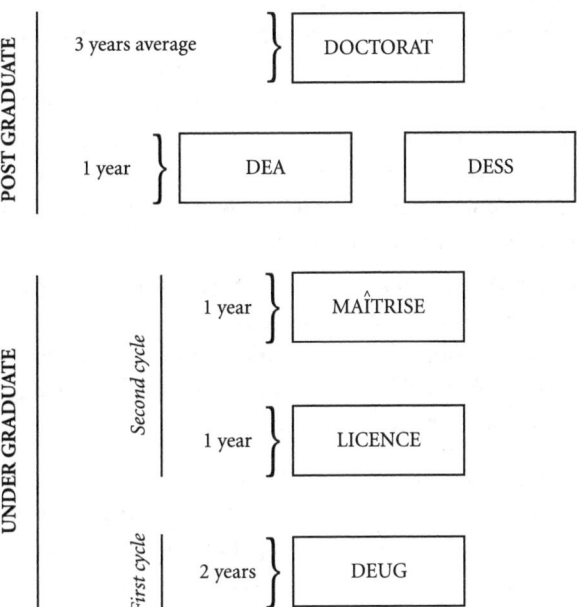

Fig. 10.1 Stages of legal education in France

curriculum, which over the years has undergone considerable changes, is devised by each law school, in accordance with governmental regulations. Under the current law, the so-called 1997 Bayrou reform (from the name of the then minister of education, and consisting of two major statutory texts: ministerial *arrêtés* of 9 April 1997 and 30 April 1997), French law schools operate on a semester and modular system with a strongly interdisciplinary approach to law. This approach is plainly to be seen in the first year of the law degree, as the description that follows will show. Thus, each semester of the first year of teaching is organised in the form of *unités d'enseignements*, as follows:

(i) *Unité d'enseignements fondamentaux* (foundation subjects). This *unité* must occupy not less than 40 to 55 per cent of a student's work load in the first semester and not less than 50 to 60 per cent in the second. *Enseignements fondamentaux* include a historical introduction to legal studies, private law, civil law, public law, constitutional law and, either history of law or, political science.

(ii) *Unité de découverte de disciplines complémentaires* (subjects in complementary disciplines). Aimed at introducing students to law related disciplines such as economic science and modern social and political history, this *unité* must represent not less than 30 to 40 per cent of a student's load, in the first semester only.

(iii) *Unité de méthodologie* (methodology). This *unité* must consist of not less than 15 to 20 per cent of a student's work-load in the first semester, and 20 to 25 per cent in the second. In the first semester this *unité* is also known as *conférence de méthodologie* and takes the form of a one and a half hour weekly tutorial applied to the learning of practical legal skills such as using a law library, looking for learned sources, learning how to take notes, learning how to read and summarise legal texts, carrying out legal research and working in groups. *Unité de méthodologie* also includes, in the first semester, an introduction to the institutions and the legal terminology of a foreign legal system. In the second semester, *unité de méthodologie* is geared towards developing students' intellectual skills through the study of a particular discipline. These disciplines may include, by way of example, an introduction to international law, sociology or political science.

(iv) *Unité de culture générale et d'expression* (general knowledge and self-expression). This *unité* must occupy at least 20 to 25 per cent of study time in the second semester only. The objective of this *unité* is principally to develop skills such as oral communication, in particular through the study of a foreign language, and this is supplemented by information technology skills.

In terms of teaching hours this represents, in the first year of studies, a total of approximately 450 hours; the minimum requirement for the first two years of the law degree (DEUG) being 1,000 hours of teaching, of which 20 per cent has to be carried out in teaching groups (*Arrêté* 30 April 1997, art. 6).

10.1.3 Abstract concepts and methodology

A further characteristic feature of French legal education is the high level of abstraction that pervades the teaching. As will be shown in the course of this chapter, the emphasis is on theoretical rather than practical knowledge, to which a strong methodological component must be added (as seen at Chapter 10.1.2.2 above). Legal education in France is primarily aimed at providing a sound knowledge of general principles together with the development of a capacity to manipulate abstract concepts and construct logical arguments. This emphasis on abstract concepts and methodology associated with French legal education is historically based and has, in part, been ascribed by legal historians to the dominant role played, in the past, by the systematic study of Roman law in law schools. In England, as will be seen, it is rather a strongly organised and dominant legal profession, with its attendant specific needs and habits, which has conditioned the teaching method of the country. Although the character of the legal system has developed away from these origins over the years with a consequent significant transformation of the system of legal education in both countries (see Chapter 10.2.3 below), abstraction has remained a strong feature of French legal education. The following headings develop this point further.

10.2 Cultural and historical context

A French law teacher invited to teach in an English law school might be struck by the students' interest in the practical aspects of a given problem, their propensity to engage in policy discussions, and the fact that, when a principle is set, they will always question whether this principle is capable of effective application and, if so, in what defining circumstances. French law students, in contrast, used as they are to thinking of law in terms of principles rather than practice and procedure, might barely question the effectiveness of the rules and principles they learn. Moreover, when asked to develop an argument, they would rather tend to display a deductive mode of syllogistic reasoning from given principles, similarly to the syllogistic reasoning they have already seen when instructed to read and analyse judicial decisions and scholarly articles in their classes. It has been suggested that this complete difference of approach is the consequence of two distinctive frames of mind. This point is examined in a first subheading.

10.2.1 Two ways of thinking

It is commonplace to say that the French excel in the formulation of general ideas and worship logic. Reason is their guide and beacon. Their taste for logic is such that, in some circumstances, they would even disregard experience if it is in conflict with and contradicts the rational system they have conceived and carefully constructed. By contrast, the English are empiricist, being concerned primarily with acting rather than understanding. As long as the results are satisfactory, it matters little that they have been obtained in a way that reflects a partial or total absence of logic. They shrink from systematisation and mistrust both generalisation and, above all, ideologies. They practice the method of 'wait and see'. They wait for problems to arise, and then solve them, not according to what 'logic' would dictate but to what experience suggests, circumstances permitting. Lord Macmillan (1938), in a masterly lecture delivered at Oxford, contrasted these two ways of thinking by using the description, given by the authors of a book on the Surrey landscape, of the two main countryside roads in that county. Whereas, he said, the typical Surrey countryside road snaked down to the plain, the Roman road cut across the countryside in a straight line. The difference in shape between the two roads was accounted for, he added, by the fact that, whilst the former had formed itself naturally, moving from one agglomeration to the next, following the layout of the landscape, by contrast, the latter had been built up following a plan established in advance. Transposed into a legal context, this figurative comparison is particularly revealing, not only of the distinctive mode of thought, but also, by extension, of the form of legal system adopted respectively by each country. Thus, the empiricist pragmatic case-by-case approach to legal problems, a reminder of the Surrey road, is typical of the common law; the ability to establish in advance general principles aimed at application to an infinity of cases, as with a planned Roman road, has of necessity given rise to a system of codified law.

Resorting to a predetermined mind-set, or national psychology, when accounting for the differences that exist between common and civil law systems, may at first glance be appealing, but it is not conclusively verifiable, since it rests on the questionable general assumption that different people have an innately different cast of mind. French comparative lawyer J. Lambert (1961) asserted the view that the reason for the difference between the two systems is not to be found in a quasi-biological predisposition but, rather, in the methods of teaching law that each system has been applying over the centuries. Without neglecting the role played by social and political factors in this respect, Lambert's main argument was that devotion to principles and to logic in one case, to practice and experience in another, does not mirror a difference of mind but, rather, a difference of 'task'. Indeed, from early on, French lawyers have been educated in law schools by teachers who, though they may often also have been practitioners, have nevertheless been compelled, by the nature of the didactic role conferred on them, to organise their material and present the law in an orderly, methodical and systematic manner. By contrast, English lawyers have traditionally been mainly trained in the courtroom by a class of practitioners whose field of investigation and basis for legal argument were previously applied court solutions. From this perspective, English lawyers developed their own system of legal education independently of that provided by the universities.

The relevance of teaching method to the mode of legal thinking can be illustrated in the current experience of teaching law in England on courses which include one or two years of studies in France. This shows that when, together with their English fellow students, French students start their legal education in English law schools as is usually the case, they find it as difficult as their English fellow students to adapt to the French methods of teaching once they return to France in order to complete the French leg of their course of studies. The observable fact that English students seem to struggle more in France can be ascribed to the problem of language which their French counterparts in turn suffered in the English part of their course of studies. Setting aside the language difficulty common to both groups of students, there is nothing in the work produced to indicate that, these students find the law of their counterpart legal system more alien to their mode of thought than their own. This appears to support Lambert's argument that, of the two, it is the method of teaching that matters when accounting for differences between the two systems, and not the national mind. The following subheading briefly traces the historical factors, in this respect, that have contributed to making French law 'a teacher's law' and English law 'a practitioner's law'.

10.2.2 Teacher's law v. practitioner's law: an historical outline

10.2.2.1 The study of Roman law in the law schools of medieval France

The landmark in the intellectual development of French jurists is the revival, at the dawn of the twelfth century, of the study of Roman law, based on the Emperor Justinian's compilation of Roman law, the *Corpus Juris Civilis*, in Northern Italy and Southern France. In France, Roman law had been in force in the '*pays de droit écrit*', the Southern part of the country, since about the end of the eleventh century. It is to this early study of Roman law in law schools, which arose out of the acceptance, in most Continental countries, of Justinian's *Corpus Juris* as authoritative, that A. Watson (1981: 32) is referring when attributing the tradition of formal rationality to the civil law systems:

To sum up, when the *Corpus Juris* is treated as authoritative, Roman law, regarded as being in force, is taught systematically; the rules of law, especially of substantive law, are emphasized; local variations in law are minimized; the rules are not obscured by consideration of the interest, financial or otherwise, of practitioners; and the law is set out independently of the practical problems which occur in actual cases.

This description accurately reflects, to this day, the civil lawyer's approach to law.

The earliest method of studying Justinian's books, especially the Digest (a compilation of the writings of the great Roman jurists), consisted of a literal examination of these texts by the scholars of the twelfth and thirteenth centuries, the so-called 'Glossators'. The Glossators, and this is the origin of their name, used to insert short notes or glosses, first between the lines, and then in the margins of the text being studied, in their attempts to ascertain its meaning. The most famous members of the Glossator school of thought, were Irnerius (1055–1130), and later Accursius (1184–1263); it is to the latter that we owe an impressive compilation of the work of the Glossators. Mainly based at the Italian law schools of Bologna and Ravenna, the most eminent Glossators, apart from their writings, used to lecture on their work for students coming from all over Europe. Following them, in the later medieval period, came the Post-Glossators or Commentators, the most well known of whom was the Italian Bartolus (1314–1357). Glosses came to be more substantive commentaries on Justinian's *Corpus Juris*, all this with a view to adapting Roman law principles and rules, as clarified by the Glossators, to the conditions and legal environment of medieval life.

The Glossators and Commentators of the medieval period paved the way for those scholars who, in France, as in Germany, carried forward in the following centuries the systematic study of Roman law, drawing principles and developing concepts which through to the present day have shaped the mind-set of the civil lawyer. The work of these scholars culminated in the systematic legal treatises of the seventeenth and eighteenth centuries, which, like the series of treatises written by Pothier (1699–1772) in France, survived the French Revolution to influence the content and structure of the Napoleonic codes, and thus became the prelude to codification.

It is interesting to note that the method used by the Glossators and Post-Glossators still continues to appeal to some scholars who, like Professor J. Carbonnier (2000: 128–132), find it a rational way of explaining and commenting upon the concept of ownership as set out in today's art. 544 of the Civil Code. Using definitions and classifications that are found in Roman law, Carbonnier, in following the style of the Glossators, is able to elucidate in a methodical way each single term of art. 544, with particular emphasis on the grammar of the text (*glose*). Turning to a more substantial, but nevertheless concise, commentary on the text as a whole, Carbonnier, in keeping with the Post-Glossator style, uses a more critical and contextual approach, applying in particular political, sociological and socio-economic considerations (post-glose). At a time such as the present when Roman law is barely studied and hardly figures at all in the law curriculum, Carbonnier's approach is still evidence of the continuing validity of the ancient Roman law based method of instruction in the legal education of today's generation of law students.

10.2.2.2 The Inns of Court as centres of legal education in England

Although Roman law was also studied in England at the time of the Glossators, and has had some influence on the history and development of the Common law, especially through the influence generated by the works of Bracton, it has never played an educational role in shaping the mode of thought of English lawyers. Legal historians generally attribute this to the fact that the *Corpus Juris* was never 'received' in England in a way similar to that in which it was received on the Continent. The main reasons put forward for this lack of a full acceptance of Roman law in England were the early establishment of a Common law throughout the country, and the early existence of a centralised legal system and of a strong and active legal profession. Unlike Continental lawyers whose techniques have been derived from a meticulous analysis of the Roman texts, English lawyers have constructed their law and shaped their collective mind principally on the basis of court cases. And whilst Continental lawyers have, from early on, been educated at universities, English lawyers have received their training at the Inns of Court which were the first centres of legal education in England. It has been recorded that, even before organised legal education began in the Inns of Court, young apprentices of the law, sitting in a 'crib', used to spend their time eye-witnessing practitioners arguing their cases in the courtroom. From the middle of the thirteenth century until approximately 1553, student advocates started taking notes in 'Year Books' during court cases. In spite of being recorded in a random manner, these Year Books later became a valuable source of information on how the law was being made in the courts. In his *History of English Law*, Sir William Holdsworth (1936: Vol. II pp. 507–508) stressed this dominant role played by the Inns of Court in English lawyers' education as well as highlighting the influence played by the Year Books on legal teaching and, more generally, on the development of the common law:

The training which they [the Inns of Court] gave was intensely practical, and no doubt it kept practical, the argumentative, the procedural side of law prominently to the front – perhaps sometimes to the exclusion of legal theory. It produced the men who wrote the Year Books – the men who made the common law a system of case law.

Thus, whilst from very early on the French legal system has relied on academic study as a means of educating its lawyers, the English legal system, within the same time frame, has relied on apprenticeship. This complete difference in training could not help resulting in variance in the mode of thinking, and therefore in the respective methods of teaching that characterise each of the two systems today.

However, legal education in both systems has, over the years, undergone consider-able transformation. New trends have emerged on both sides which have notably resulted in greater emphasis being placed on theoretical knowledge in English legal education and in more attention being paid to the practical aspects of the law in French law schools.

10.2.3 Transformation in both systems

10.2.3.1 England

Today in England, as Professor Bicks (1994) puts it, 'the explanation of the law and its systemisation have become the responsibility of the university jurists'. Referring to this change as the 'intellectual transformation' of the English system of education, P. Bicks traces it back to Lord Selborne's campaign for scientific legal education in the 1870s and to the influential role played later by authors like Dicey, Anson and Pollock in transforming law into an academic discipline. It is in the light of this development that, following the path paved by the 1971 Ormrod Committee, one of the main recommendations of the recent Lord Chancellor's Advisory Committee on Legal Education and Conduct (ACLEC) in its First Report on Legal Education and Training (1996) was that 'the degree course [in England] should stand as an independent liberal education in the discipline of law, not tied to any specific vocation' (recom-mendation R 4.1). The ACLEC also emphasised the need to 'return to basics' in the education and training of lawyers, recommending in this respect that more attention should be paid in future to legislative material instead of confining teaching to case law material only. An over-emphasis in English legal education on case handling, to the detriment of other legal sources, has also been the subject of criticism in the work of an eminent Oxford scholar, the comparative law professor O. Kahn-Freund. In a lecture devoted to legal education, Professor Kahn-Freund (1966: 127) reflects on the model of legal education based on case law offered by English law schools, in the following terms:

Is legal education based on case law not like a medical education which would plunge the student into morbid anatomy and pathology without having taught him the anatomy and physiology of the healthy body? More than that, is the concentration on decided, and especially on reported, cases not like a clinical education which would enable the doctor to diagnose and to treat some complicated brain tumor without ever telling him how to help a patient suffering from a simple stomach upset?

The foregoing would suggest that there has been, in England, a significant shift of attitude in respect of what law schools are for.

10.2.3.2 France

In France too change has come about. Legal instruction is no longer confined to teaching abstract concepts drawn from legal texts. Increasing attention has been paid over the years to case law. The resulting effect is that today's French law students spend as much time as their English counterparts studying case law. Although the method of case study differs between the two countries, case analysis has now become a common way to 'discover' the law in France. In the last 25 years there has also been a noticeable increase in the number of published cases and case notes. However, this substantial growth in the number of readily available reports of judicial decisions and the consequential effect of a widespread knowledge of the work and decisions of the courts have had the opposite effect of placing more emphasis on cases than on statutory instruments, which provoked French Professor Atias' (1980) heated anger with the comment that 'one day a (French) student who is not aware of the latest court of appeal decision is likely to be labelled a shirker'. Furthermore, contemporary academic textbooks, despite a continuing strong emphasis on theory and concepts, pay more attention than previously to the practical aspects of the law and to its effectiveness in social life. They also generally take a more contextual and interdisciplinary approach to law rather than just focusing on the rules themselves (the latter being labelled the 'black-letter' approach). Two currently widely used academic textbooks can be quoted to illustrate this new contextual approach in the area of property law, a subject where, traditionally, a conceptual and 'black-letter approach to teaching has been prevalent. Firstly, in the preliminary part of Professors F. Terré and P. Simler's *Droit civil-Les Biens*, 5 edn, Paris: Dalloz, 1998, a lengthy paragraph entitled 'les influences', considers property law in the context of economic welfare, social psychology, tax law, public policy, planning and zoning law, and the natural environment. Moreover, in its introductory chapter (Chapter 1, section 1), this book puts property law in a comparative, sociological and philosophical perspective. Procedural aspects are also included with appropriate descriptions of the types of available remedies, together with useful technical details and a multitude of case references throughout. Similarly, in the second example, J.Carbonnier's *Droit Civil-Les Biens*, 19 edn, Paris: PUF, 2000, contains, for each chapter, a section separate from and following the main text, in which the author provides readers with an informative and contextual analysis of questions related to the subject-matter of the particular chapter, along with relevant case and bibliographical references. Thus, each question is approached first in its historical and sociological context, then from an economic viewpoint, and finally from a standpoint of legislative policy, as well as legal theory and judicial practice.

However, despite these changes, in both traditions each system of legal education has retained its own intrinsic features. These may be summarised as follows:

10.2.3.3 Summary

In England:

(a) law teaching remains very specialised and is still oriented towards the vocational stage of education for becoming a solicitor or barrister

(b) law reports still remain the primary source of teaching material

(c) when teaching their subject, law teachers still tend to show some reluctance towards the construction of logical argument and the abstract manipulation of complex ideas, and instead show a marked preference for policy discussions.

In contrast, French law schools still place a strong emphasis on:

(a) theoretical knowledge, consisting primarily of the systematic exposition of existing rules and principles

(b) the definition and analysis of the main concepts to be found in the codes, concepts which have been further developed by the courts

(c) argument based on a logical and formal, rather than on a discursive, analysis of legal problems, both in oral presentation and legal writing.

These distinctive characteristics of French legal education are particularly reflected in the main teaching methods used to impart legal knowledge and skills to law students. These teaching methods are the *cours magistral* and the *travaux dirigés* to which this chapter now turns. At the end of the chapter a short section describes the examination technique specific to French law schools.

10.3 *Cours magistral*

Lectures in France, known as *cours magistraux*, consist of a formal and systematic oral presentation of a subject by a teacher. Their main purpose is to provide the background theoretical knowledge which will then be applied to particular exercises in tutorial groups (see Chapter 10.4 below). As the word *magistral* suggests, this form of teaching has always been considered as a superior method of teaching in French law schools. In the past, *cours magistral*, then called *leçon de droit*, had the peculiarity of bearing a degree of resemblance to a court hearing. Law teachers used to wear a gown similar to that of a judge and the audience was composed of students as well as members of the general public. Each group had to sit separately in a designated area and do so quietly. Both were there only to listen to what the teacher had to say, and any sign of approval or disapproval was strictly forbidden. In short, equal similar respect was due to the law whether it was applied by a judge to a case, or taught in a law school by a law teacher. Although this similarity of respect due to both court hearings and law lectures has completely disappeared today, the French law lecture still remains very formal. This is now examined in more detail.

10.3.1 General organisation of a *cours magistral*

Law lectures in France are given by *professeurs* and *maîtres de conférences*. Both hold doctorates, but unlike the latter, the former have successfully passed the *concours d'agrégation*, a highly competitive examination open to doctorate holders only. In the form in which it is presented, the *concours d'agrégation* foreshadows the *cours magistral* in the sense that it consists of a series of four formal oral presentations (called *leçons*) by the candidate, delivered to a jury. Whereas the first presentation focuses on the candidate's research output, the second is held on a general topic relating either to the sources of law or to the civil law. The third presentation is held on a topic aimed at testing the candidate's general knowledge of the law (the subject of which is given 24 hours in advance of the oral hearing) and the fourth presentation revolves around a topic drawn from the candidate's own specialised field of law.

Cours magistraux take place in very large lecture halls (*amphithéâtres*) where students are lectured to in large groups of several hundreds. Class size obviously makes interaction between teachers and students during lecture time very difficult, if not impossible. However, this lack of exchange also reflects the tradition of the French *cours magistral* in which law students are expected to listen and take notes during lectures. In the past, it was even made compulsory for law teachers to dictate the text of their lecture, as a preliminary to further development and explanation on the subject (Decree 21 September 1804, art. 70)! This rule of dictation has fortunately disappeared but the *cours magistral* is still a very formal monologue delivered without any possibility for discussion or exchange of views between teacher and students. This tradition can be put forward when accounting for the fact that French law teachers are not inclined to apply a method of instruction based on questioning similar to, for example, the Socratic method that is applied in most American law schools. However, it has to be said in support of the French tradition of lecturing that the digressions, potential conflicting arguments, and more generally the open debate generated by the questioning method, do not promote clarity and considerably reduce the available time left for completing the programme that has to be covered.

The formal nature of French law lectures is further reflected in the fact that they follow a rigid abstract structure, called *plan de cours*, with multiple headings and subheadings. In the nineteenth century, following laws on legal education enacted under Napoleon's rule, this *plan* had to follow the structure adopted by the codes (Loi of 13 March 1804, art. 2). Today, the structure is free from such constraints, but still reflects the traditional generalised technique of deductive logic, from the general to the particular, of which French jurists are so fond. By way of illustration, this is how a first lecture on the law of obligation is likely to begin in France, following a *plan* probably similar to this one:

Partie 1- Les Sources des Obligations
Livre 1-Le Contrat
Titre 1-La Formation du Contrat
Chapitre 1- Conditions de Validité
Section 1- Le Consentement
§ 1-L'Existence du Consentement
A- Offre
1-Conditions de l'Offre
a) L'Offre doit être Précise
b) L'Offre doit être Ferme

This way of presenting a lecture is not merely a reflection of the French tendency towards orderly arrangement and categorisation. It is also intended to fulfil at least three precise purposes:

(i) First, it acts as an aid to understanding the subject, by approaching it as a coherent whole rather than as a piecemeal succession of legal aspects of any particular question. In the same vein, it provides an appropriate structure for a better exploration of the links between general principles and particular circumstances.

(ii) Second, it is a convenient way of covering, in a minimum and measured time-scale, the maximum required of a subject's syllabus which has to be covered by the end of the semester.

(iii) Finally, it is intended as a memory aid. Each heading of the so-called *plan de cours* operates as a mnemonic device, in the sense that it helps to trigger the memorising of each following heading, and thus assists in bringing each step to mind with the attendant detail of the teacher's lecture. One must, in this context, bear in mind that the law curriculum in France is much larger, and lectures are far greater in number than in England. For example, first year students are on average required to attend for 18 teaching hours per week. Thus, French law students have a lot to memorise, especially if it is borne in mind that teachers base their examinations on what they actually teach during lectures, and that examinations are, by tradition, not open-book examinations.

10.3.2 Lecture notes

Note taking constitutes one of the most important activities in student life, whether it arises out of the reading of legal material or, as here, during the course of attending lectures. Yet, few students are prepared to take this exercise as seriously as they should and to follow the necessary steps to improve their skills in this respect. It should be noted with respect to *cours magistral*, and in view of what has been said above, that it is essential, as soon as possible, to acquire a good note-taking technique. Lecture notes are a very good learning tool and this must be considered from two points of view:

(a) being a first approach to a subject, they form an excellent basis for further development, since they can be supplemented by the reading of other legal material

(b) with the examination in mind, they are an effective way of remembering the content of a lecture. What one writes down oneself is better remembered.

Because of the specific features of French lectures and to make best use of lecture notes, it is advisable to take the following steps:

(i) The plan of the lecture must be apparent. At the beginning of the lecture, as well as at the beginning of each section, the lecturer announces the structure which is to be followed. Students must note this down straight away, if they wish to benefit from the lecture and do not want to get lost!

(ii) All definitions given by the teacher must be noted in full. French law students are expected to be able to define the concepts on which any legal argument is based.

(iii) Pages must be well spaced out and the content must be clear. This will make for easier subsequent reading.

(iv) For greater efficiency within the time constraints, sentences must not be taken down in full but in abbreviated form.

(v) A margin must be left for adding more detail at a later dated if necessary.

(vi) As they will later be used for exam revision, these notes must be re-read within two or three days of taking them, in order to alter or improve them.

(vii) Above all, students should make an extra effort to concentrate on what the teacher is saying and note only what is essential. There will always be time to fill in with more detail later. Taking notes is more than the mere mechanical act of a pen scratching paper!

10.3.3 Supplementary course material

Lecture notes are an essential, albeit insufficient, source of legal material for covering a course. They must be supplemented, in each subject, by other course material. There are a certain number of legal literary sources available if one wishes to go more deeply into a particular subject. Only the most significant – *polycopiés*, textbooks and legal encyclopaedias – are considered here. However, a few words should nevertheless be said about *Mélanges* in view of their original contribution to French legal literature. These are edited works made up of a series of essays on a common theme and written in honour of a distinguished scholar by colleagues, who may also have been this scholar's students and who wish to pay tribute to their former *maître*. The high quality of the work produced make *Mélanges* a valuable and much sought after source of scholarly writing. Amongst the classics in this range of literature are *Mélanges Roubier* (1961) and *Mélanges Raynaud* (1985).

10.3.3.1 *Polycopiés*

Law teachers' lectures may also be available in printed form called *polycopiés*. However, *polycopiés* should not be used as a substitute for lecture attendance. On the contrary, they should be used in conjunction with lectures. In this respect, they have a certain number of advantages:

(a) They provide a support for oral teaching. Notes are not always reliable. Students may have missed important points through not paying attention during the lecture.

(b) They allow students to 'think' about what they hear instead of focusing only on making sure they put down everything the teacher is saying.

(c) Students can better identify the key points and instead of taking notes on everything, they can concentrate on noting down the main points.

(d) It is less tiring, as students can take brief notes during lectures and come back to the subject-source later if more detail proves necessary.

10.3.3.2 Textbooks

Alongside *polycopiés* there are the traditional textbooks. In French law, a distinction is made between *traités* (treatises), *manuels* and *précis* (both handbooks). The latter two are less detailed and more student-friendly than the former. Indeed, treatises are impressively researched works of scholarship written by leading academics and providing a critical and informed analysis in a particular area of law. They are usually made up of a number of individual volumes intended to cover a whole branch of law. The civil law treatise by Demolombre, Professor at the University of Caen, was started in 1845 under the title *Cours de Code Napoléon*, and consisted finally of 31 volumes! Other classic civil law treatises include Aubry et Rau's *Droit Civil Français* (13 volumes) and Planiol et Ripert's *Traité Pratique de Droit Civil* (14 volumes). Treatises are not intended for use by first or second year students, owing to the highly theoretical nature of the work they contain. Another drawback is that they are not regularly updated. However, more recent treatises are regularly updated, for example, Ghestin et Goubeaux's *Traité de Droit Civil* (14 volumes) and Mazeaud's *Leçons de Droit Civil* (9 volumes). Treatises cannot replace the traditional, more accessible and easier to use student textbooks as produced in the form of *manuels* and *précis*. The *manuel* provides a less exhaustive analysis than a treatise, and is in turn a more detailed work than is to be found in a *précis*. An example of a *manuel* is Carbonnier's *Droit Civil* (four volumes). *Précis* are concise textbooks aimed at providing a condensed and objective description of a subject. The presentation is student-friendly and they are regularly updated. The most widely used *précis* are *précis Dalloz* (published by *Dalloz*) and *précis Domat* (published by *Montchrestien*).

10.3.3.3 Legal encyclopaedias

These are weighty, collective works made up of a series of volumes and designed to provide a complete statement of the law, in a particular branch, in a clear, exhaustive and accessible manner. The two most widely used French legal encyclopaedias are the *Dalloz* encyclopaedia, known also as *Répertoires* (cited as Rép. civ. for *Répertoire de Droit Civil* or Rép. pén. for *Répertoire de Droit Pénal et de Procédure Pénale*), and, the Editions techniques' *Juris-Classeurs* (cited as J.-Cl). They both have a similar presentation apart from the fact that, whereas in the *Répertoires*, topics covered are arranged, as in any ordinary encyclopaedia, alphabetically, *Juris-Classeurs* follow the articles of each of the codes in numerical order. To facilitate research, there is in both an alphabetical index under each topic, in addition to each volume's own main index. Both are also regularly updated by a biannual (*Répertoires Dalloz*) or, quarterly (*Juris-classeurs*) loose-leaf supplement. Both encyclopaedias provide, each in its own way, a description of the relevant rules and court rulings in a specific area of law. The approach is rather practical, especially in the *Juris-Classeurs*. The emphasis is more on detailed information than on detailed analysis, as reflected in the large number of quoted bibliographical and case references they supply readers with, the implied intention being to allow readers to acquire a quick and precise answer to any particular point they may have. However, some contributing authors have succeeded in producing valuable scholarly studies on particular topics with both a strong theoretical and contextual emphasis, yet without neglecting detail and references traditionally associated with legal encyclopaedias. A striking example, by way of illustration, is the *Jurisprudence* section, in the *Dalloz Répertoire de Droit Civil*.

10.4 *Travaux dirigés*

10.4.1 General organisation

Just as in English law schools, tutorial groups in France, called *travaux dirigés* (abbreviated to TD), are linked to a lecture programme and consider problems and exercises arising out of the material distributed in advance in the form of a *fiche de travaux dirigés*, the French equivalent of the English handout. This *fiche* does not merely consist of a reading list supplemented by a series of points to be considered at the next tutorial but rather a set of photocopies of full court judgments, case notes and learned articles that are to be read and prepared in advance of the tutorial. In this respect, French law students' life is, in one sense, made easier since they do not, at least at the beginning of their studies, have to hunt around in the law library for cases as much as their English counterparts have to do. There are further, more significant differences between the two systems of tutorial teaching groups, especially with regard to work assessment and in terms of general organisation. There are more students in teaching groups in French law schools than in English ones, with roughly 25 to 30 students per class (compared with fewer than ten in England). TD last one hour and a half each week for each core subject taught (for those other than core subjects, see Chapter 10.5 below). Attendance and class preparation are rigorously enforced as both are taken into account for the final mark, the reason for this being the existence of a generalised system of continuous assessment (*contrôle continu*). Since the introduction of a semester system in 1997, subjects are examined at the end of each semester. Under this system at the end of each semester students receive a TD grade out of 20 for each subject. This grade is subsequently added to the three-hour end of semester examination result for each subject to produce a total out of 40 (marks in foundation subjects are weighted by a factor of 2 or 4). However, some core subjects are only assessed by the students' performance in TD. In this case, students receive a TD grade out of 40 in the relevant subject. The TD grade, in all cases, is determined not only by regular attendance, but also by the quality of the written work handed in, on written tests carried out during classes and on overall participation. The weight accorded to TD performance in course assessment explains why regular attendance and preparation for classes by the reading of assignments specified in the *fiche de travaux dirigés* is to be highly recommended in order to achieve success in the French system.

10.4.2 Purpose of *travaux dirigés*

Travaux dirigés are intended to develop students' legal skills using a set of traditional legal exercises that are described in the following chapter. However, it should be noted that whereas in *travaux dirigés* the objective is to teach students to think and speak like lawyers, it is not intended that students should, in class, reflect personally on what they are learning, or express their own personal views about law or legal issues. Indeed, in keeping with the tradition and spirit of French legal education, the knowledge of substantive law is considered to be more important than legal imagination or creativity. Furthermore, the aim of TD is not to prepare students for the courtroom. As a consequence, there is little scope provided in the TD programme for testing the ability of students to present a legal argument, let alone to argue both sides of a case. This is to be regretted in view of the central role that dispute and contention play in the life of a lawyer. However, this was not always the case. It should be noted, first of all, that controversy, as a method of expounding the law, has always been present in scholarly works (see, in particular, the survey of French scholarly works carried out by Professor C. Atias in *Annales des Facultés de Droit*, 1985, pp. 107–123). Historically, it was also a widespread method of teaching the law in the French law schools of the fourteenth and fifteenth centuries. In this respect, French legal historians recount how students at that time used to argue in class each side of a case in debates, called *disputationes* or, alternatively, in a more specific exercise called *quaestio disputata*, similar to the moots organised at about that time by the Inns of Court in England. This *quaestio* took the form of a fictitious case with two speakers each arguing one side of a case and concluding with a *solutio* given by the teacher, sitting for this purpose as a judge. Unlike English law schools, where mooting is still practised and is, indeed, a very popular exercise, French law schools have long since abandoned this method of teaching law by way of arguments *pro* and *contra*. Confronted in the sixteenth century with new methods of teaching based on deductive logic advocated by legal humanists, the controversy-based teaching method gradually disappeared from law schools supplanted by a legalistic approach to the law and its attendant belief that the true law is the law set out in authoritative form, cleared of any doubtful elements.

However, the importance of being articulate is nevertheless acknowledged in French law schools and is addressed in the form of oral presentations called *exposés*. *Exposés* are made by individual students, usually at the beginning of each TD, on a topic determined in advance with the tutorial instructor. They are intended to help develop and test students' abilities in basic research and oral presentation skills. *Exposés* follow the same basic structure as *dissertations* (see at Chapter 11.2.2 below). They must, however, be presented within a strict time limit (usually ten minutes) and should not be read out verbatim from notes. *Exposés* are important because they offer an opportunity to gain some experience in public speaking and to become generally more familiar with legal material and terminology, qualities very much relevant to, and required for, lawyers' professional work.

10.5 Examinations

In French law schools, core subjects are assessed in part by written examinations and in part by continuous assessment of TD performance (on the latter, see Chapter 10.4.1 above). Written examinations are dealt with in the next chapter together with legal exercises for both of which similar skills are required.

Other subjects (usually optional) are assessed by way of oral examination. Oral examinations, apart from being a very good way of testing students' memory and presence of mind, also contribute to the development of their oral communication skills. Students are asked, within a restricted period of time, to answer a question they have drawn at random, which has been covered in the *cours magistral*, and for which a ten minute preparation period is usually allowed. The mark awarded will generally be dependent on a capacity to exhibit certain skills such as:

(a) giving an exhaustive answer to the question

(b) structuring in the general presentation of the answer

(c) being articulate, in particular ensuring that sentences are finished with thoughts worked out to their conclusion, together with a correct use of legal terminology

(d) being able to discuss the question in context, particularly in view of new related developments.

Owing to staff shortages and to lack of time, this tradition of oral examination has tended to disappear from some French law schools. In recent years it has, in part, been replaced in some subjects by short written examinations, in the form of either short essays, or multiple choice questions.

Chapter references

Annales des Facultés de Droit et de la Science Juridique, Vol. 2, *Les Méthodes d'Enseignement du Droit*, 1985.

ATIAS, C., 'La Mission de la Doctrine Universitaire en Droit Privé', JCP 1980, I, 2999.

BIRKS, P., *Reviewing with Legal Education*, Oxford University Press, 1994.

BIRKS, P., *Pressing Problems in the Law*, Vol. 2, 'What are Law Schools for?', Oxford University Press, 1996.

BORKOWSKI, A., *Roman Law*, London: Blackstone Press, 1994, pp. 336–347.

BOULANGER, F., 'Réflexions sur les Problèmes de Formation des Etudiants dans les Facultés de Droit', JCP1982, I, 3077.

DAINOW, J., 'The Civil Law and the Common Law: Some Points of Comparison', *The American Journal of Comparative Law*, 1967, Vol. 15, pp. 419–435.

DAWSON, J.P., *The Oracles of the Law*, The University of Michigan Law School, 1968, pp. 34–65 and 122–134.

HOLDSWORTH, W.S., *A History of English Law*, Vol. 2, 4th edn and Vol. 4, 3rd edn, London: Sweet and Maxwell, 1936, 1945.

KAHN-FREUND, O., 'Reflections on Legal Education', *The Modern Law Review*, 1966, Vol. 29, pp. 121–136.

LAMBERT, J., 'Le Rôle de l'Enseignement dans la Différenciation du Système Juridique de Common Law et du Système Juridique de Droit Civil', *Mélanges Roubier*, 1961, pp. 295–303.

Lord Macmillan, 'Deux Manières de Penser', *Introduction à l'Etude du Droit Comparé*, Vol. 2, part 3, Paris: Sirey-LGDJ, 1938, pp. 3–17.

MERRYMAN, J.H., *The Civil Law Tradition*, 2nd edn, Stanford University Press, 1985.

VAN CAENEGEM, R.C., *Judges, Legislators and Professors*, Cambridge University Press, 1987.

VINOGRADOFF, P., *Roman Law in Medieval Europe*, 2nd edn, Oxford: Clarendon Press, 1929.

WALL, S., 'Legal Education in France', *Journal of the Association of Law Teachers*, 1992, Vol. 26, pp. 208–214.

WATSON, A., *The Making of the Civil Law*, Harvard University Press, 1981.

11

Legal exercises

A further central feature of French legal education is the time spent in the learning process in testing students' ability to apply to their written work the knowledge and mode of reasoning they are acquiring from theoretical teaching and from the reading of cases. This practical aspect of legal education is achieved through a set of well-defined formal legal exercises known as *cas pratique, dissertation,* and *commentaire d'arrêt,* for each of which this section provides a method to follow when answering, together with practical applications.

11.1 *Cas pratique* (problem question)

Cas Pratiques closely resemble problem questions in English law. Thus, similarly, as with a problem question, what is required in a *cas pratique* is the analysis of a fictitious factual situation raising a certain number of legal issues. More specifically, the aim of the exercise is to examine and discuss each of the issues identified in the *cas pratique* and arrive at a solution which is the outcome of a logical chain of reasoning. The main difficulty in answering *cas pratiques* is to correctly 'justify' the answer. Indeed, in constructing their answer, students must not only show that they have a sound working knowledge of the relevant law, in particular by identifying the facts which have legal significance and applying them to the appropriate rules of law; they must also display in their work a logical sequence of reasoning when formulating and presenting their answer.

11.1.1 What does a *cas pratique* look like?

By way of illustration, two examples of *cas pratiques* (Problem 1 and Problem 2) are set out in Box 11.1). *Cas pratiques* usually start with a request such as 'Traiter' or 'Résoudre le cas pratique suivant' followed by either:

(i) A detailed account of a series of events interspersed with, or followed by, a series of specific questions, each concerned with a distinct legal point, (following the model of Problem 1).

or,

(ii) A more condensed story, followed by a general request addressed to the student, such as '*Que lui conseillez-vous?*'; '*Que vaut le point de vue défendu par X?*'; '*Quelles sont les chances de succès de son action?*' (following the model of Problem 2).

Although, *prima facie*, students may be asked to do a variety of things in a *cas pratique*, ranging from determining one party's rights and liability to predicting the possible outcome of a court case, whatever the question asked, the same technique needs to be applied in constructing an answer. The basic techniques of answering *cas pratiques* are summarised below.

11.1.2 Answering *cas pratiques*

Answering *cas pratiques* entails that students put themselves in the place of a judge delivering a judgment or, of a practitioner advising a client. Thus, what has been said previously about legal reasoning in Chapter 7, particularly with respect to syllogistic logic and the process of *qualification des faits* (Chapter 7.2 and 7.3.2 above), is highly relevant here and will only be briefly touched upon in this section. A certain number of steps should be followed when constructing an answer to a particular *cas pratique*; these are described below. Although this method of answering may appear time consuming, especially when used for examination purposes, one must bear in mind that within the standard three hours duration of a French law exam students are generally asked to answer only a single problem, thus allowing plenty of time for them to sort out and assess the facts.

The steps for answering *cas pratiques* are:

(a) *Identify the facts which are relevant* Relevant facts are those which have legal significance. In French they are known as *faits utiles* or, *faits pertinents*. The legal significance or, relevance of a particular fact, is dependent on the context. For example, in Problem 1(a) the way the statues are displayed on the terrace, whether in a niche or on a base, is relevant when determining whether or not they are included in the sale of the house, as the Civil Code (art. 525) and the courts take these facts into account when deciding in similar situations.

(b) *Translate facts into legal terms* Facts and questions related to these facts are generally formulated in non-legal terms in *cas pratiques*. Here, prior to identifying the legal issues, and then, establishing the rules applicable to the problem, one must first 'translate' the facts into legal terms. This step is clearly crucial since without it, no correct move towards the answer can proceed. Using the two examples of *cas pratiques* provided, here are simple examples of 'legal' translation.

Problem 1 states:

'M. Josserand a acheté une villa entourée d'un immense parc avec de magnifiques statues ornant la terrasse. Lors de son installation, en octobre, il s'aperçoit que le vendeur, M. Planiol, a emporté avant son départ non seulement les statues, mais encore. . . .'

In legal terms this becomes:

'A la suite d'une vente portant sur un immeuble (la villa et le parc), l'acheteur constate que certains meubles (les statues . . .) ont été enlevés par le vendeur.'

Problem 2 states:

'Il se voit dès lors contraint de procéder à l'abattage de tous les animaux de sa ferme, soit 400 bovins, 100 moutons et 100 porcs. D'après lui le fautif est M. Seguin qu'il veut trainer devant les tribunaux comme il le mérite.'

This can be translated into legal terms as:

'Un fermier a subi un préjudice matériel résidant dans la perte de son cheptel et tient le fermier voisin civilement responsable du dommage occasionné. Il désire le poursuivre en justice.'

(c) *Identify the legal issues* (in French, *problèmes de droit* or, *problèmes juridique*) This step is the follow-up to the preceding one. It is also a vital move in the process of answering a problem and indeed the hardest one, since the whole construction of the answer rests on it. In a French *cas pratique*, there may be either a series of major legal issues, each giving rise to a separate question, as in Problem 1 or, a single main legal issue with a number of related legal points, as in Problem 2. Again using the two illustrations given, the legal issues, can be identified as follows:

Problem 1:

Issue 1 (a): Les statues et autres objets mobiliers sont-ils, au sens de la loi, des immeubles par destination, faisant ainsi partie de la vente de l'immeuble auquel ces objets sont attachés?

(Are the statues and other movable property *immeubles par destination*, thus being part of the sale of the house to which these objects are attached?)

Issue 2 (b): La surélévation de l'immeuble constitue t-elle un trouble anormal de voisinage donnant droit à réparation?

(Does the raising of two further storeys on the neighbouring house constitute a *trouble anormal de voisinage* creating thereby a right to compensation?).

Problem 2:

Main issue: Y-a-t'il un lien de causalité entre le dommage subi par M. Durand et les évènements qui ont eu lieu dans la ferme de M. Seguin, y compris l'action de son fils Benoît, rendant ainsi M. Seguin responsable de la perte subi par M. Durand?

(Was M. Durand's loss caused by the sequence of events that took place at M. Seguin's farm, including the acts of his son Benoît, thus making M. Seguin legally liable?)

Related legal issues: (i) Si ce lien existe, M. Seguin peut-il se retourner contre les restaurants qui ont confectionné la pâté et le boucher qui a fourni la viande avariée?

(If this sequence of events is to be regarded as having caused the damage, can M. Seguin claim against the restaurants and the butcher who both contributed to M. Durand's loss?).

(ii) Peut-il aussi invoquer comme moyen de défense le jeune âge de Benoît qui, n'étant pas capable de discerner les conséquences de ses actes, n'a pu de ce fait commettre une faute?

(Can M. Seguin use as a defence the fact that Benoît is a very young child and that, therefore, he cannot be guilty of contributory negligence?)

(d) *Apply the relevant rules* Once the facts have been translated into legal terms and the issues identified, it becomes possible to state the relevant rules and to apply them to the issues of the case. In Problems 1 and 2 the relevant rules are as follows:

Problem 1:

Issue 1 (a): Articles 524–525 of the Civil Code (both defining the notion of *immeubles par destination*. On this notion see *Ville de Genève et Fondation Abbeg v Consorts Margail* at Chapter 8.3.1 above).

Issue 2 (b): The so-called doctrine of *troubles anormaux de voisinage* whereby a neighbour cannot impose on another a degree of nuisance more than what is reasonably considered to be a normal standard of inconvenience.

In Problem 2:

Main issue: Article 1382 of the Civil Code, the key provision describing the conditions for civil liability, i.e. fault, damage, causation. Also, of relevance are the particular rules governing causation in the French law of tort, as they arise in the two approaches adopted by the courts, namely: *équivalence des conditions* (any event without which the loss would not have been incurred is the cause of this loss) and, *causalité adéquate* (only the event which is regarded as being the determining cause of the damage is to be treated as a cause in law). Regarding the animal feed, art. 1384 al. 1 (see 4.3.2.1 below) is also relevant.

Related issues: (i) The doctrine of subrogation under which the defendant is entitled to pursue any claim that the plaintiff would have had against third parties in respect of the loss. The doctrine of *obligation in solidum* may also be of relevance here: where the damage is the result of the combination of the fault of others the plaintiff can sue any one of the joint defendants for the whole amount of the damage. (ii) Article 1384 al. 4 of the Civil Code, on parental liability, as well as the relevant case law, especially *Gabillet v Noye* and *Fullenwarth v Felten* (1984) JCP II, 20255, the two landmark decisions of the Court of Cassation where it was decided that there was no further need for an injured party seeking damages to show, as had previously been the case, that a young child who caused harm had the capacity to discern what she/he was doing at the material time.

Whatever their sources, these rules must be examined and discussed at length prior to their application to the facts. Thus, students must describe and explain the relevant code and statute provisions (or general principles of law), as well as the relevant case law. Academic writing must not be neglected, especially in controversial areas or, in areas where at the source of a judicial solution is a particular doctrine which has been developed by recognised academic lawyers. Such is the case in the law of tort with the two main approaches to causation adopted by French courts (referred to above) originating from the works of the German jurists Von Kries and Von Buri. Thus, in *cas pratiques* which raise an issue of causation (such as Problem 2), these authors must be cited when answering with their contributions to this area of law being discussed.

(e) *Propose a solution* The solution to a *cas pratique* must arise out of the application of the relevant rules to the facts, following a line of reasoning similar to the syllogistic approach as that adopted in judicial decisions (see Chapter 7.2.1 above). A good problem solving technique cannot do without showing this logical link between facts, rules and the solution proposed. Furthermore, in circumstances where there is more than one possible solution to the legal issue raised, either because the situation is not clearly dealt with by statute or code provisions or, because case law is not consistent on this issue, it is important that all these possible solutions are stated, for what students are primarily judged on is not so much the choice of a particular solution but, the reasoning which has led them to that particular solution. However, this does not prevent students being more specific when necessary, especially when they have been specifically asked in a *cas pratique* to 'advise' a plaintiff. In such a case, students might indicate their solution and, as long as this choice from possible options is correctly justified (by a new trend emerging in case law or in academic writing, call for reform on the issue. . . .), their answer will be considered acceptable and marked accordingly.

11.1.3 Presentation of the answer

There is no pre-determined formal presentation as is the case with essay writing when answering a *cas pratique*. Students are expected to discuss the various issues or legal points in succession following a short introduction briefly stating the facts. However, in French law a number of basic writing skills are expected. These are considered in the next section which is devoted to essay questions but which apply equally to problems as much as to essays.

11.2 *Dissertation* (essay)

Dissertation is the French equivalent to 'essay question' in English (note that the closest equivalent to the English term 'dissertation', in the context of French legal education, is *mémoire*, a very long essay that postgraduate students are asked to write as part of their course work). In the context of an examination *dissertation* is also referred to as *sujet théorique* and is of three hours duration, the usual time given for a law exam in France. When compared to an essay question in English law, *dissertation* is a longer and much more formal written exercise also requiring much more than the basic techniques usually involved in English legal essay writing. Indeed, a French legal

Box 11.1 Problems (or *cas pratiques*) 1 and 2

Problem 1: *Josserand v. Planiol and Ripert*

En avril, M. Josserand a acheté une villa entourée d'un immense parc avec de magnifiques statues ornant la terrasse. Lors de son installation, en octobre, il s'aperçoit que le vendeur, M. Planiol, a emporté avant son départ, non seulement les statues, mais encore les outils de jardinage entreposés dans le garage, la balançoire et le toboggan qui avaient fait la joie de ses enfants lors de la visite de la villa, et les poissons tropicaux aux couleurs chatoyantes qui nageaient dans le petit étang du jardin.

(a) En novembre, M. Josserand vient vous consulter et vous demande s'il dispose en droit d'une action pour récupérer ces différents objets. Si oui, sur quel fondement cette action peut-elle être exercée?

Quelques mois plus tard, M. Josserand apprend que son nouveau voisin, M. Ripert, a décidé de surélever son pavillon de deux étages, ce qui aurait pour conséquence, selon un rapport d'expert, de priver de lumière sa nouvelle propriété au sud et à l'est. M. Josserand vous consulte de nouveau pour savoir s'il pourrait assigner en justice M. Ripert si celui-ci menait à terme son project de construction.

(b) Dans cette hypothèse, quel serait le fondement d'une telle action? Quelles seraient ses chances de succès compte tenu du fait que M. Ripert était installé sur les lieux bien avant M. Josserand et, de plus, a obtenu toutes les autorisations nécessaires pour la surélévation de sa construction?

Problem 2: The foot-and-mouth case

Le 28 février dernier la ferme de M. Seguin a été déclarée zone contaminée et interdite à toute circulation humaine ou animale suite à la découverte d'un cas de fièvre aphteuse parmi les animaux qui composent son cheptel. Quelques jours plus tard, M. Durand, le fermier voisin, donne à son tour l'alerte. Deux de ses porcs présentent des signes manifestes de la maladie. Il se voit dès lors contraint de procéder à l'abattage de tous les animaux de sa ferme, soit, 400 bovins, 100 moutons et 100 porcs. D'après lui le fautif est M. Seguin qu'il veut trainer devant les tribunaux comme il le mérite. Il est prêt à invoquer les faits suivants:

(i) La pâtée servie aux chèvres de M. Seguin a été identifiée comme étant la source probable de l'épidémie.

(ii) Cette pâtée a été confectionnée à partir des restes de viande avariée provenant de deux restaurants de la ville voisine, 'Le Relais' et 'La Petite Chaumière'.

(iii) Ces restaurants ont l'habitude de se fournir en viande chez le boucher local, Raoul, réputé pour ses installations insalubres.

(iv) Le fils du fermier Seguin, Benoît, âgé de 4 ans, s'amuse depuis fin février à faire l'aller-retour sur la bicyclette entre la ferme de son père et celle de M. Durand, contribuant ainsi à propager le virus.

Quelles seront, à votre avis, les chances de succès d'une action en justice engagée par M. Durand à l'encontre de M. Seguin?

essay has a particular format in that it must comply with a number of specific requirements. In this respect, the layout of the discussion must be brought out by the use of headings and subheadings, each of which being clearly indicated in the answer. What follows is some guidance on how to write a good legal *dissertation*.

11.2.1 *Le Sujet, tout le Sujet, rien que le Sujet* (the topic, all the topic and nothing else but the topic)

This is one of the golden rules of essay writing. This suggests that only what is relevant to the topic should form part of the essay. It further entails that, before starting to write, the scope of the question posed has been carefully thought out and defined. This is not an easy task especially in view of the fact that essay questions, in French law, are very often worded in general terms similarly to chapter or lecture headings. Thus:

Essay 1: *Le Droit au respect de la vie privée*

Here, the generality of the question might suggest that all topics that fall within the right to privacy are relevant. However, this cannot be the case for it would only lead to a mere recital of that relevant part of the course the question addresses. This is not the object of the exercise. In fact, what students are expected to do when facing this type of question is to bring to the surface the underlying problematic aspects of the question for consideration and discussion. In Essay 1 this might be boundary to privacy. Indeed, this boundary is particularly problematic when viewed against the competing right of freedom of expression. A further problematic aspect of the question of privacy could be: can privacy be adequately protected and how (legislation, self-regulation. . .)?

Defining the scope of a question to be answered is equally difficult with two further frequently employed forms of essay question. The first, which follows now, refers to questions which are formulated with a question mark such as:

Essay 2: *Peut-on dire de la jurisprudence qu'elle est une source de droit?*

Here the problem raised is more identifiable than in the former type of essay question (Essay 1). This implies, with greater force than formerly, that students limit the scope of their answer to what is asked for and only for what is asked for. Again answering successfully requires a careful delimitation of the boundaries to the question put so that students do not end up writing everything they happen to know on the various aspects of the general subject, in this case *jurisprudence*. Full general knowledge on a topic can never make up for the necessary thinking required to tackle an essay question. Hiding behind a question mark a controversy is very often to be found or, more generally, an important question which is open to debate. It is this hidden controversy or debate that, once again, needs to be brought out for consideration and discussion. This does not mean, however, that students are to take sides in this debate. French essay writing is concerned with presenting the law in an objective way, not standing up for one's own personal opinions! Thus, what students are asked to do is to state both sides of the legal argument raised by such a question, refraining from getting personally involved in the controversy one way or another or to start a great debate on the question.

Another common kind of essay question causing difficulty, is when students are asked to compare and contrast two notions or concepts. For example:

Essay 3: *Distinguez la règle de droit et la règle morale*

Here, students must be careful not to treat the notions side by side or, one after the other such as: I- *La Règle de Droit* / II- *La Règle Morale.* Indeed, such a way of answering will only result in two separate mini-essays on each notion rather than in the comparison asked for. The process of comparing inevitably implies the juxta-position of the two notions involved but with a view to bringing them into relief, to establish their similarities and dissimilarities. Successful comparison can, thus, only be effectively achieved by approaching the question from various perspectives or, alternatively, by structuring the answer around a number of relevant characteristics common to each of the two given notions. Thus, in Essay 3 above, law and morals could be contrasted from each of the following points of view:

(a) source

(b) content

(c) objective.

Alternatively, comparison can be achieved by using themes common to both concepts, such as:

(a) law and morals as rules of conduct in society

(b) law and morals as rules aimed at achieving justice.

11.2.2 *Plan* (layout)

Planning an answer is essential to essay writing. However, in French law, it is not an overstatement to say that the structure of the answer is as important as its content. In this respect, French legal essays are expected to display a very formal structure called *plan* supporting the argument developed in the discussion. A good *plan* is made up of the three following elements:

(a) introduction

(b) two part discussion

(c) conclusion.

Introduction. The introduction is an important part of the French legal *dissertation* in that a good introduction will not only immediately create a good impression upon the person marking but will also strongly influence the quality of the discussion that follows.

A good introduction firstly should put the question in context, from the general to the particular. This is known in French law as the technique of *entonnoir* (funnel). Taking as an example Essay 2 on *jurisprudence*, the introduction should firstly ascertain the meaning of the phrase *source de droit* (source of law), then consider generally the different sources from which French law arises, namely, legislation and custom, before moving on to consider the actual question asked, whether precedent constitutes a source of law. More specifically, an introduction is intended to answer three questions: What? Why ? and How?

What? Consists in defining the scope of the question and explaining its meaning. Thus, in Essay 2: begin by defining the concept of source of law and then state what are the official sources of law in France.

Why? Is concerned with presenting the significance of the question asked. This would include showing its relevance in a sociological, historical and, comparative perspective. Thus, in Essay 2: show the relevance of the question asked in view of the particular status ascribed to precedent in France since the 1789 Revolution and of the French doctrine of separation of powers, as well as in the context of an absence of doctrine of binding precedent similar to that found in Common law systems.

How? Is showing the way in which the question will be discussed, namely by outlining a *plan* which will then be used to develop the argument (see, below the proposed *plan* for Essay 2).

It is advisable to write the introduction only when all the various points of the argument have been thought about and drafted in rough, the reason being that it is only at this stage that it becomes possible to appreciate the full ambit of the question asked and to figure out the component parts of the answer.

Two part discussion. A French legal essay is usually constructed around two well defined parts. Unlike arts subjects, where the practice is to develop an argument in three parts (known as *thèse / antithèse / synthèse*), French jurists are very attached to the two-part *dissertation*, probably reminiscent of the fact that there are always two sides to a legal argument! These two parts form the core of the *plan* and should be clearly numbered on the essay or exam paper with a formal title for each of them. They should be further subdivided into paragraphs where the various elements of the discussion are arranged in separate subheadings, preferably two, clearly labelled A, B, etc . . . if required (see below the practical applications provided under '*plans d'idées*'). This writing format is often a cause for astonishment, or even derision, amongst students who, when first introduced to it, think that it is a rather 'schoolish' way of approaching academic legal writing. However, they very quickly change their attitude when they realise that, not only, is this format the one adopted by academics and practitioners when writing learned articles and case notes, but also, the absence in their papers of any visible *plan* as described above leads to poor marks. This format actually serves a twofold purpose. Firstly, from a teacher's or examiner's point of view, it conveniently allows, at first glance, an appraisal of the structure of the answer given, making the marking of a paper much easier and less time consuming. Secondly, from a student's point of view, a two part *plan* with headings and subheadings provides the main threads for an essay which, once put down in writing, prevents him/her from straying too far from the subject. Having said this, the extreme emphasis law teachers usually place on the requirement for a *plan* often leads students to mistakenly think that a 'good' *plan* can be a substitute for lack of content. This is never the case since a 'good' *plan* is not one that merely exhibits attractive headings but, more importantly, is the one that accurately reflects what is being discussed.

French law usually distinguishes between two kinds of *plans*: *plan technique* and *plan d'idées*.

(a) *Plan technique* adopts the technical subdivisions that are usually used in legal writings to describe a notion, an institution, a right or, a particular court. Thus:

I- Definition/Application (for a notion, such as *bonne foi* i.e., good faith)

I- Conditions / II – Effets (for an institution such as marriage)

I- Formation / II – Execution (for a right such as the right of ownership)

I- Composition / II – Rôle (for a court such as the Court of Cassation).

(b) *Plan d'idées* is built up around the main issues (ideas) taken from the question. For example, in Essay 1, a *plan d'idées* would be:

I – Faut-il protéger la vie privée?

A – Les difficultés à délimiter la sphère de la vie privée.

B – Les intérêts en conflit.

II – Les solutions adoptées en droit français.

A – Par le législateur.

B – Par le juge.

In Essay 2:

I – La jurisprudence n'est pas une source formelle de droit:

A – En raison du principe de la séparation des pouvoirs.

B – En raison de la prohibition des arrêts de règlement.

II – La jurisprudence est une source effective de droit:

A – De par l'existence d'une hiérarchie judiciaire.

B – Grâce à sa mission d'interprétation.

The choice between *plan technique* and *plan d'idées* is dependent upon the nature of the question itself. Some questions, as those given above, lend themselves to a *plan d'idées* on account of the problems they raise or, the controversy they generate. Questions more related to technical and working aspects of a notion, an institution or a right, with a view to describe, compare or contrast, call for *plans techniques*. Such is the case with Essay 3 which fits a *plan technique* such as: I-*Distinction quant au domaine* / II-*Distinction quant à la finalité*.

One thing to bear in mind is that there is no 'ideal' plan. Thus, all the examples

illustrated above are mere suggestions. As long as the *plan* adopted is correctly justified and covers all the relevant aspects of the question asked it will pass as a 'possible'
plan. Also, *plans* are not found in lucky bags! Students need a good working knowledge of the subject, a lot of thought and some practice before being able to find a *plan*
which is acceptable. Whatever *plan* is finally adopted, the two parts must be well
counter-balanced. A part which is too long or too detailed as compared with the other
one, is a sign that the *plan* chosen is defective and needs to be reconsidered. Furthermore, each of the headings and subheadings should be connected to each other by a
transition linking the different parts of the discussion.

Conclusion. In a French legal *dissertation*, a conclusion is not compulsory. In fact,
some teachers even advise students not to conclude since a conclusion, not being
intended by definition to add anything to the discussion, is therefore redundant.
Furthermore, there is sometimes a tendency on the part of students to introduce in
their conclusion points that have been earlier missed out in the discussion or that they
did not find time to consider in the main body of the text. This produces a very bad
effect, which explains why in this case a conclusion should be avoided. A conclusion in
fact is only useful if it serves to sum up the points made in a long and complex
discussion or, to open up a discussion towards other perspectives not specifically
addressed or contained in the question being considered.

11.2.3 Style of writing a *dissertation*

The first thing to bear in mind is that French law teachers and examiners attach great
importance to formal presentation. A piece of work that looks untidy is very often
thought of and judged by teachers as unmethodical or unsystematic. It is therefore
essential for students to write a first draft and then to check the detail in the final copy
of the work prior to submitting it for marking. During examinations, as they do not
have time to draft out answers in full, students should, before writing their final
answer, write down in rough in bullet point form the *plan* they have decided upon
with some brief notes on the main points to be addressed. The preparation of a rough
copy of the full introduction is also recommended, as this is considered to be a very
important part of the paper. Students must refrain from writing their rough work on
the actual exam script which they then cross out when the final copy has been written.
Plenty of rough paper is provided during French law examinations for the students to
use!

As regards content, students must also make sure they adopt, in the process of
writing their *dissertation*, a strict legal approach to the subject under consideration.
Philosophical considerations, for example, should not form part of the discussion. A
philosophical approach to a legal question very often makes the whole discussion
pompous and woolly when what is required is simplicity and rigour. However, the
introduction may briefly consider extra-legal implications of a question as long as this
is relevant. Personal comments, value-judgements and even criticism are to be

avoided. Such personal statements as '*Je pense*', or, '*à mon avis*' are viewed in a very bad light by teachers and examiners alike who expect students to answer the question put to them in an impersonal non-partisan way. Personal opinion is left to senior jurists such as law teachers who, in France at least, like to think that they know better than the students themselves! Having said that, some degree of criticism in essay writing is permitted as long as it reproduces an accepted view and is conveyed in non-personal objective terms. Finally, the writing content should be shorn of needless repetition complying thereby with the norms of the ideal style of legislative and judicial drafting as described earlier in Chapters 1 and 8 of this book.

11.3 *Commentaire d'arrêt*

Commentaire d'arrêt consists of a detailed analysis of a judicial decision, usually a decision of a highest court (Court of Cassation, *Conseil d'Etat* and *Conseil Constitutionnel*), with a view to evaluating this decision and assessing its legal implications. This is an important exercise in that it enables law students to assess the true meaning and scope of legal rules, through the interpretation made of them by the courts. French law students, with some justification, particularly fear this exercise in view of the hermetic jargon and peculiar structure featured in French judicial decisions. These particular features forcefully point up the main difficulties of *commentaire d'arrêt*: how can anyone comment meaningfully on a text saying so little and in a style so unfavourable to further discussion? There is no magic recipe for overcoming such difficulties. Mastering *commentaire d'arrêt* is a long process which may take years of study and is achieved gradually through the ongoing process of acquiring knowledge and the practical experience of reading cases. There is, however, a set of guidelines on the basic techniques to be applied to the reading, analysis and discussion of a French judicial decision that each generation of law teachers has passed on to the next. These guidelines now follow.

11.3.1 Reading a French case

This section should be read in conjunction with the descriptions in Chapters 7 and 8 of the grammatical and logical structure of French judicial decisions. The present chapter looks only at the way judicial decisions are laid out in law reports. By way of illustration, two decisions (referred to as Arrêt 1 and Arrêt 2) are set out in Box 11.2, both being reported in the 1995 *Bulletin de la Cour de Cassation*. The choice made here of two Court of Cassation decisions is justified by the fact that, in French law schools, students usually start their apprenticeship in *commentaire* by analysing decisions of the Court of Cassation. These decisions are usually short and do not require for the first year students who have not yet acquired the necessary expertise, the technical knowledge and skill involved in the reading of a *Conseil d'Etat* or a *Conseil Constitutionnel* judgment.

French law reports usually follow a standard more or less similar to that illustrated in Box 11.2. Thus, running down these two cases are to be found (the numbers after each heading below correspond to those in the illustration):

(a) The *abstrat* (1) This is a short paragraph made up of a series of keywords aimed at identifying at first glance the subject-matter of a case.

(b) The *sommaire* (2) Similar to a headnote in English law reports, it contains a summary of the court's decision. Its size may vary (and can, indeed, be longer than in the cases provided in illustration) according to the length of the decision and the number of legal points raised by the case. The *sommaire* is drafted by the case reporter, not by the judge who gave the decision. It is, therefore, not part of the judgment and cannot be used as a substitute for reading the case.

(c) The date of judgment (3) In law reports other than the *Bulletin* the date is usually preceded by the name of the court in which the case was heard, a detail not needed in the *Bulletin* since this publication only includes Court of Cassation decisions.

Note that in our illustration *abstrat, sommaire* and date are common to both cases involving similar issues but different circumstances and parties.

(d) The text of the judgment (4) This is discussed below at Chapter 11.3.2.

(e) The names of the parties (5) This starts with the name of the appellant (or plaintiff in the lower courts), followed by the name of the respondent (or defendant in the lower courts). Thus in Arrêt 1: *Mlle X.* contre *Société Transport agglomération Elbeuvienne.* The term *contre* is sometimes abbrieviated *c.* and is the French legal equivalent of 'versus' but, unlike 'versus', *contre* is not spoken in French differently from the way it is written. In other law reports, names generally appear, not at the end of the judgment like in the *Bulletin* but, after the *sommaire* and before the judgment.

(f) The composition of the court, together with the names of counsel appearing in the case (6) Although these details are important, in French law reports they only appear as footnotes to a decision and in small print. Yet, it should be noted that the status of the presiding judge is usually a good indicator of the importance of the issue(s) raised in a case and may influence the weight that a decision carries (this is certainly the case when the Head of the Court of Cassation presides over a case, a circumstance which is exceptional).

Unlike English law reports, in French law reports there are no identifying letters in the margin, or even numbered paragraphs providing a reference point when citing a judgment. The reason for this may lie in the brevity of French judicial decisions. However, decisions which are longer than normal, such as lower court decisions generally or, higher court decisions raising a substantial number of issues, would certainly benefit from letters in the margin in that it would make the reading of such decisions easier, especially during class-time where, currently, the only way to locate a piece of text which is being referred to is by counting the lines!

11.3.2 The judgment

Before examining in detail a Court of Cassation decision, a distinction must be drawn between the two types of decisions given by the Court, namely *arrêt de cassation* (as *Arrêt* 1) and *arrêt de rejet* (as *Arrêt* 2). The former is when the Court upholds the appeal, deciding thereby that the lower court came to the wrong decision. The latter is when the Court dismisses the appeal, having thus agreed with the decision of the lower court. The outcome of a case is indicated in the final part of the Court's judgment, the *dispositif* (see Chapter 8.2.1 above) as follows:

(a) *Arrêt de cassation*:

Casse et Annule . . . l'arrêt rendu par la Cour d'Appel de. . . (quash the decision given by the Court of Appeal of . . .), in conjunction with an indication of the lower court to which the case is referred back for reconsideration or,

(b) *Arrêt de rejet*:

Rejette le pourvoi (dismiss the appeal). It should be noted here that in appeals to the Court of Cassation the term used for 'appeal' is *pourvoi*, not *appel*. The French term *appel* applies only to appeals from a court of first instance to a court of appeal.

Arrêts de cassation and *arrêts de rejet,* also differ substantially from one another in terms of structure and content. Anyone reading a case should be aware of these differences before any attempt is made to understand what the case is about. Using the two illustrations in Box 11.2, these differences between the two are now considered.

Arrêt de cassation (Arrêt 1). This takes the following form (*the number after each heading refers to each illustration*):

(a) A *visa* (*1.1*) As discussed at Chapter 7.2.2 and 8.2.1 above *visa* is the citation of the relevant statute or code provision. It is followed usually (as in *Arrêt* 1), although not always necessarily, by a *chapeau* (on this notion see Chapter 4.2.4 above) where the Court states in the form of a principle the interpretation it intends to give to the text cited in the *visa*. This part is the most informative part of the judgment since it clearly brings to the reader's attention the principle on which the solution given by the Court of Cassation is based. This clear expression of the principle allows a comparison with the principle established in earlier similar cases, more specifically, as to whether the Court has, in the present case, confirmed this principle; whether it has been reinterpreted, or, whether it has been extended or, interpreted more narrowly.

(b) A brief statement of the facts (*1.2*) This statement refers to the parties to the case and briefly describes the procedure leading up to the hearing before the Court of Cassation. This statement takes on board the facts as established by the lower court (as the expression '*selon l'arrêt attaqué*', used in the judgment suggests), since the Court of Cassation does not reconsider facts, only law.

(c) A summary of the lower court's decision (*1.3*).

(d) The reasons why the Court of Cassation considers that the case was not correctly decided by the lower court (*1.4*) This is the determining part in the judgment which, when considered together in conjunction with the statement and the interpretation made of the rule of law, at the beginning of the Court's judgment, informs the readers as to why and to what extent the lower court has misinterpreted or ignored the applicable rule.

Arrêt de rejet (*Arrêt 2*). This is composed of:

(a) A brief statement of the facts (*2.1*) This statement is similar to the one in *arrêt de cassation*.

(b) A summary of the *moyen* (*2.2*) A *moyen* is made from the grounds on which the appeal is based. The summary of the *moyen* is typical of an *arrêt de rejet* since the Court, before dismissing the appeal, indicates what indeed were the arguments of the appellant which are now being rejected. The *moyen* always starts either with the words '*attendu qu'il est reproché à l'arrêt attaqué d'avoir*' (as illustrated in *Arrêt 2*) or, '*attendu que le demandeur au pourvoi* (i.e. the appellant) *fait grief à l'arrêt d'avoir*'. There may be a single *moyen* (called *moyen unique*) or, a series of *moyens*. In the latter case the *moyens* are numbered and are examined in rank order by the Court. However, the Court may decide to consider all the *moyens* together, usually when the issues raised are interrelated, and thus decide on them all, at one and the same time. The Court in this case will then say: '*sur les (number) moyens réunis*'(as in *Arrêt 2*). *Moyens* are subdivided into *branches*, introduced in the text of the judgment by the phrase '*alors que*', followed, when there are two or more *branches*, by '*d'une part*, '*d'autre part*', '*en outre*' and '*enfin*' (as illustrated in *Arrêt 2*). Each branch forms a separate point of criticism raised by the appellant against the lower court decision. *Arrêts de rejet* say very little on the lower court decision other than by allusion. Since the Court of Cassation agrees with the solution adopted by the lower court, there is no need to repeat in full in the text of the judgment what is regarded by the Court as being the correct answer to the case. However, it may happen that the Court of Cassation, whilst dismissing the appeal, does not agree with the reasoning of the lower court. If this is so, the Court substitutes its own reasons in place of those adopted by the lower court (*substitution de motifs*). However, even in this case, the lower court's reasoning will generally still be omitted.

(c) The refutation by the Court of Cassation of the appellant's arguments. (*2.3*) This refutation is easy to spot in the decision as it is always introduced in an *arrêt de rejet* by '*Mais attendu*'. In rare cases, the actual refutation may be prefaced by the statement of the principle on which the solution is based (as in *Arrêt 2*), similarly to a *chapeau* in *arrêt de cassation*.

The difference in structure between *arrêt de cassation* and *arrêt de rejet* can be shown in summary form as follows:

Arrêt de cassation:

Vu (*visa*)

Attendu que (*chapeau*)

Attendu, selon l'arrêt attaqué, que (facts)

Attendu que. . . .l'arrêt relève (lower court's decision)

Qu'en statuant ainsi, alors que (reasons for reversing the lower court decision)

Casse et annule

Arrêt de rejet

Attendu que, selon l'arrêt attaqué (facts)

Attendu qu'il est reproché à l'arrêt (*moyen*) . . . alors que. . ., alors
que. . . (*branches*)

Mais attendu que (refutation)

Rejette le pourvoi

11.3.3 Method of analysis and discussion of a court decision

The critical analysis of a judicial decision, which is the object of a *commentaire d'arrêt*, consists, first, of a detailed examination of the dispute leading to the case, second, of an evaluation of the decision, followed, third, by a discussion of the legal implications of the solution adopted by the court giving the decision. These three aspects of case analysis in French law i.e., examination, evaluation and discussion, are usually summarised under the following separate headings:

(a) sens

(b) valeur

(c) portée.

Before writing the actual commentary on the case, a preliminary task is to consider each of these headings and the questions they may raise. A basic recommended technique is to address each heading on a separate rough copy sheet, which will later serve as a reference when drafting the actual *commentaire* itself.

11.3.3.1 Preliminary work

Each heading is addressed in turn.

Sens (first rough copy). This first rough copy determines the general legal background of the dispute. In this respect, each of the following questions should be addressed:

(i)   What are the facts?

(ii)   What was the claim (in French '*objet de la demande*')?

(iii)   What was the legal issue at the root of the appeal (in French '*problème juridique*')?

(iv)   What was the decision of the lower court?

(v)   What are the arguments of both parties on this issue (in French 'les thèses en présence')?

(vi)   What is the rule applied by the Court of Cassation to solve the issue?

(vii) How does the Court interpret this rule?

(viii) What has the Court decided and why, in particular, what are the factors which have determined the Court to reach this decision?

Valeur (second rough copy). Here, the reasons are to be assessed why the decision reached by the Court of Cassation should be agreed or, disagreed with. Academic writing, *conclusions* of the *avocat général*, as well as *travaux préparatoires* (where the issue raised in the case has been the object of recent reform) may be used to assist students with their answer. However, during examinations, these are not provided together with the text of the decision to be commented upon. It is assumed that, prior to the examination, students have read extensively on the points raised in the case to be commented upon. When critically appraising the *valeur* of the decision the following questions should be addressed:

(i)   Has the highest court followed a logical line of reasoning when giving its decision?

(ii)   Is the solution adopted consistent with the rules and principles governing the area of law concerned?

(iii) Is it consistent with the prevalent view in academic writing?

(iv)   Is the solution adopted desirable?

(v)   Is the solution adopted fair?

(vi)   How does the decision fit into the political, social, economic and moral context?

Portée (third rough copy). Here, the legal implications of the decision are to be considered around two main questions, which are:

(i) Does this decision fit a consistent line of precedents? To answer this, the decision to be commented upon should be compared and contrasted with previous cases dealing with the same issue.

(ii) Is this decision authoritative (in the French legal meaning. See Chapter 4.2 above on factors giving weight to precedents.)?

English law students should be familiar with many of the foregoing points since English case study, in particular the search for the *ratio*, involves most of the questions being addressed here. However, owing to the differences of form and style of judicial decisions in French and English law, some points will be more difficult to determine in the one system as compared with the other. Thus, the *ratio decidendi* will, *prima facie*, be easier to determine in a French case, since the rule or principle on which the solution is based is usually stated in the judgment; however, unlike English cases, the statement of the legal issue being decided is rarely made overtly in a French case and has therefore to be identified. This is usually achieved by examining in detail the argument from both sides, in French *les thèses juridiques en présence* (i.e., each party's argument or, each conflicting court's view, lower and higher court). So, the difficulty when analysing a French case is not so much to identify the legal rule on which a case was decided but, rather, to define the legal issue to be decided in that case. In the two illustrations provided the principle serving as a basis for the decisions is clearly stated in both *Arrêts* (1.4 in *Arrêt* 1 and 2.3 in *Arrêt* 2). Thus:

(Vu l'article 1382 du Code Civil;)

L'état végétatif d'une personne humaine n'excluant aucun chef d'indemnisation, son préjudice doit être réparé dans tous ces éléments.

(The vegetative state of any human being does not preclude any claim for damages in respect of any head of loss for injury sustained, in this case the victim being entitled to full compensation for injury suffered).

However, it is to be noted that the legal issue itself is not clearly stated here. However, it may be determined from the facts, decision of the Court of Appeal (referred to in *Arrêt* 1) and arguments of the appellant (referred to in *Arrêt* 2), as follows: can a plaintiff made to fall irreversibly unconscious (and thus being incapable of experiencing pain) recover damages for pain and suffering as well as damages for loss of amenities?

Once this three part preliminary work has been done, students can proceed to the actual *commentaire*.

11.3.3.2 The *commentaire*

A *commentaire d'arrêt* adopts a structure and a writing format similar to a *dissertation* thus, an introduction and a two part *plan*. However, owing to the special nature of this exercise being based on a judicial decision there are techniques specific to *commentaire d'arrêt* which need to be specified and described.

Firstly, as is the case with any commentary on a text, a *commentaire d'arrêt* must avoid two pitfalls:

(a) a mere paraphrasing of the text under consideration

(b) the writing of an essay on the general topic without reference to the text provided.

In both cases there would, in effect, be no *commentaire* at all, this producing very poor results.

Secondly, the nature of the text to be analysed – in this case, the judgment – determines the choice of a *plan* necessarily different to that of an essay. Thus, the introduction to a *commentaire d'arrêt* will include the following elements:

(a) a summary of the facts, including the name of the court hearing the case and date of judgment

(b) a description of what the case is about

(c) a statement of the legal issue(s)

(d) a presentation of the significance of the question(s) raised by the case seen from different perspectives, such as historical, sociological, policy and comparative law.

The objective in the introduction is not to go into detail – as this will be done in the actual discussion which follows – but to present the decision briefly. As far as the discussion itself is concerned, it must adopt, as with *dissertation*, a two part structure. Here, a distinction must be drawn between cases raising only one legal issue and those raising two issues or more.

In cases raising one legal issue only, a typical *plan* of a *commentaire d'arrêt* would be:

I-Analyse / II-Discussion

Under *analyse* (I) comes an objective examination of the decision, using the answers already prepared in rough to each question addressed in the section headed *Sens* (above, at Chapter 11.3.3.1). In an *arrêt de rejet* the main thrust of the analysis is to contrast the arguments presented by the appellant in the *moyen* to the solution adopted by the Court of Cassation when dismissing the appeal. In an *arrêt de cassation*, this contrast is to be made between the lower court's decision and the Court of Cassation's decision upholding the appeal, particularly in respect of the rule applied by each of the courts and their differing interpretations.

Discussion (II) is an evaluative and critical study of the decision, using on this occasion the answers given to the questions previously addressed in the sections headed *Valeur* and in *Portée*. Thus, under *discussion* all the points listed at Chapter 11.3.3.1 above are to be considered and discussed.

Turning now to cases where two or more legal issues are being raised, the *plan* should consider each issue in turn, such as:

I-Issue 1 / II-Issue 2

adding the parts for each issue raised, as required. Within each part, subdivisions should be then made into *analyse* and *discussion*, details of which are described above.

As with what has been said about *plan* at Chapter 11.2.2, the *plan* proposed here is only a suggestion. Experience shows that, whilst during the first years of study it is advisable to adopt a simple *plan* similar to that suggested here, increased knowledge and experience in legal studies may, at a later stage, call for a more sophisticated *plan* to *commentaire d'arrêt*. In this respect, the *plans* adopted by *arrêtistes* (see Chapter 9) in their case notes may serve as a source of further inspiration for those who wish to improve their technique in this area.

Box 11.2 Reading a French case: *Arrêt* 1 and *Arrêt* 2

(1) RESPONSABILITE DELICTUELLE OU QUASI DELICTUELLE. – Dommage. – Réparation. – Personnes pouvant l'obtenir. – Victime en état végétatif.

(2) *L'état végétatif chronique de la victime d'un accident n'excluant aucun chef d'indemnisation, son préjudice doit être réparé dans tous ses éléments (arrêts nᵒˢ 1 et 2).*

(3) 22 février 1995.

Cassation partielle.

ARRÊT Nᵒ 1

(4) Sur le moyen unique :

(1.1) Vu l'article 1382 du Code civil;

Attendu que l'auteur d'un délit ou d'un quasi-délit est tenu à la réparation intégrale du dommage qu'il a causé ;

(1.2) Attendu, selon l'arrêt attaqué, que Mme Annick X... qui circulait à bicyclette a été heurtée et blessée par l'automobile de M. Y..., que Mlle Catherine X... agissant tant en son nom qu'en celui de Mme Annick X... sa mère, a assigné M. Y... et son assureur, la compagnie Norwich Union, la caisse primaire d'assurance maladie d'Elbeuf et la société Transport agglomération Elbeuvienne en réparation de son préjudice ;

(1.3) Attendu que pour exclure Mme X... de la réparation de son préjudice personnel l'arrêt relève que, salon l'expert, la victime, réduite à l'état végétatif, n'est absolument pas apte à ressentir quoi que ce soit qu'il s'agisse d'une douleur, d'un sentiment de diminution du fait d'une disgrâce esthétique ou d'un phénomène de frustration des plaisirs comme des soucis de l'existence ; que la cour d'appel en déduit qu'il n'existe pas la preuve d'un préjudice certain ;

(1.4) Qu'en statuant ainsi, alors que l'état végétatif d'une personne humaine n'excluant aucun chef d'indemnisation son préjudice doit être réparé dans tous ses éléments, la cour d'appel a violé le texte susvisé ;

PAR CES MOTIFS :

CASSE ET ANNULE, mais seulement en ce qui concerne le préjudice personnel de Mme X..., l'arrêt rendu le 25 juin 1992, entre les parties, par la cour d'appel de Rouen ; remet, en conséquence, quant à ce, la cause et les parties dans l'état où elles se trouvaient avant ledit arrêt et, pour être fait droit, les renvoie devant la cour d'appel de Paris.

Rejet.

Box 11.2 *Contd.*

ARRÊT Nº 2

Sur les deux moyens réunis :

(2.1)   Attendu, selon les arrêts attaqués (Colmar, 7 juin 1991 et 15 janvier 1993), que le mineur Eric Z..., qui circulait à bicyclette, a été blessé dans un accident de la circulation par l'autocar que conduisait M. Y..., préposé de la société nouvelle X... (la société) ; que les parents de la victime, tant en leur nom qu'en celui de leur fils, ont assigné ceux-ci en réparation de leur préjudice ; que la Caisse nationale militaire de sécurité sociale militaire a été appelée en déclaration de jugement commun ;

(2.2)   Attendu qu'il est reproché à l'arrêt d'avoir indemnisé le préjudice ainsi qu'il l'a fait, alors, selon le moyen, que, d'une part, la cour d'appel n'a pas répondu aux conclusions par lesquelles la société et M. Y... avaient demandé expressément la confirmation du jugement entrepris et soutenu que l'état d'inconscience dans lequel se trouvait la victime ne permettait pas de lui allouer une indemnité dont elle ne tirerait aucun avantage ni amélioration de son état (cf. conclusions d'appel, page 2) et, encore, que l'indemnité de son incapacité permanente partielle reviendrait en l'occurrence à lui verser un salaire dont elle ferait l'économie (cf. conclusions d'appel du 22 mai 1992, page 3) ; que l'arrêt attaqué, qui laisse ces chefs péremptoires sans réponse, a violé l'article 455 du nouveau Code de procédure civile ; alors que, d'autre part, l'arrêt qui liquide le préjudice corporel de la victime en fonction de son maintien en milieu hospitalier et qui justifie par ailleurs sa décision de mettre en compte une indemnité supplémentaire de 800 000 francs par le fait que l'incapacité permanente partielle a pour but non seulement de réparer les conséquences pécuniaires de la diminution de la capacité physique, mais également les répercussions physiologiques dans la vie quotidienne réalise un double emploi et a violé ainsi l'article 1382 du Code civil ; alors qu'en outre, la société et M. Y... ayant expressément conclu à la confirmation du jugement entrepris (cf. conclusions d'appel, page 5) du 22 mai 1992, les motifs donnés par le jugement se trouvaient intégrés dans leurs conclusions d'appel et constituaient autant de moyens auxquels la cour d'appel était tenue de répondre ; qu'ainsi, l'arrêt, qui s'absient de réfuter les motifs suivant lesquels l'état d'inconscience dans lequel se trouvait la victime ne permettait pas, en ce qui concerne le préjudice esthétique et le préjudice d'agrément, de lui allouer une indemnité dont elle ne pouvait tirer aucun avantage ni amélioration de son état (cf. jugement entrepris, page 8 *in fine*) viole l'article 455 du nouveau Code de procédure civile ; alors qu'enfin, l'arrêt, qui alloue réparation d'un préjudice esthétique et d'un préjudice d'agrément dont il n'est nullement établi qu'ils aient été réellement ressentis par la victime, a violé l'article 1382 du Code civil ;

Box 11.2 *Contd.*

(2.3)   Mais attendu que l'état végétatif d'une personne humaine n'excluant aucun chef d'indemnisation, son préjudice doit être réparé dans tous ses éléments ;

Et attendu que l'arrêt, après avoir relevé l'existence chez la victime de périodes de conscience toute relative même si, par ailleurs, elle reste à l'état purement végétatif, évalue, répondant aux conclusions, dans l'exercice de son pouvoir souverain d'appréciation des modalités et du montant de la réparation du dommage, les préjudices esthétique et d'agrément ;

D'où il suit que le moyen n'est pas fondé ;

PAR CES MOTIFS :

REJETTE le pourvoi.

(5) Arrêt n° 1
N° 92-18.731.   Mlle X..., *ès qualités d'administrateur légal*
de Mme X...
contre société Transport agglomération
Elbeuvienne et autres.

Arrêt n° 2
N° 93-12.644.   *Société nouvelle X... et autre*
contre consorts Z... et autre.

(6) *Président* : M. Zakine. – *Rapporteur* : M. Michaud. – *Avocat général* : M. Monnet. – *Avocats* : la SCP Boré et Xavier, M. Copper-Royer (arrêt n° 1), la SCP Célice et Blancpain (arrêt n° 2). M. Blanc (arrêts n°s 1 et 2).

Source: Civ. 2, 22 février 1995, Bull. Civ. II, n° 61.

Chapter references

ANCEL, P., *Travaux Dirigés d'Introduction au Droit Civil*, Paris: Litec, 1994.

DEFRÉNOIS-SOULEAU, I., *Je Veux Réussir mon Droit*, 3rd edn, Paris: Armand Colin, 1998.

GRIDEL, J. P., *La Dissertation, le Cas Pratique et la Consultation en Droit Privé*, 4th edn, Paris: Dalloz, 1996.

MENDEGRIS, R., VERMELLE, G., *Le Commentaire d'Arrêt en Droit Privé*, 6th edn, Paris: Dalloz, 1996.

Index